A NEW WORLD
JERUSALEM

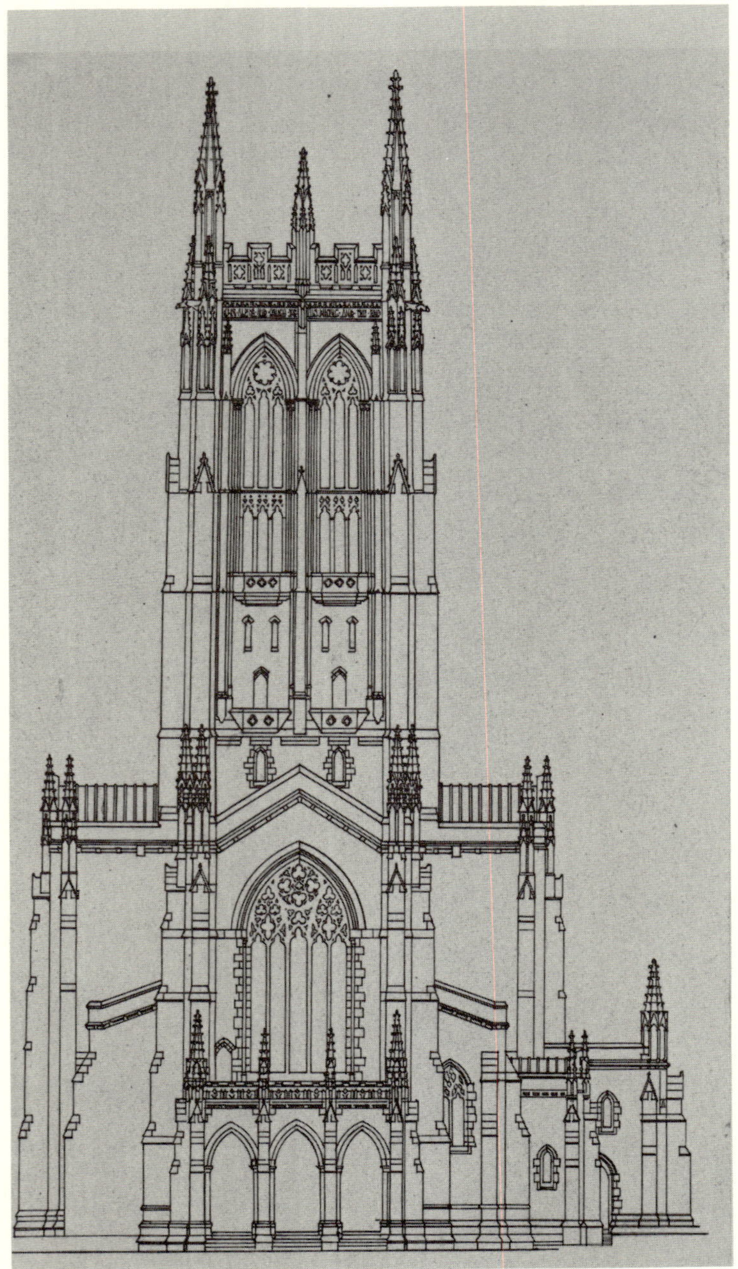

Bryn Athyn Cathedral. A line drawing by Frank Snyder of the west facade of the cathedral captures its beauty and strength. *Courtesy of the Academy of the New Church.*

A NEW WORLD JERUSALEM

The Swedenborgian Experience in Community Construction

MARY ANN MEYERS

CONTRIBUTIONS IN AMERICAN STUDIES, NUMBER 65

GREENWOOD PRESS

WESTPORT, CONNECTICUT • LONDON, ENGLAND

Library of Congress Cataloging in Publication Data

Meyers, Mary Ann.
    A New World Jerusalem.

    (Contributions in American studies, ISSN 0084-9227 ;
no. 65)
    Bibliography: p.
    Includes index.
    1. New Jerusalem Church.   I. Title.   II. Series.
BX8721.2.M48   1983   289.4   82-11997
ISBN 0-313-23602-X (lib. bdg.)

Library of Congress Catalog Card Number: 82-11997
ISBN: 0-313-23602-X
ISSN: 0084-9227

First published in 1983

Greenwood Press
A division of Congressional Information Service, Inc.
88 Post Road West, Westport, Connecticut 06881

Printed in the United States of America

10 9 8 7 6 5 4 3 2 1

For
Harold Galpin Dye
1901-1982

Contents

Illustrations

Preface

Philadelphia perches on the Pennsylvania bank of the Delaware in the shape of a high-crowned, broad-brimmed hat. Its principal suburban neighborhoods stretch west along Lancaster Pike (U. S. Route 30), the first turnpike in the state, and north along Old York Road (U. S. Route 611), built in 1693 and extended in the early eighteenth century as a highway to New York. Setting out from Wynnewood for Bryn Athyn, I head northeast. The route I follow leads along Penn Valley roads quite like the one on which I live. In the 120 years since the Pennsylvania Railroad laid double track from Philadelphia to Paoli, the Main Line has emerged as the archetype of the affluent, cosmopolitan suburb. Dwellings are gracious and shade trees line my way.

Crossing the Schuylkill River into Manayunk, I pass modest brick and stucco houses built on the steep slopes of this working-class city neighborhood which has changed little in six generations. It blends physically, ethnically, and economically into blue-collar Roxborough. Saint John the Baptist Roman Catholic Church has dominated the landscape since 1831. But descendants of the original Irish, Polish, and Italian settlers are now more likely to drive trucks or walk beats than work in the textile mills and box factories that employed their ancestors.

A bridge over Wissahicken Creek brings me to Germantown. Settled 300 years ago by Dutch and German Protestants, it is probably the oldest real suburb in America.[1] During the yellow fever epidemic of 1793, many wealthy Philadelphians fled to Germantown; afterwards, they built country estates there as summer havens. Forty years later, the coming of the railroad and another epidemic accelerated the pace of permanent settlement by commuters who worked in the city. Since the 1960s Germantown has been a predominantly middle-class black community. As I continue north, its large rambling houses, well built of Wissahicken schist, give way to block after block of row houses on the drab, monotonous streets of West Oak Lane. It is an area which underwent an extraordinarily rapid racial transition. Four years ago, Temple Sinai on Limekiln Pike was reconsecrated as the West Oak Lane Church of God.

In Chelton Hills, a condominium rises from a rolling lawn along one side of the road by which I leave the city. On the other side, "Lynnewood Gardens," an apartment complex, is built on land where once the Wideners raced horses on their private track. As I head briefly eastward, a sign tells me the Congregation Keneseth Israel was founded in 1847. It moved to Elkins Park from Philadelphia 109 years later. Originally settled by Victorian entrepreneurs, the Old York Road suburbs closest to town began drawing German Jews of wealth and social standing just before World War I. After the Second World War, there was an exodus from the city, and the synagogue I pass now serves 1,500 families.

Turning north again onto suburban lanes, I drive by the seventh and eighth holes of Abington Country Club in Jenkintown. Then there is a Quaker school and meeting house, in use since 1700, an art center, and further on, Rydal Country Club. Many corporate executives who work in the industrial northern part of Philadelphia have made their homes in the Huntingdon Valley. On Second Street Pike I pass shops, banks, and Lutheran, Presbyterian, and Baptist churches that serve them. Only for the last few minutes of my three-quarter-hour drive do I escape into patches of open country. A crossing-guard booth, like a silent sentry, marks my arrival in Bryn Athyn. There are houses here more grand than any I have seen on my way. The granite for them was quarried on the banks of Pennypack Creek; the timber is from trees felled in adjacent woodlands. At the heart of the community, and towering above it, is an architecturally magnificent church which proclaims the Lord in His Second Coming.

Given the spiritual distance between its residents and the rest of the world, there is a fitting symbolism in the space remaining physically between Bryn Athyn and surrounding Lower Moreland Township, even as fingers of development stretch toward the borough from every direction. Curiosity about the nature and extent of the social and psychological separation the Swedenborgians have maintained between themselves and their neighbors was what took me to their community.

It proved a rewarding journey. Many people aided me along the way. In Bryn Athyn, those who were especially helpful included: Eldric S. Klein, the late archivist of Academy of the New Church; his former assistant, Rosanne Grubb; Leon S. Rhodes, editor of the *Post;* and E. Bruce Glenn, Academy director of research and resources. Closer to home, there were Martin Meyerson and Renée Fox, who believed my travel notes would make a book, and three who graciously endured the writing of it: Katie, Andrew, and John.

A NEW WORLD
JERUSALEM

1

An Upper Middle-Class Sect

The cathedral-church of Bryn Athyn rises in Gothic splendor from the crest of a hill overlooking Pennypack Creek. Visually and psychologically it is the focal point of the small community which was carved out of rolling Pennsylvania farmland more than three-quarters of a century ago. Bryn Athyn is the episcopal seat of the General Church of the New Jerusalem, a religious body whose central doctrine fulfills for its votaries a hope which has glimmered, and on occasion flamed, in the hearts of men since the beginning of the Christian era.

For members of the General Church, the Second Coming is not a future event. Alone among all sectarian groups, they believe it already has occurred, having come to pass in the Writings of Emanuel Swedenborg. Since the 1890s, when the founders of the General Church removed from Philadelphia to a rural part of adjacent Montgomery County known as Huntingdon Valley, the sect has maintained a degree of cultural isolation primarily as a result of its emphasis upon a distinctive education and social life. Transmission from generation to generation of a common stock of ideas and values was perceived by the group as essential to its survival, and like other religious bodies before the, the Swedenborgians adopted vicinal separation as a means of mitigating outside interference and influence.

Religious tolerance and the availability of land facilitated the

New Churchmen's move, and it was in large measure financed by plate-glass industrialist John Pitcairn. Bryn Athyn's ties to the marketplace always have been strong, and economic independence never has been perceived by the community as a vehicle which would further its religious goals. It was rather social separation from what the Swedenborgians came increasingly to describe as the "vastated" world, which constituted their principal method for maintaining their peculiar version of reality and legitimating it in the eyes of their children on whom they counted to keep the faith.

An analysis of the process by which the New Churchmen preserved and justified their truths forms the core of *A New World Jerusalem*. But by way of introduction, I should like to emphasize an aspect of the group's separateness which makes it virtually unique among religious sects.[1] Preceding, indeed, a primary cause of the Swedenborgians' effort to set themselves apart from the world spatially, was a recognition of the fact that the cardinal tenet of their belief system set them apart temporarily. Because members of the General Church hold that the Second Coming was accomplished in the theological treatises produced by the Swedish seer Emanuel Swedenborg over a period of more than a quarter-century, they follow a different calendar; that is, they believe the world has arrived at a further stage in redemptive history than those who look forward to Christ's return in glory as the consummatory event in God's salvific plan. For Swedenborgians, the "holy city" about which John dreamed on the Isle of Patmos has descended out of heaven. It is the New Church, and its geographical locus is a lushly wooded community fifteen miles north of the center of Philadelphia. For its residents, Bryn Athyn is the "new earth" of Revelation, and in their wholly realized eschatology, longings are satisfied, which have affected adherents of Western religions since the destruction of Solomon's kingdom.

Ancient yearning for an earthly manifestation of divine favor and power found focus and unity in the New Testament concept of Parousia.[2] The application of Jesus' eschatological language to a history-terminating occurrence was the work of early Christian writers, and it can be accounted for in both theological and sociopsychological terms. The tendencies which produced the entirely unprecedented notion of a messianic drama in two acts are evident in the first Pauline Epistles, and they emerged as decisive elements in the Church's thinking by the later stages of the Gospel development. The increasingly pervasive idea of a second coming distinct from the first was the product, according to a persuasive study by John A. T. Robinson, of "an unresolved crisis in the Christology of the primitive Church, centering in the problem whether or not the messianic event had taken place."[3] The Crucifixion must have shattered the disciples' hopes that Jesus was indeed "the one who should come," and if the Easter miracle restored them, it did not settle the question as to whether the events initiating the age of fulfillment had occurred, or if some final, future act would set in motion the consummation of God's purposes in history. These unsettled and unsettling theological issues had to be faced by a Church beset by persecution, and it expectantly embraced the idea of a proximate Parousia. Writing during the oppressive reign of Domitian, the author of Revelation utilized the hope that Christ would return in glory as a means of encouraging nascent Christian communities in their hour of tribulation, and for centuries thereafter, his vision of a New Jerusalem "let down from heaven as a dwelling place for Saints" functioned in times of social unrest as balm for the afflicted.

Despite eventual condemnation of millenarianism by the Council of Ephesus in 431, chiliastic expectations persisted, as Norman Cohn has shown, "in the obscure under-world of popular religion."[4] The oppressed, the dissatisfied, and the disturbed were quick to read apocalyptic signs into all manner of of political events. Indeed, a characteristic common to virtually all historic groups given to chiliasm is that their membership was drawn from what Cohn describes as "the neediest strata of the population" living "on the margin of society."[5] H. Richard Neibuhr, in his classic study of *The Social Sources of Denominationalism*, says that among the untutored and economically disfranchised classes, "intellectual naivete and practical need combine to create a marked propensity toward millenarism, with its promise of tangible goods and the reversal of present social systems of rank. "From the first century onward," he writes, "apocalypticism has always been at home among the disinherited."[6]

As A. Leland Jamison, Werner Stark, and Sydney Ahlstrom

have suggested, however, the Niebuhrean term "disinherited" can refer to more than economic status.[7] The educationally deprived, geographically uprooted, and psychologically disturbed also may be eager purchasers of the sectarian solution to the problem of meaning. Indeed, empirical studies often have shown that sects function, as Thomas O'Dea puts it, to "reconcile the disinherited to their situation through the various compensations of this-worldly community and other-worldly expectations."[8]

My own research suggests, however, that the New Church has always attracted men and women whose education, occupation, and, in some cases income, place them considerably above the social mean. The seeds of Swedenborgianism were sown in America by a university-educated planter, James Glen, who lectured on the Writings in Philadelphia in 1784 en route to his home in Guyana. Among those who heard him was Francis Bailey, editor and publisher of the influential *Freeman's Journal.* Bailey was an elder of the Pine Street Presbyterian Church, but when, after Glen's departure for a lecture in Boston, a box of Swedenborg's books arrived in Philadelphia from London, he bought all the English editions and began to study them. Within a few months the publisher had convened a small circle of readers, including: Myers Fisher, a Quaker lawyer who had purchased the original Latin editions of that first shipment of the seer's works; John Young, a law student who became the presiding judge of Western Pennsylvania; and the Reverend Michael Slatter, a Presbyterian minister sent to the Colonies years earlier as a missionary from Switzerland. In 1787 Bailey printed at his own expense the first New Church publication ever issued in America, John Clowes's *A Summary View of the Heavenly Doctrines;* the next year, with the aid of the fifty subscribers including Benjamin Franklin, financier Robert Morris, and Pennsylvania Governor Thomas McKeen, he brought out the first volume of *True Christian Religion.*

By 1808 about twenty receivers of the heavenly doctrines were meeting regularly, and if the group was numerically small, it consisted in the main of men of some distinction. In addition to the poet Philip Freneau, there was Frederick Eckstein, a sculptor whose father was the court sculptor for Frederick the

Great; Daniel Lammot, a wealthy merchant, painted by Thomas Sully, and the father of Alfred V. DuPont's wife, Margaretta; the lawyer Jonathan Condy, who was a graduate of the University of Pennsylvania, clerk of the House of Representatives, and the husband of Elizabeth Hopkinson, daughter of the jurist and composer Francis Hopkinson, who signed the Declaration of Independence; and Condy's nephew, the young Condy Raguet, who became a founder of the Philadelphia Savings Fund Society, served as president of the Pennsylvania Life Annuity Company and the Philadelphia Chamber of Commerce, and was United States consul in Rio de Janeiro.

Largely through Raguet's efforts, Philadelphia believers organized The American Society for Disseminating the Doctrines of the New Jerusalem Church in 1815 and two years later sent out a call to all "receivers of the doctrines" to convene in Philadelphia "for the purpose of consulting together upon the general concerns of the Church."[9] A pattern of annual meetings of delegates continued until 1840 when, again through Raguet's efforts, the emerging concept of a "general church" existing at all times was reflected in the organization of a new polity known as the Central Convention.

Its leader was Richard de Charms, a New Church clergyman who was the son of a Huguenot physician and had been educated at Yale. Other lay signers of the convention's constitution, in addition to Raguet, included such prominent Philadelphians as Lammot; Dr. Constantine Hering, a recent German immigrant who had graduated from the University of Leipzig and, as one of the great oracles of homeopathy, was to found Hahnemann Medical College; and Benjamin Franklin Glenn, then a dry-goods merchant who went on to establish a successful real estate firm and play a role of continuing importance in the affairs of the New Church, as did his descendants in each succeeding generation.

These New Churchmen were all members of the Philadelphia First Society, and for five years de Charms served as their pastor. When he accepted a call to the Baltimore Society in 1845, he was succeeded by his protégé, William Henry Benade, the son of a Moravian bishop. By that time, new names on the congregational roll included: Timothy Shay Arthur, the editor of the *Home Gazette* and the author of the famous temperance ditty

'"Ten Nights In A Barroom''; Dr. Richard Gardiner, a prominent local physician; and the mathematician William Chauvenet, superintendent of the United States Naval Asylum then located in Philadelphia, which he reorganized as the Naval Academy and was instrumental in moving to Annapolis the next year. A founding member of the National Association for the Advancement of Science, the Yale-educated Chauvenet was the son of a New Churchman who had come to America from France, and he kept up an active interest in the affairs of Philadelphia Swedenborgians until just before the Civil War, when he went to Washington University, an institution he served as chancellor.

When Benade's pastoral relationship with the Philadelphia First Society was severed in 1854 as the result of a growing disparity between the High Church views of the priest, who attached considerable symbolic significance to vestments and ritual, and the so-called Quaker preferences of his congregation, his sympathizers formed a new society. Foremost among these was the realtor Glenn; Louis C. Iungerich, a Swiss merchant; Dr. David Cowley, a physician; and two newcomers to Philadelphia, twenty-eight-year-old Francis E. Boericke and twenty-three-year-old Rudolph Tafel. The son of a German wool merchant, Boericke emigrated after the 1848 Revolution; on arriving in Philadelphia, he met a professor's son, Rudolph Tafel, who had come to the United States at fifteen and already was launched upon a career as a teacher and translator. At Benade's urging, the two young men opened a depository for the sale of New Church literature in 1853, and the next year they established a homeopathic pharmacy. After six months, Rudolph left to accept a professorship at the Naval Academy, later followed Chauvenet to Washington University, then entered the New Church ministry and went to Sweden where he inaugurated the work of making photolithograph copies of Swedenborg's manuscripts. Boericke carried on the pharmaceutical business alone, earned a medical degree at Hahnemann Medical College, and in 1869 formed a partnership with Rudolph's younger brother, Adolph. Boericke & Tafel became one of the largest drug manufacturing firms in the country, significantly enriching its founders.

The new society created by these enterprising gentlemen not only subscribed to Benade's ideas about the use of representatives in worship, but also accepted his view of the preeminence of education among church functions. In 1857, members opened a school on Cherry Street, which survived only until the outbreak of the Civil War. During four years of operation, however, it served as a launching pad for a movement that was to reach full bloom with the inauguration of Bryn Athyn's comprehensive educational system.

But even in those early years Benade had ambitious plans. He was the founding member of a *sub rosa* organization of New Church scholars formed for the purpose of explicating Swedenborg's works, propagating their belief in the Writings' divine origin, and training young men for the priesthood who would perpetuate their views. Of the half dozen original members of the group, Benade had no stauncher ally than a former Presbyterian minister named James Park Stuart, who was a graduate of Illinois College and had studied at Yale before entering the New Church ministry. Another ally, who became his successor, was William Frederic Pendleton. A physician, the Georgian was descended from gentlemen freeholders in colonial Virginia. His great-great uncle was the statesman Edmund Pendleton, speaker of the House of Burgesses, who was among the wealthiest men in the new nation. His grandfather, Coleman, was born in Culpepper County and migrated to Georgia in 1807. Coleman's son, Philip Coleman, studied law, turned to publishing, and played a leading role in the establishment of Georgia Female Seminary, now Wesleyan College, which was the second college in the United States to grant degrees to women. In 1840 he undertook the publication of a literary monthly, *The Southern Ladies Book*, in which he called for a distinctive Southern literature. Moving the journal headquarters from Macon to Savannah, he changed its name to *Magnolia*, began to publish the work of William Gilmore Simms, and married Catherine Tebeau, whose forebearer's included the first governor of Georgia.[10]

William Frederic Pendleton was born in 1845.[11] He studied with private tutors until the outbreak of the Civil War when his father sent him to the Georgia Military Institute. The boy spent the next year pleading to join the Confederate forces. Finally Phillip, a major in the Fiftieth Georgia regiment, relented, and in 1862 William began his military career. Elected a company officer, he was made a captain within a year and took part in a dozen major battles. On returning home after Lee's surrender, he was introduced to the heavenly doctrines by his father who had become acquainted with them during the war. Philip now undertook a new publishing venture, *The South Georgia Times,* and William joined his younger brothers at a private academy, the Valdosta Institute. As a special student, he remained in the school until the end of 1866, then accepted a teaching post himself to earn money for college, as the harsh policies of the Reconstruction government deprived him of any hope of further financial support from his family. In the spring of 1868, he began studying medicine with his uncle, Dr. Edmund Pendleton, and in the fall entered Savannah Medical College. There he wrote plays, read Swedenborg, and upon completing his courses was graduated with an M.D. in March of 1870, some eight months after his father had been killed in a riding accident. William then went off to New York to take clinical work at Bellevue Hospital, but soon decided to study for the New Church ministry, entering the theological school at Waltham, Massachusetts in June. It was not a move which was well received by his family, for he writes to his mother:

I am very sorry to hear that you allow the letters of Uncle Edmund and Grandmother to disturb you. . . . We ought not to care so much about other people's opinion. . . . I feel that our noble father, who is now an angel in heaven, approves our course. . . . We have in our possession the leaves of the trees that are for the healing of the nations, we have the medicine that can cure all spiritual diseases. . . . Even if you look at the thing from merely a natural or worldly standpoint, you need have nothing to fear. The barriers of prejudice are fast being swept away. Here in the North . . . it is quite a respectable thing now to be a Swedenborgian.[12]

It was respectable, perhaps, but presented no immediate avenue by which Mrs. Pendleton's eldest surviving son could be of practical assistance to the younger members of the family. So when typhoid fever killed one brother and affected the mind of another, he extended a school holiday into more than a year's leave of absence, during which he took over the management of the paper and practiced medicine in Valdosta. In the late spring of 1872 he married Lawson Young, the well-educated daughter of a still wealthy planter, and with his bride returned to theological studies. William began his ministry in Wilmington, and after being ordained by Bishop Benade in 1873, he served briefly as pastor of the Cherry Street Society in Philadelphia until censured by the chancellor for his liberal views. In 1874 he accepted the pastorate of the more congenial Philadelphia First Society, but as he continued to study the Writings during the next two years, he came at length to share many of Benade's theological ideas, and was elected to membership in the academy. From 1877 to 1884 he served as pastor of Immanuel Church in Chicago, then returned to Philadelphia as a professor in the Academy's theological school. On that occasion, Benade wrote to a friend: "I am glad to have him with us, particularly glad because he enters so fully into the spirit of our order and work."[13]

But the uses of the Academy could not be carried out by the clergy alone. The support of research and the publication of books, to say nothing of the establishment of schools, were costly ventures. Financial backing was essential, and for it Benade turned without hesitation to laymen. Naturally he cultivated the support of those who had money, but given his belief in the propriety of mediating divine authority through a hierarchical ministry, there was a great if gratuitous advantage in making common cause with men who had no need of compensating for lowly secular status by seizing sectarian power. Benade needed associates who because of their commanding position in the world would not contest their subordinate position in the Church, and no one, as it turned out, was better suited to such dual roles than John Pitcairn.

Born in 1841 at Johnstone, county of Renfrew in the southwest of Scotland, the future manufacturer came to America with his family at the age of five.[14] His father, John Pitcairn, Sr., was a man with a marked talent for mechanics who had first emigrated in 1835 with his wife Agnes (McEwen) and two eldest children. He settled briefly in Brooklyn, then in Paterson, New Jersey, returned to Scotland, and in 1846 left his native land forever and made a new home just outside of Pittsburgh. Something of a skeptic, John Pitcairn, Sr., had failed to accompany his wife to kirk when she took their son John to be baptized by a minister of the Church of Scotland. The stern Presbyterian therefore refused to administer the sacrament, and the child was never baptized, until he was received into the New Church with his whole family shortly after their arrival in western Pennsylvania. John attended Sunday School with his erstwhile friend Andrew Carnegie, and he received elementary secular education in the public schools of Allegheny City. At fourteen he left to earn his own living.

John Pitcairn's remarkable business career fell into three distinct phases, involving railroads, crude oil and natural gas, and plate glass. His first job was in the office of the superintendent of the Pennsylvania Railroad in Altoona, where he learned telegraphy and, guided by the superintendent's wife, read Pope, Byron, Dickens, and Scott and committed long passages of Shakespeare to memory. In 1858 he went to Fort Wayne, Indiana as a telegraph operator and, in short time, was appointed assistant to the superintendent of the Western Division of the Pittsburgh, Fort Wayne and Chicago Railroad. At the age of nineteen, he came to Philadelphia as secretary to the superintendent of the Philadelphia division of the Pennsylvania Railroad. There he associated himself with the New Church society on Cherry Street under the direction of Benade, whom he probably had met previously on the occasion of the pastor's visits to New Churchmen in Pittsburgh.

After the dissolution of the Cherry Street School, Benade actually divided his time between the two cities until 1864 when he accepted the pastorate of the fledgling Pittsburgh Society. Young John Pitcairn also was a busy traveler during these years. Having proved himself worthy of significant railroad assignments, in 1861, amid rumors of an assassination plot, he had been given charge of the special train that carried Abraham Lincoln from Harrisburg to Philadelphia en route to Washington for his inauguration. During the Civil War he was involved in the transportation of Union troops, and advancing steadily in his career, he was appointed superintendent of the middle division of the Pennsylvania Railroad in 1866. Pitcairn remained in this post for three years, and though his headquarters were in Renovo, a little town on the Susquehanna, his diary indicates that occasionally he journeyed to Philadelphia to take part in New Church social life and attended assemblies of the General Convention in Boston and Portland, Maine.

The young man continued to pursue these avocations when in

1869 he became general manager of the Oil Creek and Allegheny River Railroad, which connected with the oil-rich districts of northwestern Pennsylvania. He was engaged in constant traveling, but again his diary shows time out for dinner with the Glenns, an evening party at the Iungerichs, and a doctrinal lecture by Benade. The pastor was enjoying considerable success about this time in building up the Pittsburgh Society, and as he wrote to Stuart, he was particularly encouraged because "some young men of prominent families and of bright intelligence . . . have come boldly forward and united with the Church by Baptism."[15] On the day they were received, Pitcairn met the new members— Walter C. Childs and Franklin Ballou. The two had been boyhood friends, educated together in Pittsburgh private schools. Childs had prepared for Yale at Phillips Andover, but when his father had agreed to let him try for West Point in lieu of joining the Union Army, he had gone to Rensselaer Polytechnic Institute to study engineering. The desired Academy appointment failed, however, to come through, so he stayed on at the Troy, New York college until 1866, when he left before graduation to accompany an older brother on a European tour. Returning to the United States, he formed a partnership with Ballou, a metallurgist, for the manufacture of a patented furnace grate for steam boilers and nonconducting asbestos cement for blast furnaces. Eventually they both moved West and then to New York, where Ballou became the vice-president of a smelting company and Childs entered a brokerage firm. In the early seventies, however, they were gay young men about Pittsburgh, and soon became fast friends with John Pitcairn. The young railroad executive also was forming a close relationship with Benade, twenty-five years his senior, whom he he looked to as a spiritual mentor and intellectual guide. The minister had separated from his wife when he came to Pittsburgh in 1864, though they were not divorced until 1877. Entering upon a welcome period of quiet study, yet lonely for his children, he undoubtedly enjoyed the younger man's company, quite apart from his growing understanding that upon the financial resources of laity depended his hopes for the New Church.

In the rugged hill country of northwestern Pennsylvania in the decades after the Civil War, large sums of money were made (and lost) more quickly than ever before in American history, and it was in the exhilarating atmosphere of the "oil boom" that John Pitcairn lay the foundation for his fortune. The young Scot had the good luck to be in the right place at the right time, but he also was spectacularly shrewd, and his success can be accounted for in terms of his drive, his imagination, and his daring. In 1871 he began to invest his savings in oil property, and at the same time became interested in the development of pipelines, the recently proposed solution to the critical problem of transporting petroleum. He built the Imperial Refinery at Oil City, and in 1872 left the railroad business to become an active partner in Vandergrift, Forman and Company, which was engaged in the distribution of crude petroleum. The firm built the first pipeline for conveying natural gas to Pittsburgh steel manufacturers, and it controlled the Natural Gas Company, Limited. Just as Pitcairn was embarking on this second stage in his career, John D. Rockefeller was organizing the South Improvement Company, a combination of a number of major oil producers who got together to force railroads to carry their petroleum products at lower rates than those imposed on their competitors. By accident, news of the infamous rebate contracts became public knowledge almost immediately, and independent producers in Oil City were in an uproar. Already many of their counterparts in Cleveland had joined forces with Rockefeller's organization, and the critical question, as framed by the local newspaper, was: "What will Mr. Pitcairn say about it?"[16] According to his diary, the New Church Scot said no when approached by the combine, although he also noted that had he agreed to a consolidation, he "would have gotten millions."[17] Instead, he helped the independent oil men to secure the same rates as had been given to the South Improvement Company. Later, after a congressional investigation, the combine lost its charter.

The third and crowning phase of John Pitcairn's business career was inaugurated in 1882 when he began to withdraw his interests from petroleum and natural gas and transfer them to the nascent plate-glass industry. Early in the year he was consulted about piping gas to a plate-glass factory which was to be erected in Creighton, Pennsylvania by a New York firm controlled by Captain John B. Ford. Interested in the project, Pitcairn invested in the company's stock, and in 1883 he joined with Ford and others to reorganize the enterprise as The Pittsburgh Plate Glass Company, with capital of $600,000. It represented the first successful attempt to produce plate glass in America, and Pitcairn served initially as vice-president of the firm. A dozen years later it had nine factories and capital stock worth $10 million. Pitcairn bought out the Ford family in 1897 and served as president of the company until 1905, when he was elected chairman of the board of directors. Under his direction Pittsburgh Plate Glass was established firmly as the leading supplier of plate glass to the American market. In 1902 it acquired the factory of the Courcelles Plate Glass Company in Belgium, and during the first few years of the twentieth century the giant corporation expended more than a million dollars on research—with the result that it developed the Lehr annealing process, a manufacturing procedure involving the slow, controlled cooling of sheet glass, which revolutionized the industry. At his death in 1916, Pitcairn's personal fortune was estimated at $60 million, and he had given uncounted millions to the New Church. Today his descendants turn over a third of their annual income to the uses of the sect.

Why has the New Church appealed consistently to the well-to-do, the educated, often to those of a scientific bent? I believe there are three reasons. In the first place, high-status persons find it easy to identify with Emanuel Swedenborg (1688-1772) whose lineage was indisputably upper class. He is, moreover, a role model for intellectual achievers. The product of a society where authority was well defined and institutionalized, he readily assumed a place of leadership in eighteenth-century Sweden. His father, Jesper Swedberg, was the bishop of Skara, and his mother, Sara Behm, was the daughter of a wealthy mine owner who served as a government official.[18] Swedenborg was educated at the University of Upsala and there immersed himself in science. After a further period of prolonged study in England, during which he read Newton and visited with the royal astronomer John Flamstead, he returned home by way of the continent and undertook the publication of a scientific journal. He then served as civil engineer, and eventually was appointed an assessor on the Board of Mines, a position he used to help build up the material sources of a country exhausted by a hundred years of war. In 1734, at the age of forty-six, he published his great three-volume work on mineralogy. The first volume, known as the *Principia,* is a mechanical and geometric account of the origin and structure of matter, which won its author a place in the first ranks of the learned men of his time. Swedenborg also displayed a sense of civil obligation and was active in Sweden's parliamentary affairs as a member of the House of Nobles. But at midlife a dramatic shift was evident in his goals. Thenceforward the scientist-statesman's attention was focused on what he called the "science of the soul."[19] (See Figure 1.)

The philosophical and theological treatises Swedenborg produced during the last half of his life are the source and basis of New Church doctrine, and their intricacies, as well as their scientific aura, are a second reason why the sect's appeal has been largely limited to people with an intellectual turn of mind. The nature of the belief system underpinning the Bryn Athyn community is the focus of the next chapter, but it seems appropriate to emphasize here that Swedenborg believed it was among men of learning that his ideas would initially take root. He wrote in Latin because it was the language in which educated Europeans of his day communicated, and, as Marguerite Block has suggested, he disseminated his theological works where he thought they would be most likely to be understood—among scientists, scholars, the nobility, and the higher ranking members of the Protestant clergy.[20] The Swedish seer was not a man of the people. He did not walk among the poor and simple, and it is hardly surprising that his ideas have not attracted them.

But if Swedenborgianism's appeal has been to those given to book learning, it is also true that the sect's stress upon schools has served to perpetuate an educated membership. Risking a tautology, I would argue that a third reason for the attractiveness of the New Church to those who value education is the guarantee implicit in its social practice that the value of education will be inculcated in future generations.

Residence in Bryn Athyn can be seen as a kind of hedge against downward mobility. The sense of elitism which the Swedenborgians' social status engenders is strongly reinforced by their belief that their religion gives them a superior perspective upon history. What caused their immediate forebearers to

Figure 1. Scientist and seer Emanuel Swedenborg claimed to have been constantly in touch with the spiritual world for more than a quarter of a century. Members of the General Church of the New Jerusalem believe the Second Coming was accomplished in his Writings. *Photo of painting courtesy of G. V. Wachenfeldt.*

disengage themselves from society at large was the radical answer they formulated to the question: What shall we do to be saved? It was arise and go.

Apart from members' social origin, however, the General Church does share many characteristics traditionally ascribed to sectarian movements. It is a voluntary association whose votaries regard themselves as a people set apart. Possessing a sure sense of its own integrity, the Church imposes certain standards of behavior upon adherents of its doctrines and possesses procedures for expelling the wayward. Claiming complete and conscious allegiance, it demands a loyalty of its members which then transcends other loyalties, whether to kin groups or class or state. Successful in maintaining its identity in opposition to worldly values for more than three-quarters of a century, the General Church seems to fit modern sociology's definition of an established sect, that is, a religious body which endures beyond the founding generation without making the accommodations to secular society characteristic of the religious denomination.[21] Of course the very theory of routinization, associated with increasing wealth and respectability for members of the sectarian group, is predicated upon the conviction that sects originate on the social periphery, which was not true of the General Church.

Swedenborgian theologians, it should be observed, would protest the classification of the General Church as a sect.[22] Indeed, despite common usage in the community, they object to the adjective "Swedenborgian" and the noun "Swedenborgianism." Emanuel Swedenborg was not the founder of their faith, but, in their view, the vehicle used by the Lord to make His Second Coming in the spirit of truth. The New Church, then, is "a new and distinct dispensation."[23] It is not seen by its members as one more variation upon a Christian theme. They do not believe it was given to revive Christianity, but to supplant it. While members of the General Convention have as their distinguishing social identity a shared admiration for the Writings, which they consider a source of new truth and hope will gradually permeate the world, members of the General Church regard the "old church" as spiritually dead. Without holding to the view that outside the New Church there is no salvation, they believe that the best hope for individual regeneration and the only hope for the redemption of the race is to be found in the heavenly doctrine given by God to an eighteenth-century Swedish nobleman.

In many respects my own ethnographic research in Bryn Athyn has been an adventure in map making.[24] A central problem was that sects,by their very nature, are closed societies. Hostility toward those who come not to pray and praise but to record and analyze is common, and the extant descriptive literature about sectarianism is a tribute to the patience and diligence of researchers in many disciplines. The Swedenborgians' rich tradition of scholarship, however, mitigates the altogether natural enmity characteristic of people who feel their values are being dissected if not questioned, and I have found New Churchmen remarkably tolerant of an outsider's persistent inquiry. Given their views of marriage and family life, the significance of which will emerge, I trust, on many of the following pages, the fact that I was married and the mother of two children proved a clear advantage throughout the course of my work, earning me a degree of receptivity in the community that would not so easily have been accorded to a person with a different social identity. For my part, I found the group's extraordinary self-consciousness, manifested in doctrinal treatises and historical studies, of inestimable value.

Despite their economic involvement with the world, political activity, and support of cultural organizations, the residents of Bryn Athyn regard themselves as constituting a distinctive community, set apart from the world in space and time on account of their religion, which they believe "is a matter, not of faith, but of life."[25] Support for this view is to be found outside the Swedenborgian tradition in the work of Clifford Geertz. The anthropologist writes that "religious concepts spread beyond their specifically metaphysical context to provide a framework of general ideas in terms of which a wide range of experience—intellectual, emotional, moral—can be given meaningful form."[26] Because, as he so eloquently phrases it, "the moods and motivations a religious orientation produces cast a derivative, lunar light over the solid features of a people's secular life," my task in *A New World Jerusalem* has been in large measure a matter of tracing the extent to which New Churchmen's notions of the " 'really real,' and the dispositions these notions induce in them, color their sense of the reasonable, the practical, the humane, and the moral."[27] If, as Geertz does, one defines culture as "a set of control mechanisms—plans, recipes, rules, instructions (what computer engineers call 'programs')—for the governing of behavior,''[28] what exists in Bryn Athyn is a distinctive American subculture.

2

Intellectual Structure: The Heavenly Doctrine

The community on the banks of the Pennypack rests on an intellectual foundation constructed of the theological ideas posited by Emanuel Swedenborg during the last half of his life. Born in Stockholm in 1688, the seer grew up in Upsala where his father was a professor of theology, then rector of the University and dean of the Cathedral. As a university student, Emanuel devoted himself to mathematics and natural science, graduating in 1709. During the next few years he continued his studies in London and at Oxford, traveled to Holland and France, wrote poetry and an algebra textbook, worked on mechanical inventions for better utilizing Sweden's water power, and published *Daedalus Hyperboreus,* the first scientific magazine ever issued in his native land. He then turned to metallurgy and won appointment as an administrator of the Board of Mines.

Launched upon his new career at thirty-five, Swedenborg visited Swedish mining districts and turned out a series of technical reports on forest conservation, hoisting machines, blast furnaces, and the market value of sulphur, while in his spare time collecting material for his philosophical masterwork. Printed in Dresden and Leipzig in 1734, the first volume, the famous *Principia,* propounds a nebular hypothesis well before Kant and Laplace published their theories of the evolution of the solar system.[1]

Swedenborg's contribution to cosmology brought him to the

attention of the scientific world and earned him a place of distinction in it. But his real interest seems even then to have been theology. The *Principia* posited the existence of something beyond space and time which he called Unmanifested Energy, and in the first chapter of this volume, which he wrote last, the Swedish scientist hints that the connection between infinite and finite is Jesus Christ.[2] His research goal from his mid-forties onward was to explore the realm of the soul, and he said that for this "all the sciences are required that the world ever eliminated or developed."[3]

In the more than twenty theological works Swedenborg wrote before his death in 1772, his logic remained the inductive logic of scientific discovery. In collecting data through observation, he reasoned from the particular to the general, only then drawing deductions from his data, which he tested by further observation—not, however, in the natural world, but in the world of spirits. More than simply an idealist for whom ultimate reality lay in a realm transcending phenomena, the Swedish seer believed that all natural objects and events are effects, therefore the expression, of spiritual causes. It was these determinants of the material universe to which he claimed to carefully attend by divine permission, "not granted," he said, "to any one since the creation, as it has been to me."[4]

The cosmogony expounded by Swedenborg as "heavenly doctrine" attempts to reconcile the concept of a transcendent God distinct from the universe with the concept of an immanent Creator. He argues that the Divine can flow into created things, but they can never become part of the Divine because God, spiritual causes, and natural effects constitute entirely separate planes of existence, that is, discrete degrees incapable of resolution one into another.

The essence of Swedenborg's dualistic ontology is that as cause is unimaginable without effect, the existence of this spiritual universe would be impossible without the existence of a natural universe. By such reasoning, then, did the seer who was first a scientist dignify matter. In his view, man is a distinct creation, though his teachings, formulated more than three-quarters of a century before Darwin published *The Origin of the Species*, do not appear to preclude the possibility that an existing form of animal life was used as a matrix for a new embryonic form. Nevertheless, he portrayed humankind as *sui generis* and wrote that man is a "form receptive of life from God."[5] The Creator fashioned him to exist coterminously in the spirit world and the world of nature. Indeed, the very purpose of creation is man's conjunction with God, which can be accomplished only by the right exercise of human reason and human freedom.

In sharp contrast to the theologians of his day who identified Adam with the *first* man, Swedenborg argued that perfection always has been an achieved characteristic. He taught that the preadamites were simple, food-gathering creatures who responded instinctively to Divine emanations, grasping intuitively their benefit.[6] As every revelation was accepted in their wills and consequently embodied in their lives, a further stage in the moral and intellectual evolution of the human species was attained, making possible yet more progress. At length there developed in the land of Canaan an exalted race, which Swedenborg termed the Most Ancient Church. This religious community was signified in Genesis by the Hebrew word for Adam, and while it was characterized externally by a still simple, nomadic life-style, internally the members of the first "church" had reached a state in which they were so exquisitely attuned to the will of God that there was nothing to subvert the operation of Divine Providence for their welfare. Because the people of this "golden age" could think in correspondences—that is, immediately recognize the inner significance and use of exterior objects in relation to the life of the spirit—they could converse with angels, and they lived in peace.

The nature of the Fall is portrayed in the Writings as a gradual decline precipitated by man's action in "turning away from God toward himself."[7] His independence, which Swedenborg taught was an illusion, began to seem real to him, and he came to regard the virtues he possessed from the Lord as his own. The external manifestation of this tragic act of self-deception was a lust for power and the goods of others; internally it effected a cleavage of the intellect and will as to function, so that man no longer opted automatically for goodness and truth, but weighed them against the pleasure of giving himself up to his material and corporeal loves. At length influx from the Divine became abhorrent to him, and he inverted his mind, closing it to the light and heat of heaven and opening it to the darkness and chill, which is the absence of God or the influx of hell. While the Fall represented a catastrophe for the religious community called the Most Ancient Church, Swedenborg specifically rejected the idea that it corrupted the whole human race in the Augustinian sense of depriving subsequent generations of the ability not to sin and justly subjecting them to damnation. Rather than a legacy of guilt, he taught that the adamic inheritance is a tendency toward evil which is not condemnatory in itself. But the effect is cumulative, and the seer suggested that again and again the total destruction of all human forms of life was averted only by the Lord's mercy. Individual salvation depends, however, upon man's voluntary cooperation with God, and for this reason, Swedenborg argued that the Creator would never revoke or nullify free will no matter to what extent man abused it. He could assert, therefore, an apparent paradox: "Evils are permitted for a certain purpose, which is salvation."[8]

Discovering a model for the history of race itself in the Biblical story of creation, the philosopher observed that the collective perversion of divine gifts led in the first instance to the Flood, which he believed signified the inundation of falsity from which God saved a remnant called Noah. The post-deluvian race constituted the Ancient Church in which a new faculty, conscience, replaced intuition. Open intercourse with the spiritual world was no longer possible, but the reconstruction of the human mind allowed man to control his wayward will by means of his understanding. With the loss of knowledge of correspondences, however, idolatry and polytheism were generated by the multiple images of the Divine, which contained a legacy of wisdom from the Most Ancient Church, but came to be regarded by members of the Ancient Church as things holy in themselves and at last were worshipped as deities. The decline of this generation was symbolized by the Egyptian captivity, and its replacement, dating from the promulgation of the Decalogue, was what Swedenborg called the "Israelitish" Church and characterized as a religious community whose sole virtue was obedience. In it the truths of religion were preserved in the form of external compliance with moral laws and ceremonial observance. But the Jews, like their predecessors, "falsified the meaning or understanding of the Word,"[9] inviting annihilation and necessitating the radical intervention of the Lord into history.

Swedenborg's explanation of the purpose and nature of the Incarnation resides in his distinctive doctrine of the Divine Human—the keystone in the arch of his theological system, which represented a fundamental challenge to the orthodoxy of his day. The seer's experiences in the spirit world confirmed him in the belief that the effects of successive apostasies among the guardians of religious truths were not limited to the natural world. So closely linked were the two realms, he said, that the noxious effusions of the declining churches surged up into the heavens and they were "suffocated by them as by a flood of Stygian waters."[10] Retention of angels in their integrity as well as the salvation of men and women were a function, then, of the Advent. Redemption, according to Swedenborg, involved a judgement in the spiritual world by means of which the Lord separated good from evil spirits, subjugated the hells, and put the heavens into order, thus preparing for the establishment of the Christian Church. But because the infinite cannot approach the finite, it was necessary for the Lord to assume a human form.

Swedenborg taught that the Son, much less the Holy Spirit, did not exist until the Incarnation, but that Jesus and the eternal Father are one. When the seer viewed them in relationship to each other, he saw no distinctions. Christ was not a party to the Trinity; it resided in Him who was at once Creator, Redeemer, and Comforter. It is the second identity which Swedenborg emphasized, however, in formulating his doctrine of the Divine Human. He said that the child born in Bethlehem took His soul from the Father and His body from Mary, and through her derived the tendency to evil which afflicts all men. Jesus' life was filled with temptations, and in overcoming them, even the last which was the cross, He glorified His Human and made it Divine. The process was completed with the Resurrection when, the Swedish philosopher wrote, the Lord "put off everything derived from the mother, and put on everything belonging to the Father."[11] He even said that he had chanced to speak with the Virgin in the spirit world, and she had told him she was "unwilling that any one should acknowledge [the Lord] as her Son, because the whole Divinity is in Him."[12] The philosophical difficulty inherent in this view, of course, is the inescapable conclusion that God, who is changeless, realized potential through the glorification of His human nature, and became what He was not before. Nowhere did the seer attempt to resolve this paradox, but taught it as a truth from the Lord.

The "fundamental error" of Christianity was not only a conception of the godhead as "three Divine Persons from eternity," Swedenborg said, but also the orthodox belief that "the passion of the cross is redemption."[13] Eschewing any idea of a vicarious atonement, he declared that the Incarnation and Glorification made possible human conjunction with the Lord, and through Him with God the Father, and in this relationship resided the possibility of eternal life. Calling Calvin's concept of predestination a "pernicious doctrine" and a "cruel notion," he also rejected the Lutheran teaching that faith alone is sufficient for salvation. With Rome, he argued it must be expressed in works, and further observed that "there is no faith without charity, and no charity without faith."[14] Because man's adamic inheritance precludes complete success in resisting temptations, moreover, Swedenborg insisted that neither genuine charity nor true faith is attainable without repentance.

But turning from sin and amendment of life is not accomplished by contrition or sacramental confession. It is a matter, the philosopher declared, of having, in the first place, a knowledge of sin, then the examination of conscience, which involves scrutiny not only of one's acts, but also one's intentions; recognition and acknowledgment of sins; prayer to the Lord for help in avoiding temptation; and, finally, the beginning of a new life. He said that repentance promotes reformation, which consists of desire to attain the spiritual state, and regeneration, which is its attainment effected by the Lord with man's cooperation. The human part involves doing good actions that are of use to the neighbor, which is the second aspect of charity. It is noteworthy that Swedenborg's interpretation of the second commandment in relation to the first led him to teach that "the degrees of love toward the neighbor ought to be estimated by love towards the

Lord, and thus by how much of the Lord or from the Lord the neighbor really possesses."[15] The duties of charity he defined as giving just and faithful service in whatever office one fills be it that of prince or plowman, while the benefactions of charity involve "helpful services which are rendered outside the ordinary duties of one's occupation."[16] The latter is voluntary; the former mandatory, for it is inextricably linked to the fulfillment of a person's "use," that is, the sum of the individual's responsibilities to others in all relationships of life. "To love the the Lord," Swedenborg said, "means to do uses from Him and for His sake."[17] In a sense, then, the useful person is a regenerated person. As such he is in communion with heavenly angels, and when he dies, the seer declared, he enters into their company. He acknowledges them as kinfolk, and they know him for one of their own.

Swedenborg's demystifying of death and the life men and women can expect thereafter has gained more attention than any other aspect of his work. He taught that heaven and hell are not simply future states; nor are they places. The spiritual world is, he implied, a psychological realm, of which death makes men conscious, but in which every human being has some standing throughout the whole course of his earthly existence. Writing in language as explicit as that found in the reports he prepared for the Board of Mines on the phosphorous content of iron bars, the seer described the postmortem state in elaborate detail. He scrutinized what Christianity had found, at the last, inscrutable. He claimed to have been—not occasionally nor intermittently, but constantly—in touch with the spiritual world for more than a quarter of a century, all the while maintaining full possession of his rational faculties. "In company with spirits and angels, hearing them speak and in turn speaking with them," he was allowed to glimpse "wonderful things in the other life which," he said, had "never before come to the knowledge of any man, nor entered into his [imagination]."[18]

Death for Swedenborg was a passage, and he said that when man dies, "he carries with him everything that belongs to him as a man except his earthly body."[19] Memory is retained, and spirits can recall everything seen, heard, read, learned, felt, or thought through all their mortal existence. He reported that he had actually been permitted to undergo an experience simulating death, which revealed to him that when the heart ceases beating, the Lord immediately draws forth the spirit from the body, a process he said could be called resurrection because the form of the spirit is the human form. Indeed, in the first state a man enters after death, which is an intermediate realm between heaven and hell, he initially has the same face, manner of speech, and disposition he had on earth, so that unless he is closely observant, he will think he is still in the world. Reunions with relatives, friends, and acquaintances will take place at this stage, which lasts from a few days to as long as a year, depending on the degree of harmony between an individual's external and internal nature, but at length his ruling loves are revealed, all appearances shed, and he passes into a second phase of spiritual life. A man's true character now is manifested in countenance and form, all superficial ties are severed, and he associates only with kindred spirits. It is at this point that the wicked cast themselves into hell in search of congenial company, while the regenerate are received into the highest realm of the intermediate state where they are made ready for heaven. Instruction in doctrine drawn from the Word is given them by the Lord through the instrumentality of angels, and when their preparation is complete, angelic societies receive the newcomers with joy.

Throughout the Writings, Swedenborg uses physiological analogies in explaining points of theology, and a kind of methodological crescendo is reached in his description of heaven. It is where God dwells, and in the aggregate, the seer declared, heaven reflects a single man, which he called the *Maximum Homo* or Grand Man. The concept is a logical inversion of the Judeo-Christian idea that God created man in His own image, but in anatomical detail Swedenborg goes far beyond the simple correspondence Paul suggested between the Church and the body of Christ or, for that matter, the symbolism developed by Thomas Hobbes in the *Leviathan* when he described the commonwealth as an artificial man. Swedenborg's teaching is that the uses performed by the innumerable angelic societies of which heaven is composed correspond to the functions of the human body. "In general," he wrote, "the highest or third heaven forms the head down to the neck; the middle or second heaven forms the breast down to the loins and knees; the lowest or third heaven forms the feet down to the soles, also the arms down to the fingers."[20] This tripartite division reflects a more general separation into celestial and spiritual realms, the former consisting of angels who receive emanations from the Divine more interiorly, and consequently surpass in wisdom and love and are more closely conjoined to the Lord than the spiritual angels. The two kingdoms constitute the highest and middle heavens. In the lowest heaven are angels who receive influxes from both the celestial and spiritual realms, but in contrast to their inhabitants who admit truths more or less quickly into their wills, the angels of the lowest heaven simply live morally and believe in God without having any interest in further instruction. Swedenborg observed that there was no social intercourse between the three heavens and that furthermore, each was divided into societies according to the angels' interior affections. "All who form the same angelic society resemble each other in countenance in a general way," he said, "but not in particulars."[21] The garments of angels correspond to their intelligences, as their dwelling correspond to their rank, thus it seems that the heaven of one spirit is never identical with that of another.

The dynamic quality of the afterlife is stressed over and over again by Swedenborg, and nowhere in his portrait can one spy languid harpists plucking strings around the throne of God. "It is impossible to enumerate the employments in the heavens, still less to describe them in detail," he wrote, "for they are numberless, and vary in accordance with the functions of the societies. . . . Everyone there performs a use, for the Lord's kingdom is a kingdom of uses."[22] Indeed, angels find in their daily occupations the chief source of their happiness, and the seer observed that the many forms of service available inlcude ecclesiastical, civil, and domestic affairs. Spirits who as men loved the Word are called to be leaders in public worship, those who loved their country to the degree of putting the common good above personal need function as governors, and female angels who in the life of the body loved children tenderly are entrusted with the care and education of the youngest spirits. "Every child," Swedenborg was careful to point out, "wherever he is born, whether within the Church or outside of it, whether of pious parents or impious, is received when he dies by the Lord."[23]

He also declared that there is marriage in heaven, although not necessarily between men and women who were earthly consorts. Partners generally meet after death and live together for a time, he said, but only "if their inclinations are concordant and sympathetic do they continue their conjugial life."[24] When genuine spiritual union does not exist between those who contract marriage on earth—as in the case, the philosopher said, of partners who desire dominion over each other, belong to different religions, or engage in polygamous relationships—then the Lord provides suitable spouses, as He does for those who remain single in the world. Good people who truly prefer perpetual celibacy are escorted to the side of heaven because for Swedenborg the center belongs to those in conjugial love. He believed that such profound psychological differences exist between men and women, the former acting from reason, the latter from affection, that neither can attain his potential for perfection outside of a complementary union. Indeed, in the relationship between husband and wife he finds an analogy for the realtionship between love and wisdom in God. Whether Swedenborg believed that the physical aspects of earthly marriages are incorporated in celestial ones is unclear, however, as in *Heaven and Hell* he described the latter as "conjunctions of minds," while a decade later in *Conjugial Love* the seer said he overheard an angel tell curious newcomers that although heavenly unions were similar to those on earth even to "the ultimate delights," they were "much more blessed because angelic perception and sensation is much more exquisite than human."[25] In any case, the seer firmly declared that in heaven the fruits of marriage are not offspring, whose procreation is among the chief ends of earthly unions, but good and truth. As they return in appearance and vigor to the springtime of their youth, celestial couples advance in blessedness. With the help of their evils, which they are permitted to reexperience from time to time that they may take more intense delight in divine influx, angels make constant spiritual progress, but the process is never completed, for regeneration continues to eternity.

Reformation, however, is impossible for individuals who cling to their evil ways, and the Writings teach that hell is made up of those who revere falsity. The Lord sends no one there, but "it is man who condemns himself because he rejects good."[26] Swedenborg emphasized that "no one in the other world suffers punishments on account of the evils that he has done in this world, but only on account of the evils that he does [there]; although it amounts to the same thing," the seer observed, for "man continues the same as he has been in the life of the body."[27] As with the inhabitants of heaven, the character traits of the infernal spirits—in this case, contempt for others, envy, hostility, hatred, revengefulness, cunning, deceit, unmercifulness, and cruelty—are reflected in their appearance. "Hideous and void of life like those of corpses" is how Swedenborg described the faces he saw in hell, adding that some were "black, others firey like torches, others disfigured with pimples, warts and ulcers." The bodies were monstrous, but of the Lord's mercy, he said, the denizens of these regions do "not appear as loathsome to one another as they appear before the angels."[28] In its entirety, the form of hell is that of a single devil, but its geopolitical structure corresponds to that of heaven with three general regions in which are located the infernal counterparts of every celestial society. The Lord is the governor of all the hells, Swedenborg taught, and through His angels checks insanities and restrains uprisings. For demons who break the heaven-imposed law, punishment is swift and sure, and it is meted out by their fellow citizens who gladly avail themselves of any opportunity to inflict suffering. As crime deprives the evildoer of God's protection and lays him open to the assaults of his associates, fear usually serves to maintain the boundaries of acceptable behavior. The Lord's concern is to keep the hellish emanations of falsity and evil from overwhelming the heavenly outflow of good and truth, because man's precious freedom of choice can only be maintained in a spiritual equilibrium. Its destruction necessitates God's personal intervention, as occurred at the First Advent and again, the Writings boldly declare, at the Second.

A public, if anonymous, hint of his chiliastic expectations was given by Swedenborg as early as 1751 when, in the third volume of the *Arcana,* he interpreted the twenty-fourth chapter of Matthew, which attributes to Jesus certain predictions related to the consummation of the age, as referring to the end of the Christian Church. Seven years later, in the book entitled *The Last Judgment,* he declared that the eschatological courtroom drama had been enacted in the spiritual world in 1757, and that he had witnessed with his own eyes pronouncement of the divine sentence. In the vigorous prose of a war correspondent, the seer described how first Roman Catholics, then Mohammedans, Gentiles, and lastly, Protestants, were driven from their strongholds in the region between heaven and hell where, as the result of infernal emanations into the worlds, chaos reigned, thus obscuring the divine light intended for men. The judgment rendered against each group of spirits in turn involved exploration of the inner character of their evils, separation of basically well-intentioned individuals from the wicked, and their removal to a place safe from the cataclysmic upheavals which shook the intermediate realm prior to the descent of the unregenerate into hell. Benevolent spirits were then lifted up into what Swedenborg called the "new heaven," and with their assumption all things were "brought into order with a consequent restoration of the spiritual equilibrium which exists between good and evil."[29] The concomitant restoration of freedom of choice to men brought great joy to the angels, but the philosopher cautioned his readers against expecting any dramatic external manifestations of the reinstitution of spiritual liberty. The Last Judgment did not in itself make the frail strong nor mitigate the drag of hereditary inclinations toward evil. And yet, for those willing to accept it, Swedenborg shortly brought fresh hope.

Within the year he declared "the New Church is at this day being instituted," and presented, in short form, heavenly doctrines drawn from the Word, which explain how men should conduct themselves on earth if they seek admission to the new heaven.[30] In 1763 he declared that a new church was being established because the old church had falsified or set aside God's truth.[31] Three years later, he announced that from the new heaven a new church would descend to earth, and that together they would constitute the New Jerusalem.[32] It was in 1769, however, that Swedenborg's millenarianism flowered, and he wrote of his recently published *Brief Exposition of the Doctrine of the New Church:* "This book is the Coming of the Lord, predicted in Scripture! In the spiritual world there was inscripted on all my books, 'The Lord's Advent.' The same I also wrote by command on two copies in Holland."[33]

But this treatise was only a precursor of Swedenborg's great last work, *The True Christian Religion.* It was completed in June of 1770, and on the nineteenth of that month, he added a final paragraph:

After this work was finished the Lord called together His twelve disciples who followed Him in the world; and the next day He sent them forth into the whole spiritual world to preach the Gospel that the Lord God Jesus Christ reigns, whose kingdom shall be for ever and ever, according to the prediction in Daniel (VII, 3, 14) and in the Revelation (XI, 15) . . . . This took place on the 19th day of June, in the year 1770.[34]

The date marked a kind of second Pentecost—the occasion on which the New Church was established in the spirit world, after its descent from heaven. Its institution on earth would depend upon man's reception of the truths from the Lord upon which it must rest. These were communicated, according to Swedenborg's unequivocal declaration, by his own theological writings, in which was accomplished the Second Advent. His explanation of why the Lord cannot come again in person was that "since His ascension into heaven, He is in His glorified Human; and in this He cannot appear to any man unless the eyes of his spirit are first opened . . . therefore . . . He will appear in the Word, which is from Him, and is thus Himself."[35] The seer then left no doubt about whose pen God had made the instrument of His return.

This Second Coming of the Lord is effected by means of a man . . . who cannot only receive the doctrines of . . . [the New] Church with his understanding, but can also publish them by means of the press. I testify in truth that the Lord has manifested Himself to me His servant, and sent me on this duty; that He then opened the sight of my spirit, and thus introduced me into the spiritual world, permitting me to see the heavens and the hells and also to converse with angels and spirits, and this now continually for many years. I also testify that from the first day of my call, I have not received anything pertaining to the doctrines of that Church from any angel, but from the Lord alone while reading the Word.[36]

If the function of the Second Advent was to make possible the establishment of a new church among men, the timing of this eschatological event, as Swedenborg often repeated, was determined by the spiritually moribund condition of the Christian Church. Analysis of what he considered its errors was inextricably linked to his explication of the "heavenly doctrines" in his last book. He dates the onset of the decline of the old order from the Trinitarian proclamation of the Council of Nicea, but he is careful to incorporate in his teachings everything of spiritual value he felt remained in Christianity, including the sacraments of baptism and the Holy Supper, which he described as "two gates, through which a man is introduced into eternal life."[37] The former he considered a sign of the individual's introduction into the Church that he might know and acknowledge the Lord as Redeemer and be regenerated by Him. The latter is portrayed as "a signature and a seal" to "those who worthily approach it . . . that they are sons of God," but Swedenborg also wrote that "conjunction with the Lord is effected by the Holy Supper."[38] To the righteous and unrighteous alike He is present in the Sacrament, but this observation amounts to little more than a notation, and it pales beside the emphasis on the Lord's presence in the Word found throughout the Writings. As the end of his long life approached and the completion of what he considered his unique mission was at hand, the seer recounted a vision of a magnificent temple within which "lay the open Word, surrounded with a blaze of light." Gazing at the radiance, he perceived that the edifice was a symbol of the New Church and the book unfolded there a sign of the revelation of the internal sense of the Word. When he came nearer, he noticed an inscription above the temple gate reading: *"Nunc licet,* which signified," he said, "that now it is permitted to enter intellectually into the mysteries of faith."[39]

3

Intellectual Structure: The Separatists

But the divine dispatch which characterized the establishment of the New Church in the spiritual world was not replicated on earth. Indeed, Swedenborg had no illusions about the skepticism that would greet his claims. While declaring that the "New Church is the crown of all the Churches," he also observed:

That the Christian Church, as it exists today, . . . consummated and vastated, cannot be seen by those on earth who have confirmed themselves in its falsities, because a confirmation of falsity is a denial of the truth. . . .Every lunatic believes his own folly to be wisdom, and wisdom to be folly.[1]

To the inevitable "how long" question posed by an impatient subscriber to his teachings, the seer answered that "by degrees, as that [new] heaven is being formed, the New Church likewise begins and increases."[2] As the Rev. Mr. Collin explained to the readers of the *Philadelphia Gazette*:

Though persuaded of being commissioned from heaven to establish a new system of religion, Swedenborg had no desire to see it enforced by violent measures, nor did he exert himself in making proselytes, except by his writings. . . . He never intimated a wish to be the head of a sect, but indulged the fond hope that the ecclesiastical establishment would, by a tranquil, gradual illumination, assume the form of his New Church.[3]

Interest in Swedenborg's ideas developed among people of wealth and learning in Sweden, France, and Germany, but in the eighteenth century the soil most hospitable to sectarian seedlings was English. Even before the seer's death, a Quaker chemist William Cookworthy, who founded the British porcelain industry, the Reverend Thomas Hartley, a Northamptonshire vicar, and Dr. Husband Messiter, a prominent London physician, undertook at their own expense the translation of several of his treatises into English.[4] Many translations of the theological writings into French flowed from the pen of another London resident, Dr. Benedict Chastanier, a French surgeon who had first read Swedenborg in Avignon, and in his adopted country was the first to assemble a group of readers. An early English convert with ties to America was the Reverend Jacob Duché, a Tory exile from Philadelphia, who had served as rector of Christ Church and on the faculty of the College of Philadelphia (which became the University of Pennsylvania). In Manchester yet another Anglican clergyman, the Reverend John Clowes, became a receiver of the new doctrines, and for more than sixty years he preached them from within the Church of England, stoutly maintaining that Swedenborg's teachings were destined to permeate the established order.[5]

The question of separation from the "old" churches has been the most divisive issue in the history of the New Church. Ideologically, the General Church is descended from Clowes's English opponents who believed the Writings intended a distinctive ecclesiastical organization with its own authority structure, criteria for membership, and behavioral expectations. The leader of the separatists was Robert Hindmarsh, the young owner of a successful London printing business, who had been honored by an appointment as Printer Extraordinary to the Prince of Wales. The son of a Methodist minister, he had become acquainted with Swedenborg's teachings through reading *Heaven and Hell,* whereupon he formed a small circle for the purpose of translating and publishing the Writings. Initially, the group worshipped at Mr. Duché's chapel, but sentiment for separation gradually increased, and in 1787 the London Society adopted a constitution proclaiming that "introduction into the New Church is solely through the spiritual correspondent, baptism, performed in that church." It added that "conjunction with the Lord, and consociation with the angels of the New Heavens, are effected by the Holy Supper, taken in the New Church, according to its heavenly and Divine correspondent."[6] But a model for the institution of a priesthood to administer the sacraments was nowhere provided, and even after procuring a dissenter's license, members deliberated at length over the method of securing an ordained clergy. They counted within their own ranks several Anglican priests and Methodist ministers, but to grant the power of ordination to them was an impossibility. To do so, as one historian has written, would have been "a case of death giving life";[7] therefore, the little band of London New Churchmen seized what seemed to them the only viable option. At a historic meeting in 1788, they selected by lot twelve male members of the society to act as representatives of the rest in laying hands upon two old church clergymen and, by this rite, inaugurating them into the ministry of the New Church.

The society rented a chapel in Great East Cheap, and it prospered for a time. In 1789 members played host to their co-religionists from elsewhere in England, from Sweden, and even as far away as Jamaica, at a general conference. Those in attendance managed to agree on some thirty resolutions setting forth the beliefs of the New Church, and they established a custom of meeting regularly to consider ecclesiastical affairs. At the next conference, questions of catechetical instruction and liturgy were considered, and in 1791 a resolution was adopted giving clergy and laity equal voting power. Reacting against the democratic polity thus institutionalized by the conference, a minority, led by Hidmarsh, drafted a proposal for a hierarchical form of government, and when it was roundly voted down, withdrew from the conference. But the episcopal faction was never able to create a successful organization of its own. Indeed, its political ideas appeared stillborn until revived a hundred years later in America.

The initial growth of the New Church in the New World was coterminous with the Second Awakening (1795-1835), and as evangels like Lyman Beecher and Charles Finney extended westward their Puritan heritage, Swedenborgian missionaries like Jonathan Condy carried translations of the Writings beyond the

Alleghenies to Tennessee, Kentucky, Ohio, and Illinois. But the twin loci of power remained in the East, in Philadelphia and Boston, and the fundamental issue separating adherents in the two cities was the authority of the Writings. Inextricably linked to this question were others about the state of the Christian world and the importance of New Church education. As early as 1822, Philadelphian Daniel Lammot had written to Bostonian Samuel Worcester:

For my part I consider the theological works of Swedenborg . . . do not contain one contradiction or untruth. To believe otherwise is to deny that he was divinely commissioned; and to deny this is to place his claims to credibility on a footing with Joanna Southcote [sic] and Jemima Wilkinson.[8]

Neither the illiterate "woman clothed with the sun" nor the Universal Friend was as likely, however, to attract a New World Brahmin as the Swedish philosopher, and Worcester wrote to Lammot in reference to Swedenborg's theological treatises: "We read them for instruction and not for authority . . . . His works . . . are only an exhibition of such truths as the elevation of his mind enabled him to perceive. They are perfect in the same degree that regeneration was perfect in him."[9] And so the debate raged, but no American before Richard de Charms stated the sectarian position quite so forthrightly as the Yale-educated priest. In 1837, he wrote:

I am rationally convinced that Swedenborg was fitted and commissioned to teach the Doctrines of the New Church from the Lord immediately, therefore his doctrines are the Lord's doctrines, and are to be received with the Lord's authority. If Swedenborg is not what he says he is, then there is no New Church—the millennium is not at hand—the New Jerusalem has not descended—the Last Judgment is still in prospect; and we are once more afloat without chart or compass amidst all the conflicting theological elements in which the church has been and still is upturned, and shaken to its very center. All is once more guesswork. But if Swedenborg is what he says he is, then there is a totally different state of things. The Doctrines which he has taught are the Lord's, are to be taken on the Lord's authority, and are to be lived if we are ever to come to the Lord in His Word.[10]

In time, the acceptance of the divine authority of Swedenborg's writings was bound to transform the everyday existence of New Churchmen. Their religious beliefs would become the source of a distinctive conception of the world, the self, and the relations between them. Transmission of their perception of reality to their children would become a paramount value; indeed, it emerged as a central, if ultimately unrealized, goal of the first organizational expression of their distinctive views.

As a direct rival to the Boston-dominated General Convention, a body known as the Central of "Middle" Convention was formed in 1840 largely through the efforts of de Charms, then pastor of the First Society of Philadelphia. He argued persistently for day schools, and as a result of his efforts, they were established by a few societies. But more significant in the long run were de Charms's personal missionary efforts. A trip in the autumn of 1844 took him to Lancaster where he met William Henry Benade, a twenty-eight-year old Moravian minister who was destined to play a prophetic role in the affairs of the New Church, leading the people he had chosen for brethren to Canaan, while he remained on the Moab plains.[11]

Benade's paternal forebears were long and prominently connected with the *Unitas Fratrum,* a sect which traces its origin to the persecuted remnant of fifteenth-century Hussites. His father, Andrew Benade, came to America from Germany in 1795 to teach in the Moravian School at Nazareth, Pennsylvania, and married Maria Henry, the daughter of a wealthy Lancaster armorer, in 1811. Five years later, while the Benades were living in Lititz, Pennsylvania, where Andrew served a Moravian congregation as general pastor, William Henry was born. When he was six, his father was made bishop, and the family moved to Salem, North Carolina for four years, then returned to Lititz, and in 1836 removed to Bethlehem where Andrew was called to preside over the governing body of the Moravian Church. The year before, William had graduated from the Moravian Theological Seminary, and in preparation for his ordination, went to teach at the Brethren's Nazareth school, where he remained until 1841, the year following his reception of holy orders.

The young minister began to study the Writings in 1843 upon

having his attention called to them by several prominent lay members of the Lancaster New Church society. When he met de Charms the following year, the older man seems almost at once to have become his spiritual director. Late in 1844, Benade preached the Second Advent to a Moravian congregation in Philadelphia, whereupon the Brethren locked him out of their church. Shortly thereafter he was baptized and licensed to proclaim the gospel of the New Jerusalem. Called to the Philadelphia First Society as de Charms's successor, the priest began to take an active part in the affairs of Central Convention, and during its final years, leadership passed to him. Although he brought its members back into the General Convention, in 1852, after that body restored autonomy to individual societies, the chasm which separated his from more liberal coreligionists grew deeper.

The issues between them turned on the nature of the Writings, and in a striking analogy, Benade compared the "natural womb of the Virgin and the mental or internal sensual scientific and rational womb or matrix found in the mind of Emanuel Swedenborg."[12] The Swedish seer, then, played the same role in the eighteenth century as that played in the first century by Mary of Nazareth. Swedenborg "was called into a new and unheard office and miraculously fitted for it," his friend and correspondent Stuart said, and with an emerging sense of elitism he wrote to Benade: "When I declared . . . the Doctrines set forth by Swedenborg to be DIVINE, the word came as a clap of thunder on all *half and half sort of people,* and I knew it would."[13] Responding in the same vein, Benade declared: "Some of us have reached Mt. Sinai and others have not." He warned Stuart that "this game must be fought out to the end," and acknowledging the centrality of the question of authority, he predicted the New Church would "divide upon it."[14]

Brightly as Academy ideals burned in the hearts of men who found themselves in doctrinal harmony, the movement did not manifest itself organizationally for some fifteen years. After a while however, its underground status began to seem to its leaders morally distasteful and a material disadvantage. Referring to Swedenborg's vision of the inscription *Nunc Licet* above a temple door, Benade asked, in light of this "permission," was not ''a bold and open policy the . . . right one to follow?'' ''I for one,'' he wrote to Stuart, ''am willing to announce our policy, and to meet all opponents openly. . . . By this course, we gain a large membership and support and yet keep the helm in our hands.''[15] For his part Stuart replied that from the first he had ''felt the want of a *body* that everyone could see as well as a heart and lungs, that they could not see.'' The time had come, he suggested, for a visible organization, and he listed schools, a cathedral-church, and a publishing house, all supported by lay contributors, as proper Academy functions.[16]

John Pitcairn made the dream a reality. With Benade and two other New Church friends, he ''organized New Church Club'' on January 12, 1874.[17] Two days later he wrote a check for $500 as an initial contribution toward the expense of publishing a proposed journal, which the club members conceived as an organ of New Church scholasticism. Members of the old ''Harmony'' were invited at once to join with them, and Stuart wrote from Wyoming expressing his pleasure in being given ''a place in the—well, what do you call the body?'' ''It is well,'' he allowed, ''to keep the organization *non scripta.*''[18] But the next year, members named it ''Academy of the New Church.'' Internal propaganda was avowed as their collective purpose, and to this end a sum of $200 was appropriated to enable an Urbana student, who did not wish to take his theological training at the Convention school at Waltham, Massachusetts, to study with Benade and another minister instead. By the next summer, six young men were under the tutelage of Academy clergymen.

The year 1876 was marked, of course, by the nation's centennial celebration, and it was in Philadelphia, the site of the exposition, that the Convention delegates assembled in the early summer for their annual meeting. After its adjournment, members of the Academy remained in the city, and a quorum of twelve, who were to constitute an inner council, met at Dr. Boericke's home on the nineteenth of June. The previous day, they had given Benade the title of chancellor, elected Stuart as secretary, and appointed the two ministers together with the Pittsburgh laymen as a board of finance. Now they selected a half-dozen new associate members on the basis of doctrinal soundness and subscribed their names to a declaration of principles, prepared by Benade, which acknowledged "that the Second Coming of the Lord is not in person, but in the Word which is from Him, and . . . it is effected by means of a man, before whom He manifested Himself . . . Emanuel Swedenborg."[19] The Academicians reavowed their intention to train young men for the priesthood and to collect and publish the seer's manuscripts and the original editions of the Writings, as well as to prepare and publish collateral literature, as the purpose of their union. Listening outside the closed door of the meeting room,[20] Dr. Boericke's daughter heard the men conclude their formal organization of the Academy of the New Jerusalem with a recitation of the prayer Jesus taught the Galilean disciples He sent forth to proclaim the Good News on earth and whom, according to Swedenborg, He dispatched again in the spirit world to announce the gospel of the Second Advent on the nineteenth of June in 1770.

The councilors subsequently decided to publish a serial under Stuart's editorship and to centralize the instruction of candidates for the ministry, which Academy priests in various locations had undertaken on a private basis, by the establishment of a theological school in Philadelphia. Consequently, at the Academy's second anniversary meeting in June of 1877, application was made for a charter from the Commonwealth, which was granted in November.[21] The new journal, *Words for the New Church,* first appeared on July 30, 1877, and it caused something of a sensation on account of its forthright declaration of Academy principles.

A month later, a theological school was opened with a student body of eight. As it soon became apparent that the eager young theologs were insufficiently prepared for divinity studies, they were demoted to college work to make up missing subjects before being allowed to continue their professional course. When school opened in the autumn of 1878, the ministerial candidates were joined by several young men interested merely in collegiate studies. Together they took courses in mathematics and the classics, but also in English, modern foreign languages, and a variety of sciences, including electricity, climatology, mineralogy, astronomy, and zoology, and for many years no clear division existed between students in the college and theological school.[22]

At the commencement of 1879, the first two bachelor of arts degrees were awarded, and the first three bachelor of theology degrees were conferred the next year.[22] In addition to the recitations and orations traditionally given upon such occasions, the ceremonies were marked by the singing of Hebrew psalms.

In 1880 Chancellor Benade presided over what had become an annual nineteenth-of-June celebration, which that year was held in an idyllic country setting near Alnwick Grove, later Bryn Athyn, Pennsylvania. A trinal order of membership had been established, and initiations were now a part of the anniversary meetings. The highest order of Academicians were the twelve male members of the council, which was the governing body and included the chancellor as *primes inter pares.* The councilors could be either priests or laymen, but from the first, the latter were persons of some wealth. The middle order, created in 1880, was the college, and appears also to have consisted only of males, probably for the most part distinguished laymen, as the first initiates were a military officer, a lawyer, and two physicians.[24] At the base of the triangle were the associate members, both men and women, single and married, who were nominated by the collegians, approved by the councilors, and received by the chancellor. Badges of different colors distinguished the three orders of Academicians, and initiations were conducted as part of increasingly elaborate and wholly private worship services, which often closed with the singing in Hebrew of a ''secret'' anthem, *Shaloo Shalom,* ''Pray for the Peace of Jerusalem.''[25] The elaborate ritualism clearly functioned to heighten the members' sense of elitism as a people set apart not only from the world, but from the mainstream of the New Church in America. As one of the early initiates wrote in her diary, they saw themselves as ''pioneers,'' and as for herself, she said: ''It is . . . utterly impossible . . . to express the delight felt at being received into that body.''[26]

A small monthly journal, entitled *New Church Life* by its principal backer, John Pitcairn, first appeared in January 1881. Under the editorship of Edward P. Anshutz, brother of the painter Thomas Anshutz, it quickly became the official organ of the Academy, for the next year Stuart died and in 1884 *Words for the New Church* ceased publication. The periodicals represented an effort to reform the New Church at large, but Benade felt strongly that in the children of members lay the Academy's best hope for survival, and in September of 1881, a boys' school was opened with eleven students, ranging in age from six to fifteen under the direction of Louis Tafel. The next year, Dr. Boericke's daughter, Malvina, established an infant school, and at the same time, a private girls' school was started by Mrs. Sarah de Charms Hibbard, a daughter of Richard de Charms and an adherent of the pedagogy introduced earlier in the century by the German educator Friedrich Froebel. In 1884 Mrs. Hibbard's classes were taken over by the Academy, and the same year, Benade began a series of "conversations on education" with an eye to training New Church teachers. Reflecting his own fascination with the psychology of learning, these lectures were institutionalized in 1890 as a normal department under the aegis of the college. They emphasized Swedenborg's concepts about stages of human development and reflected characteristic New Church optimism about the perfectability of man. Rationality, liberty, and a spiritual conscience were the end results of "true" education, the chancellor said, and he placed a truly extraordinary burden on the parochial school by suggesting that its function was not merely to train students in the way they should go, but to prepare them directly for heave.

From the kindergarten through the college, religious instruction in the heavenly doctrines was an essential ingredient of the educational program. The Academy's secular curricula were distinguished from those of other late nineteenth-century schools by their emphasis on Hebrew, anatomy, and mythology. Following Swedenborg, the New Church scholastics felt that the Old Testament could best be understood when read in the language in which it was originally written. The anatomy courses were related to the Swedish seer's stress upon the correspondence of natural and spiritual forms. The perceived importance of studying classical myths was rooted in Swedenborg's teachings about the spiritual development of the race. But more important than the specific content of the curriculum at any level was a general New Church interpretation of the nature of reality and the course of history which pervaded every discipline and gave a distinctive cast to the schools.

Throughout the whole decade of the eighties, as the growing self-consciousness of the Academy was reflected in the establishment of educational institutions, estrangement increased between the Philadelphia-based New Churchmen and those allied with the General Convention. A relaxation of organizational rules in 1882 permitted considerable autonomy to state associations and opened the way for an episcopal form of government in the Pennsylvania Association, which in 1883 was reorganized as the General Church of Pennsylvania.[28] Benade was from the first its general pastor or bishop, but there also was a council of clergy and, to consider financial matters only, a council of laity, with John Pitcairn as chairman. As the result of another liberalizing Convention action, moreover, it became possible for individual societies in other states to forsake their own associations and affiliate with the General Church.[29] Groups in Concordia, Kansas, Chicago, and Brooklyn did so, and rather belatedly, the Convention began to realize that schism was inevitable.

The most immediate controversies involved wine and women. In 1887 the Convention-loyal temperance advocate John Ellis of New York published a book, *The New Christianity*, which climaxed his campaign for the use of unfermented grape juice in the Holy Supper. As Swedenborg nowhere prescribed total abstinence, and by every testimony enjoyed on occasion the fruit of the vine, members of the Academy saw no reason to eschew alcohol. They served wine at official functions, and indeed roundly defended its use. "Alcoholic preparations," it was said, "speedily reach the brains and impress the wonderful little glands, whose functions are the production of emotions and thoughts. Ideas flow more freely, the senses are more acute. As the ambrosial odor of the wine greets the nostrils, the affections are vivified, and thus form a social sphere which transforms a listless company into a chatty, brilliant and entertaining party." Swedenborg taught, it was noted, "that to imprison man's passions and appetites in the chains of enforced obedience is but to let his evils smoulder, which will burst forth in more irrepressible and direful forms when opportunity is afforded."[30]

The seer's anticipation of Freud is even more apparent in his teachings on conjugial love. While the Writings do not suggest that wine is an evil, and were interpreted by members of the

Academy as indicating that suppression of natural pleasure in wine might well be, they do say that extramarital sex is from hell, but add that it may be permissible under certain circumstances not involving adultery. The seer's teachings on fornication appear in the second part of *Conjugial Love,* and they always have been an embarrassment to some receivers of the doctrines. The academicians, however, considered it tantamount to blasphemy to disavow any portion of God's Word, and in 1888 the *New Church Life* squarely faced the issue. In answer to a reader's question, the editor declared: "It may be necessary for a true Christian to keep a concubine, and herein do we see the maxim exemplified that God looks not on acts but at ends."[31] The frank acknowledgment of the plain sense of the Writings reflected in the journal statement generated widespread reproach from those who did not regard all of Swedenborg's works of equal inspiration, and as the decade drew to a close, Benade's Convention enemies did not hesitate to accuse the twice-married chancellor, as well as other Academy leaders, of dwelling on the doctrine of permissions to excuse their own immorality.[32]

The Phiadelphia-based New Churchmen, and women, bore the calumny with dignity and grace. Far more painful than outsiders' deliberate misrepresentations was an internal quarrel which in 1888 resulted in Louis Tafel's severing his connection with the Academy he helped to found a dozen years earlier. Ostensibly the dispute stemmed from the minister's taking the part of parents who complained to the chancellor about their sons having been whipped at school. In protest, he sent his own children to a Quaker institution, and for this act of insubordination, Benade dismissed him from his pastoral duties and enjoined him from preaching in any society under the jurisdiction of the General Church of Pennsylvania. Tafel thereupon resigned from the Academy, labeling it "an intrument for the enslavement of the Church."[33] The disagreement over a case of discipline had been simply a surface manifestation of a serious subcutaneous disturbance fomented by a growing concentration of power in the hands of one man, who was both chancellor and bishop.

At the 1889 Convention meeting, sixty-three of Tafel's parishioners presented a petition protesting that he had been removed without the consent of the society and requesting a reversal of Benade's decree. Without investigating further, the assembled council of ministers ruled that the action taken by the bishop in no way affected Tafel's standing as a minister of the Convention. This decision appeared to abrogate the freedom the Convention had granted state associations, and at its meeting, the General Church drew up a resolution condemning the ruling.[34] Antagonism between the two bodies was escalated further by Benade's induction of William F. Pendleton into the third degree of the ministry in 1888, an action he described the next year as marking the establishment of the "Priesthood of the Academy."[35] Enraged by what it regarded as an audacious rite performed without its sanction and in the absence, moreover, of a request from the General Church of Pennsylvania, the 1890 Convention stigmatized the investiture as disloyal "to the spirit . . . of the Convention under which Mr. Benade holds the office of General Pastor."[36]

The crux of the controversy, of course, was that Benade and his followers no longer recognized the authority of an ecclesiastical body which did not share their view of the authority of Swedenborg's teachings. Although questions dividing the two factions were a complex of the doctrinal, the organizational, and the personal, overshadowing everything else were their irreconcilable positions on the nature of the Writings themselves. Nearly a century before, a New Church traveler had observed:

I have in my sojournings from place to place, lately met with two classes of readers of the Hon. Baron Swedenborg's work: One class holds it as a fixed principle with them that the Baron's Writings are really the Word of the Lord. . . . The other class readily allows the Baron to be a person highly illuminated by the Lord, and that his Writings are highly useful in opening the spiritual sense of the Word . . . but still they cannot allow his Writings to be upon an equal footing with the WORD ITSELF; for, say they, this would be raising the Baron and his Writings rather above their proper place, for none can be THE WORD but the Lord alone.[37]

A fervid belief in the Writings as the Lord in His Second Coming eternally present was, however, the *sine qua non* of membership in the Academy, and in the autumn of 1890, the long foreshadowed break between the two classes of readers of the Honorable Baron's work occurred to the regret of many and the relief of all. Meeting in Pittsburgh, November 13-16, the General Church of Pennsylvania adopted a resolution by a three-fourths vote which severed the slender thread which still tied it to the Convention.[38] "We had come to see," Bishop Pendleton later wrote, "that the step taken was inevitable, and that we could do our work better and in greater freedom as a separate and independent body, and consequently there was no other course to pursue."[39]

Early in 1891, by action of the council of priests and the council of laity meeting in joint session, the geographical limitation implicit in the appellation General Church of Pennsylvania was removed by changing the name of the sect to The General Church of the Advent of the Lord.[40] It was a superficial gesture which failed to address itself to the most critical problem faced by the New Church scholastics. For correcting the title designating the body which had separated itself from the Convention to correspond to horizontal reality did not bring it into accord with vertical reality. Whatever it was called, the General Church remained an external church responsible for worship. The internal church was the Academy, and its function was education, a use exaggerated, according to a priest involved, "far above . . . ecclesiastical and pastoral uses."[41] The general membership of the two bodies was identical, and some New Churchmen did venture to question the wisdom of the arrangement, but to the man at the head of both it made sense, and the joint council of General Church, meeting in 1891, and a general assembly of all its members, meeting in 1892, expressed their approval of the concept of two churches. It seemed to a participant, looking back upon the situation but a dozen years later, a matter of "man-worship,"[42] and, as it happened, the man worshipped had been felled by a stroke during a visit to London in 1889, after which his rule became increasingly autocratic. Old, ill, and recently widowed, Benade was irascible, suspicious, and intolerant of views opposed to his own. At a meeting of the council of the clergy in 1893, he offered to resign from the episcopate of the external church, then withdrew his resignation and returned to England where he married for the third time. In London the next year he presided over a meeting of "priests of the Academy" on the occasion of the visit of eight American clergymen with five colleagues residing abroad. At this session he demanded that the Church be governed not by a bishop who was the first among equals, but by a high priest responsible to the Lord alone. No appeal from his judgments was countenanced, but Benade did suggest that should the supreme ruler go "utterly wrong," members of the Church might "depart from him."[43]

It was a formula for the deposition of a tyrant that the Swedenborgians were finally to employ three years later. In the meantime, they bore with the chancellor with an external equanimity which suggests either continued enthrallment by his compelling personality or a visceral fear that a presumptive challenge would sink their sectarian ship on its maiden voyage. "The impossibility of the situation became more and more apparent," a contemporary observer noted, "but so great was the desire to maintain the peace, order, and uses of the Church, and so intense was the spirit of loyalty and gratitude to the 'grand old man' who had founded the Academy and chrystallized [sic] its principles, that no steps of a revolutionary tendency were ever taken by any of the leaders or members of the Church."[44]

The new Churchmen's anguish mounted in a rapid crescendo when, in the summer of 1896, at a meeting of the council of the clergy, the chancellor, who was then nearly eighty, announced that as high priest he alone was qualified to nominate his successor. The hollow right to accept, not to reject, his selection was left to the priesthood. Yet even in the face of undisguised megalomania, no move was made against the raving old bishop for eight months. Having left their congregationally inclined brethren behind in the Convention, the laity did not waver in its deference to the clergy in ecclesiastical affairs, and the clergy did not withhold their obedience due the primate in an episcopal polity until he turned on the one man he had himself raised to the third degree.

William Frederic Pendleton, vice-chancellor and bishop, bore the burden of his brother priests' unarticulated hope for the future of the New Church. When Benade went to England in 1893, he became head of the theological school, and during the bishop's long absence, the transplanted Georgian, along with others, established a home in the country north of Philadelphia where in 1891 the chancellor, with the approval of the council, had determined to remove the Academy. The national economic crisis two years later delayed the proposed erection of school buildings, and when Benade returned from his English sojourn, he adamantly opposed the project. Nevertheless, enough small children were residing in Huntingdon Valley by the autumn of 1896 to necessitate the establishment of a parochial school under the supervision of the vice-chancellor, and this development infuriated the bishop. To other priests Benade suggested that Pendleton was sabotaging the movement to which he had devoted a lifetime, and upon a chance meeting with the Reverend Homer Synnestvedt on January 20, 1897, he flatly accused the vice-chancellor of "hypocritical and malignant" designs. In "his usual cunning manner," the bishop said, "he is trying to break our work all to pieces," and then the old man betrayed his fear that William Pendleton was diverting the affection and admiration of John Pitcairn. When at that moment the vice-chancellor happened upon the two, Benade charged him to his face with "a devilish and malicious piece of business."[45] Two days later Pendleton sent the chancellor his resignation from the Academy, declaring he had lost confidence in his ability "to govern the Church, in his discretion as a leader, in his judgment of the character of men, and in his sense of justice in dealing with his subordinates."[46]

Meanwhile, learning of the confrontation, five ministers met with Benade and expressed their unanimous faith in the vice-chancellor's innocence. The bishop refused to withdraw any of his charges; therefore, three of them, convinced that the survival of the sect depended upon Benade's withdrawl from office, called a meeting of the full council of the clergy. When it became apparent, however, that two priests still supported Benade, they recognized that a less-than-unanimous appeal for his resignation would be hopeless, so the three ministers and two others, including Pendleton's brother, resigned from the Academy and the General Church. Benade accepted their resignations and those of three other priests who soon joined them. He then wrote to Robert Glenn, the president of the Academy corporation, stating that the "misconduct and final recalcitrancy" of certain of the priests of the church of the Academy had made it necessary for him to suspend the Academy's educational operations. Glenn replied that the authority he had exercised belonged properly to the corporation, but he would at once call a meeting of the directors. In the meantime, almost all of the members of the congregation worshipping in Huntingdon Valley withdrew from the Academy and the General Church. When the board met, it quickly decided that the disturbances warranted the immediate closing of the schools, but before the members adjourned, Benade joined them. Still an imposing figure—tall, with luxuriant white whiskers—he tallked to the men who called him "Father" about preserving the most valuable books in the library. Then the old bishop announced to them that he had substituted his own will for God's, and he resigned as chancellor.[47]

The church—not the church of the Academy nor of the Ad vent, but the *ecclesia* that was a few hundred people with shared beliefs—was not leaderless. A week before the final denouement, five ministers petitioned Bishop Pendleton to assume episcopal authority and receive them as priests. He agreed, stating: "We are not here to proclaim a new doctrine, but a new spirit and life in the doctrine. . . . There are two essential features of Church government and of Church life, without which there can be no organized Church. These are Council and Assembly."[48] Grasping each hand in turn, Pendleton constituted the petitioning ministers as a council of the clergy of the General Church of the New Jerusalem, and agreed to accept individual application for membership. Thus the sect was reorganized on the sixth of February in 1897, and in June an assembly of 152 persons would affirm it was rightly done. But no bells pealed that winter day. The launchers of the new venture were, as one later wrote, "in a state of anxiety, contrition, internal conflict and worry, amounting almost to despair."[49] Haunted by the thought of patricide, they were adamant that only in freedom could the Church prosper and awed at the enormity of the task they had undertaken. Now the reluctant revolutionaries must rebuild an ecclesiastical organization and an educational system while also constructing a community on the banks of Pennypack Creek.

4

The Physical and Social Structure: Establishment of a Community

After withdrawal from the Convention, the General Church was characterized by a great turning inward. Having severed the tenuous ties which bound them to the larger Swedenborgian body, the Academicians were compelled to confront questions about who they were, where they had been, and where they were going. A paramount necessity in the years following 1890 was the establishment of a psychosocial identity. Explicitly denying that the General Church was a sect, its leaders looked to the Writings in formulating a definition which proclaimed it ''a New Dispensation, the crown of all the Churches which have been since the beginning of the world, the glory of the latter days, in which has been fulfilled all prophecy, which can never be destroyed, but which is to last . . . through endless time, its beneficent influence, and its saving power increasing, among all the nations of the earth from generation to generation.''[1] The absolute surety about their collective relationship to God reflected in this self-ascribed identity was tempered by the New Churchmen's recognition of individual frailty. A core element in their belief system was the moribund state of the Christian world, and during the early nineties, a contamination theory was developed which portrayed residence among the mortally ill as a grave danger to the nascent religious organization. The chosen people had a need of Zion, and it was to the hills north of

Philadelphia that members of the Academy looked as they considered a site for the city of God.

That the Lord would lead them into green pastures, they had no doubt; nevertheless, as Bryan Wilson has pointed out, "a degree of tolerance and the availability of land are important facilitating circumstances for the introversionist sect to come into being as a colony."[2] Both conditions prevailed in eastern Pennsylvania at the end of the last century. Quakers, Mennonites, Amish, and Disciples of Christ had lived in the area in relative peace for many years, and while a smoldering fear and hatred of immigrant Irish Catholics flared briefly in the Natavist riots of 1844, acceptance of religious diversity represented more nearly than these disturbances the normative values of the society at large. Within a few miles of metropolitan Philadelphia, moreover, land was still plentiful. Where once the lodges of the Lenape stood among the beechwoods on the shores of a stream called *Pemapec*, Philadelphians escaped the city heat on summer outings in the years after the Civil War. Alnwick Grove in the Huntingdon Valley was a popular picnic area, and when nearby farmers could be persuaded to provide accommodations, townspeople, including some New Churchmen, would take their vacations there. Securing land, like lodgings, was mainly a matter of money which, to the enduring good fortune of the General Church, was supplied by John Pitcairn.

In 1889 the plate-glass manufacturer purchased for $14,000 his first thirty-five acres of land near the intersection of Paper Mill Road and Huntingdon Turnpike, the dirt toll road along which farmers drove wagonloads of produce to markets in Philadelphia. (See Figure 2.) Within the next four years, he acquired an additional 44 acres for $128,021, and by the time of his death in 1916, Pitcairn's real estate purchases in what was by then the borough of Bryn Athyn amounted to some 550 acres for which he had paid approximately $165,000.[3] In the early nineties the land consisted of grain fields and fallow rich with daisies and buttercups, pasture, orchards, and wooded hills. Winding through the valley was Pennypack Creek, crossed here and there by old stone bridges. Once it had powered grist mills, but as the turn of the century approached, the idle stream served only as a gentle passage for canoes in spring and summer and a solid,

Figure 2. The bridge over Pennypack Creek leads by Fetter's Mill where Welch farmers brought their grain to be ground long before the settlement of Bryn Athyn. The track in the foreground once carried nine trains a day directly between the borough and Philadelphia. Now passengers must change at an intermediate stop. *Photo by John M. Meyers.*

gleaming surface for skaters during winter months.

The decision to move the Academy schools to Huntingdon Valley was made by Chancellor Benade, with the approval of the council, in 1891.[4] Despite the reassessment of building plans and the eventual delay in construction necessitated by the Panic of 1893, a public announcement of the intended relocation was made in June of that year. The next month, John Pitcairn had two adjacent tracts of land, totaling ninety-eight acres, surveyed and laid out into fifty-five separate lots. Ground was broken about that time for his own home, a twenty-five room Norman style dwelling located on a fifty-acre estate, and in April of 1894 he sold the first of the lots. During the next twenty-two years he disposed of some thirty more to individual purchasers, realizing about $32,000 on the transactions. Pitcairn sold two-thirds of the properties for less than a thousand dollars apiece, and it is apparent that the whole real estate venture was more a colonial than a capitalistic endeavor.

Robert Glenn, the son and heir of New Churchmen Benjamin Glenn, gave up his own flourishing realty business in Philadelphia to assume general management of the settlement. In 1884 he and John Pitcairn had married sisters in a grand double-wedding ceremony, and now Glenn built his rambling Elizabethan house across the pike from his brother-in-law's estate. The rest of the residential construction in the community took place along two roads branching from a single trunk, which met again to form an oval path sloping toward the creek. Except for the philanthropist who made it possible and his executive officer, then, Bryn Athyn was initially settled by priests and laymen who lived in physical proximity analogous to their psychological unity of purpose and their spiritual solidarity. For a time, the industrialist retained the titles to nearly half the lots on which he allowed his co-religionists to erect dwellings. Families would often move to the country before their houses were finished, and an old frame structure on the Pitcairn property served them as temporary lodging. After relocation of the Academy, young bachelor teachers sometimes built one-room cottages and treehouses on another part of the philanthropist's land until they could manage more substantial residences. About a quarter of a mile down the lane that wound through Pitcairn's personal estate, in a locale known as Sleepy Hollow, were quarters mainly occupied by servants. Worship services were held at first in a grove of evergreens; then a barn on Bishop Pendleton's property served the Huntingdon Valley congregation until the autumn of 1895 when a wooden building, finished interiorly in Virginia pine and lit by a skylight, was erected for use as a chapel, school, and community center.

Only one store has ever existed in the New Church colony. It opened in 1910 when a retired actress turned part of her house into a confectionery where Breyer's ice cream cones sold for a nickel and anise-flavored candies for a penny. She later added notions and lace, but for the most part, settlers were dependent upon hucksters and a butcher, baker, and country storekeeper in the nearby village of Huntingdon. An errand boy would tour the settlement on a bicycle each morning taking orders, and deliver groceries and sundries in the afternoon by horse-drawn wagon. Almost everyone had a vegetable garden, fine fruit trees, and vines; many kept chickens, and a windmill pumped water for those in the community who did not have access to springs. John Pitcairn maintained a dairy for many years, and each New Church family's daily supply of milk was dipped from five-gallon cans brought around by wagon or sleigh, until people gradually switched to pasturized products. Coal was delivered by a drayman. While a one-track branch line of the Reading Railroad connected the settlement with Philadelphia, the nearest stop for trains on the major north-south line was a mile and a half away. But eventually, as many as nine trains a day would run directly between the New Church colony and the city, a reluctant gas company would lay mains, the tollgates would be permanently lifted, and the main highway straightened and surfaced with concrete. The fruits of technological advance, these improvements owed even more to political organization.

Recognizing the value of cooperation in the management of civil affairs, seven men owning real estate in the community met together in 1898 to form an association. They voted a local government into existence by a margin of six to one, and agreed that it should assume certain responsibilities borne until then by John Pitcairn, such as the cost of maintaining roads and the water supply system. Robert Glenn was elected president of what was called a Board of Control, and its members included, in addition, a priest and three laymen. Local taxes were levied based on the assessed valuation of property, which totaled $79,925, a village superintendent was appointed to supervise various housekeeping chores, a cemetery was laid out, and a hose and ladder were procured to ensure rudimentary fire protection. But the most significant accomplishment of the association was the adoption of a name for the New Church settlement. It was viewed as an essential prerequisite for securing a post office, a railroad station, and an express and telegraph office. The board also understood its sociocultural import. ''People like to be able to tell others where they live,'' it noted, and emphasized a name would contribute to community stability and solidarity. No agreement on one could be reached for an entire year, however, even though a committee, influenced by Bishop Pendleton, who had an affection for the Welsh language, and Samuel Hicks, who had a Welsh dictionary, submitted a list of eleven Celtic-sounding possibilities. At one point the board voted for the pedestrian ''Hillbrook,'' but it met with such widespread opposition that John Pitcairn finally dictated the choice of ''Bryn Athyn,'' a name created by the bishop for its spiritual significance. It can be translated from the Welsh as ''Hill of Cohesion,'' and so it was that the prolonged naming rite was concluded with a euphonious selection, which was confirmed on November 19, 1899 by a railroad timetable.[5]

Peter Berger and Thomas Luckmann have observed that practically the most important procedure for protecting the precarious reality of the subsociety from the nihilating threats of the world is the ''limitation of all significant relationships to fellow-members.''[6] Containment was precisely the methodology adopted by New Churchmen of the nineties in their effort to resist what another modern analyst has described as the social pressure ''against immoderate deviation from conventional religious patterns.''[7] They understood the dangers lurking equally in the Union League and the neighborhood soda parlor, and social isolation was the function of removal to Bryn Athyn. For them, as one member of the sect said, religion was ''a matter, not of faith, but of life''[8] The doctrinal basis for vicinal isolation was Swedenborg's observation that in heaven kindred spirits dwelled together

''Gatherings, where friendship emulating charity does not conjoin minds,'' he said, ''are nothing else than simulations of friendship.''[9] Life-giving relationships could only obtain, according to the Academicians, between persons with a shared belief system, and they sought to confine social intercourse, but not business, within the boundaries of church membership. An external friendship may be entertained for everyone with whom one comes in contact,'' the editor of *New Church Life* wrote in 1895. He then went on to note that:

Internal friendship can be only for the good of charity and the truth of faith, and hence for those in whom such good and truth are established, and hence, again, for those who have the true religion, and live according to it. A friendship with such as oppose, deny, or doubt one's dearest truths can have no real warmth; or, if it have, the gravest dangers threaten the soul. . . . If . . . the New Churchman enters the society of people whose religious life is opposed to his own, he separates himself to that extent from the society of the angels of the New Heaven. Can he afford to do this?[10]

Members of the General Church by and large decided they could not risk the danger, even though for some of them the move to Bryn Athyn represented the loss of a certain amount of social status. The Pitcairns, Glenns, and Starkeys all were listed in the 1890 edition of Boyd's Philadelphia *Blue Book*; indeed, between 1881, when the social register was first issued, and 1894, when the exodus to the country began, fifteen members were listed in the directory. During that fifteen-year period, six of the most prominent Phiadelphia Academicians died, one of those registered in the *Blue Book* resigned from the General Church, and one listed physician retained his practice and residence in the city. The seven who made their home in the country were dropped from the *Blue Book* after taking up permanent residence there, although other persons living within a twenty-mile radius of Philadelphia were listed under their suburban communities. The one General Churchman whose name also appeared in the *Social Register* upon its issuance in 1890 was excluded from that directory after his ordination.

Aside from those whose membership in America's inter-city

plutocracy was affirmed at one time by their inclusion in the Philadelphia edition of the national upper-class index, the initial settlers of Bryn Athyn included several physicians and merchants, a salesman, the owner of a coal company, a landscape gardener, and a farmer, as well as teachers, ministers, and other employees of the Academy. In 1900 eleven families kept a total of twenty servants, of which nine worked for John Pitcairn, who also employed a governess and a housekeeper.[11] Several members of the community were, like the plate-glass manufacturer, immigrants. For example, Carl Hjalmar Asplundh, whose sons established one of the nation's largest tree companies, left Sweden in 1882 at the age of twenty. What united these resident aliens and the men whose first American forebears crossed the Atlantic a century before the Revolution was a rational concern with religion. As an 1898 observer noted: "We have in the New Church mostly intellectual people."[12] In great measure they were men of achievement, and through the years fifteen Philadelphia readers of the heavenly doctrines have been included in such national indices of elitism as *Who Was Who, The Dictionary of American Biography,* and the *National Cyclopedia of American Biography.*[13] In their own eyes, however, the Swedenborgians' chief distinction was their affiliation with the New Church.

Academy leaders sought to create a we-they dichotomy. Tracing a lineal descent, spiritually speaking, from Abraham through Isaac and Jacob, one writer said:

Those who are from the genuine Church, who have the Word, and from it know the Lord, are in a direct line of the common stock, but those who are among the Church such as it is among the nations who have not the Word—are in a collateral line . . . [from] Nachor, Betheul and Laban.[14]

The key to their sense of elitism was not personal worth, but a conviction that they possessed a truth, which made them instruments whereby God's "purposes may be wrought in the world."[15] Christendom was described as so "tinctured with false doctrine and evil living . . . that from it exhales a sphere of contagion, calculated to spread and infect others with those falses [sic] and evils." By way of contrast, it was suggested that significant relationships with fellow receivers of heavenly doctrines could invest New Churchmen with stronger faith and surer charity. Where all are "one in the Lord, . . . the individual is perfected by the state of the whole society, and the whole is perfected from the perfection of its individual members, and thus finally with the LORD Himself."[16]

The abandonment of old customs and the severing of old ties demanded, of course, new customs which would help to cement new ties, and the Academicians evidenced a flair akin to genius for creating them. By the late 1870s, the nineteenth of June had been established as a day of special observance, marked by a worship service and social festivities, and in later years was entered on the calendar of the General Church as a distinctive festival. In 1894 the Pitcairns inaugurated the Founder's Day banquet in commemoration of the 1874 luncheon at which the industrialist, together with Chancellor Benade and Messrs. Childs and Ballou, had founded the "New Church Club." They invited all the members of the General Church in Philadelphia to a sit-down dinner in the Cherry Street hall, and after the completion of their Bryn Athyn home, they entertained members of the local congregation there at annual feasts of charity. By 1918, when the Academy had begun to generate a substantial body of alumni, a Charter Day was instituted, which combined homecoming activities with a procession in academic gowns. Following completion of the community building in 1895, Bishop Pendleton began holding a doctrinal class on Friday evenings, preceded by a church supper. Until his death, John Pitcairn donated the meat for the shared weekly meal for which the New Church diners each paid fifteen cents. Club life in the Huntingdon Valley centered from the first around the Civic and Social Club which, after the establishment of a local government organization in 1898, concentrated on providing opportunities for recreation and entertainment, including the raising of a glass with good companions. Notable among spontaneously generated traditions were summer strolls accross the fields to Willow Grove, some four miles distant, where outdoor orchestra and band concerts were led by the likes of Walter Damrosch and John Philip Sousa.

No method of more importance in forging a communitarian

spirit was devised in the early days of settlement than the rites associated with the establishment of homes. There were religious ceremonies connected with the breaking of ground, the laying of a cornerstone, and the dedication of a house, and all involved the participation of priests and people in services of song and prayer and scriptural reading.[17] Conducted sequentially, they led a family into a deeper and deeper relationship with the community. At the climactic rite of dedication, the officiating minister would charge husband and wife to declare their faith before assembled guests, which they would do by reading a passage from the Writings. The priest then would place the books of the Old and New Testaments and the Doctrine of the New Jerusalem in the sacrarium, a repository often built into the walls of Bryn Athyn homes, declaring the eternal presence of the Lord in His Word. Next he would lead the family and servants from room to room, dedicating each to its special use, and in the bedrooms he would place additional copies of the Writings. The husband and wife would acknowledge their indebtedness to God for all their endowments and possessions, and the minister would make the ritual declaration: "Except the Lord build the house, they labor in vain that build it." In closing he would bless the dwelling. Usually these ceremonies were followed by a reception for invited guests, and several weeks after the dedication of their spacious residence, the John Pitcairns extended a general invitation to all the members of the General Church still residing in Philadelphia to visit them in the country. Guests were transported to the festivities in special railway cars, then carried from the station in a procession of carriages engaged especially for the housewarming. The estate was called "Cairnwood," and the owners of even the most modest of the first Bryn Athyn residences followed the custom of naming their houses. (See Figure 3.)

The enforcement of strict endogamy was attempted in the newly established community by a barrage of sermons and articles in the *Life* stressing the dangers of exogenous unions and the importance of confining marriage within the Church. These jeremiads attested that no more critical issue confronted the fragile colony, and it underlay the emphasis upon restricting friendships to co-religionists. "Social life," it was said, "not only arises from . . . consociations beginning in marriage, but it

Figure 3. Cairnwood, John Pitcairn's Norman-style estate, serves as the residence of the executive bishop of the General Church. It was completed in 1895. *Photo by John M. Meyers.*

furnishes, as it were, soil, which . . . fosters the formation of new conjugial unions. Hence from it, as a garden and nursery . . . should be excluded with care all which does not harmonize with the conjugial, and especially whatever may injure it."[18] Swedenborg stated unequivocally that "marriages on earth between those who are of a different religion are . . . accounted in heaven as heinous; and still more so marriages between those who are of the Church and those who are outside of the Church."[19] The Academicians' literal ascription to this teaching reflected their essential differences with members of the Convention for whom endogomous marriage had no particular advantage given their hope that the heavenly doctrines gradually would permeate Christendom. By and large, their leaders remained silent on the subject of mixed unions, while the General Church declared that "to deliberately contract marriage with those who are out of the Church is to sin against the light." However faithful such relationships, they were regarded as essentially tenuous alliances disrupted at death in comparison to New Church unions which might endure for eternity. "In mixed marriages," it was said, "there can be no conjunction of minds and souls in the spiritual world, and therefore such marriages are for this world only, for the earth only, for time only, partaking of the nature of temporary marriage,—and therefore profane . . . in the sight of heaven." What General Church leaders described as the "disintegration" of the Convention was laid to its approval of exogamy, a practice the Academicians unhesitatingly labeled an "evil . . . threatening to overwhelm and extinguish the organized New Church."[20]

Apart from an instinct for survival, their vehemence was linked to their conviction that the "dire perversion of a heavenly truth" represented by mixed marriages "led to multiplied appeals to the divorce courts" and even "the condonement of unions subsequent to divorce."[21] The mid-nineteenth-century humanitarian movement to lighten the burdens of the sick, the imprisoned, the insane, and the enslaved gave impetus to a liberalization of divorce codes just as distinctive Academy positions on social issues were being formulated, and the New Church scholastics viewed with ambivalence the relaxation of civil proscriptions against terminating marriage. On the one hand, they believed that right action could not be compelled, and championed freedom of choice; on the other hand, they considered that "loyalty to the marriage bond is not only the safeguard of society, but in it lies the hope of heaven itself, and so it is to be cherished as the pearl of great price."[22] In the activities of the National Divorce Reform League, they saw "hope for no more than palliation,"[23] and from the Writings, they taught that no grounds existed for the dissolution of marriage save adultery. Swedenborg wrote that in the earthly union of husband and wife was expressed the spiritual union of truth and goodness, and the General Church maintained that "regeneration of man is not possible without the sphere of woman, nor the regeneration of woman without the sphere of man."[24] To couples caught in relationships where passion was long spent and even affection was consumed in dissensions, it sternly advised:

If conjugial love be not felt, it is to be simulated. If the marriage be not a true marriage, that is, a marriage which may endure for eternity, it is the duty of both partners to act as if it were, and by all possible means to make it appear to be such a marriage. . . . Differences, if they may not be overcome, are to be ignored, means for sympathizing one with the other and for acting as one are to be sought for and diligently used . . . the usefulness of such an attitude in marriage to the children which are born, is incalculable, for the first of birth-rights is that parents shall be united in the care and training of their children. There can hardly be conceived for children a loss more grievous than is sustained by those whose parents pull in different ways in this care and training. . . . Conjugial unions are not entered into ready made in the natural world any more than man is born directly into heaven. Such unions go hand in hand with regeneration and regeneration is a matter of growth.[25]

As early as 1889, moreover a question was raised in the council of the clergy about the propriety of New Church ministers solemnizing marriages between persons when one, or both, had been divorced for reasons deemed sufficient by civil law, but not sanctioned by the Word, and the conclusion reached was that they "ought *not* to solemnize" such unions.[26]

Swedenborg's teaching that "marriages on the earth are . . . seminaries of . . . the angels in heaven"[27] was the basis of General Church's adamant stand against birth control, a position inextricably linked to its valuation of marriage as the holiest estate. In 1894 the *Life* declared that "to imagine the conjunction of husband and wife, and at the same time an attempt to prevent conception, is too horrible and murderous and anti-conjugial to be entertained by a mind that is in possession of its spiritual freedom."[28] This view of contraception was codified in 1899 by Bishop Pendleton in his exposition and reaffirmation of "the Principles of the Academy," but in his declaration also lurked a suggestion that the practice was not unknown in Bryn Athyn. "Anything that operates against the end of creation is a sin against God, against heaven, and against society upon the earth," he said. "Such a sin is the prevention of birth in marriage. It is furthermore a sin against the conjugial itself; it is thus an abomination which is to be removed from the Church for its safety and preservation."[29] Three years later, the *Life* described contraception as a "well-nigh universal crime," a myopic view which reflected the journal's class bias, and it went on to suggest that birth control "makes a profanation of marriage itself, using it for the satisfaction of the lusts of the flesh and the defeat of the Divine End in creating a heaven from the human race."[30] The cult of Anglo-Saxonism, which pervaded American thought and politics at the turn of the century, also is an identifiable element in the General Church's opposition to interference with the arrival of offspring, and its official organ was wont to cite statistics showing the low birth rate prevailing among the native born as opposed to the high birth rate among United States residents of foreign extraction.[31]

The effectiveness of the Academicians' proscription against contraception is evidenced in the number of children born to the first settlers. John Pitcairn, whose wife died after the birth of her fourth child, had an unusually small family. Bishop Pendleton had ten children, and other households of this size were common —eight young Glenns, eight Vinets, nine Asplundhs, nine Doerings, ten Wells, eleven Odhners, twelve Homer Synnestvedts, twelve Paul Synnestvedts, twelve Roses. Nevertheless, a certain uneasiness with the apparent rigidity of the Church's position is detectable among these people who placed so high a value upon human freedom. The tension is clear in the bishop's address to a men's meeting in 1910. "Any truth made hard . . . and absolute," he said, "tends to the cultivation of a spirit of accusation, where lapse or apparent lapse is observed in others, tends to make an external rule of an internal principle of life. . . . Freedom of choice must always be present even to the extent of the permission of evil. . . . But this is not actively present if the pressure of public opinion is so strong that no choice is left but blind obedience."[32] In an undated letter to a friend, moreover, the New Church primate suggested that he had rethought his 1899 position. Acknowledging that "it is simply impossible for a woman to bear a child every year for twenty-five years," he conceded that her physical and mental health required an "interval between births, which provides that a child be born about every two years; and I am in doubt," he said, "whether the total cessation of the conjugial relation is the best means of providing for this. . . . The Church should not impose a conscience upon its members, but the members be individually responsible to the Lord . . . not only as to the delay but also as to the best method used to cause the delay—whether by total cessation of intercourse, or taking advantage of the intervals." Evidently making a fine distinction between abstinence and rhythm, the bishop concluded: "There is reasonable doubt as to the best method to pursue in this case; and in all matters of doubt let there be charity and toleration, and if we err, let us err on the side of mercy."[33]

The existence of large families within the General Church was responsible for the sect's principal charity, an orphanage. As early as the mid-eighties, a movement was initiated to provide for the nurture and education of New Church children who had lost their parents, and at the turn of the century, the Academicians seemed to be possessed with what in retrospect seems a somewhat bizarre fear that a great many orphans would become their collective responsibility. In 1899 Bishop Pendleton announced the creation of a fund which would ensure that "such children not be lost to the Church," and expressed the hope that in time it would so grow that the sect would be able to take in orphans from the world at large.[34] An immediate function of the orphanage, it was asserted, was to "bring to parents of small means a feeling of relief and security in regard to what might occur should they be called to the other world."[35] In the long run, the institution, whatever from it should take, was seen as an evangelical tool. The mass conversion of anyone but little children, to whom they could introduce the heavenly doctrines at a tender age, appeared nearly hopeless to the General Church leaders, and they confessed that "in our efforts to reach the simple we have been entirely at fault." William Pendleton's brother, Nathaniel Dandridge Pendleton, who later succeeded to the primacy, lamented that the "New Church has been distressingly 'intellectual,' " but conceded that the time had not yet come to appropriate other techniques for spreading the Gospel. Lest anyone become too anxious over the state of the unwashed, it emphasized that the present use of the General Church was "to educate the men of the Church for heaven."[36]

The distinctiveness of the Academy as a school lay in its concept of the proper goal of education. Attuned to both the voices of reason and revelation, the early New Church teachers derived from the Writings their central dogma that the two foundations of truth are nature and the Word of God. For them the separation of religious and secular education was unthinkable, as only their conjunction made it possible for a child to grow in wisdom and in understanding of man and the world. They believed in a correspondence between Latin and algebra and the lore of angels. The Convention position was that "the Church, being an ecclesiastical organization, has no more right to invade the strictly lay field of education, than it would have to go into the business of making shoes."[37] In the tradition of Richard de Charms and William Henry Benade, the Bryn Athyn scholastics eloquently maintained:

The truths of the church are as fugitives and vagabonds in a land where they are only taught perfunctorily, and where men are not willing to subordinate all to their teachings, and also to sacrifice other things to have them taught. Israel will always be a stranger in a strange land as long as children are allowed to grow up in a careless fashion among the nations.[38]

Mustering objective evidence in support of such subjective disparagement of the Sunday School system, the *Life* cited a 1902 Convention report stating that of 1,700 infants baptized since

1870, only 300 were members of a Swedenborgian society. By way of contrast, it asserted that of the more than 200 young people who had been educated in Academy Schools, only four had drifted away from the General Church.[39] "In New Church education alone," a scholar-priest declared, "is to be found the key to the . . . growth of the New Church."[40]

Acknowledgment of the propaganda value of schools was not the same, however, as equating them with the ecclesistical organization. In breaking with the chancellor, the leaders of the sect sought to clarify the relationship of the Academy to the Church. The former was to be an educational arm of the latter, and W. F. Pendleton corrected what many considered the exaggerated conception of the teacher's responsibility for the child's lot, which had been fostered by Benade. Speaking of the scope and limitations of New Church education, the bishop suggested that while it was the function of the Church to prepare souls for heaven, the function of the schools was to prepare young people for civil life and the Church.[41] Upon the reorganization of the religious body, moreover, Robert Glenn, chosen president of the Academy board of directors in 1895, became the chief executive officer of the institution, as Pendleton did not assume the title of chancellor. It was generally recognized that the financial stability of the schools during the final years of Benade's administration was attributable to lay control of the property; and while at the request of the board, Bishop Pendleton served as superintendent of the Academy, he was elected president only after Glenn's death in 1902. Ever since, the ecclesiastical leader of the General Church also has been the head of the schools, if only nominally in recent years.

A testimony to the effectiveness of the cooperation existing between clergy and layman is the fact that despite the disturbances of the winter 1896-97, classroom work was interrupted for only about two weeks. The college and boys' school resumed operation in Huntingdon Valley in the middle of February, after having been closed early in the month, and the several instructors, who had pedaled bicycles back and forth between the country and the city for more than a year, discontinued their strenuous exercise. The girls' school continued in Philadelphia until the end of the spring term, and the following October the various parts of the Academy were reunited in Bryn Athyn.

From the winter of 1894-95, primary classes had been held in the country, first in private homes and then in the community center. After the break with Benade, the lower grades of the boys' and girls' schools were combined with the local school to form the Bryn Athyn elementary school, an institution allied with the Academy, but to a degree separated from it. The college, which had been distinct from the boys' school, was merged with the secondary forms, and what became known as the seminary assumed the responsibility for educating young women. In 1904 a normal school was recognized as a distinct Academy department, but in 1914 it was merged with the college to form a separate, coeducational institution for tertiary education. The move was designed to retain longer in the sphere of the Church students who were beginning to attend secular universities in increasing numbers.[42] The theological school was continued as a graduate institution for the training of New Church clergy.

From the time of their reestablishment in Bryn Athyn, the financial position of the Academy schools was secured as a direct result of John Pitcairn's generosity. In 1899 he established a $400,000 endowment fund, and eleven years later added another $100,000 to it and an equal amount to a pension fund for teachers. In addition, during the first decade of the new century, the philanthropist financed the construction of seven handsome stone buildings on the Academy campus. The continued munificence of the Pitcairn family always has made it possible to keep tuition and fees far below cost, and a system of reduced charges and work scholarship has meant that an opportunity for a distinctive New Church education always has been available to every member of the sect living in Bryn Athyn. From the beginning, however, a portion of the high school and college enrollment has been made up of boarding students, and in 1910 the number of Canadian pupils was such that a school picnic was held on the twenty-fourth of May in celebration of Queen Victoria's birthday. The size of the total student body was eighty-two that year, an increase of fifty-seven students since 1900; and a decade later, enrollment was 118.[43] The primary requirement for admission was baptism in the General Church. (See Figure 4.)

Public worship was a part of daily activities in all the Academy schools. Courses in religion were taught at every level. The secular curricula continued to be distinguished by their emphasis

Figure 4. Academy students often found summer employment supplementing the regular domestic staffs in Bryn Athyn's large houses. Three young women, who worked at Cairnwood, are pictured on the grand stairway in a photograph taken around 1914. *Photo courtesy of the Academy of the New Church.*

upon Hebrew, anatomy, and mythology after the reestablishment in Bryn Athyn, and lectures on marriage derived from Swedenborg's teachings about conjugial love were given to upper-form students.[44] Nevertheless, a degree of dissatisfaction existed among the most thoughtful observers of the General Church educational system, which was related to a perceived lack of genuine distinctiveness in the Academy schools. "A new theology," it was said, "involves a new science, and a new science involves a new education." Possessors of the former in the works of the Swedish seer, New Churchmen had yet to develop the latter in terms of a new scholarship from the Writings. "Do we realize," one analyst asked, "the vastness of the task and the greatness of the mission?" Doubtless a few did, but the little band of dedicated teachers, including a Harvard-trained chemist who became a New Church minister and an ex-theolog who earned a Ph.D in psychology at the University of Pennsylvania, had scant leisure for the requisite research.

The cooperative spirit between priests and laity, which characterized the reorganization of the schools following the separation from Benade, also marked the process of creating an organizational structure for the General Church. By the time the first general assembly of that body was held in Huntingdon Valley in June of 1897, 287 persons, residing in Georgia, Illinois, New York, Ohio, Pennsylvania, Canada, and England, had been received as members. More than 150 of them attended the early summer meeting at which various papers were read on ecclesiastical government.[46] The atmosphere was one of conciliation, and the effort to create a new polity went forward amid a general agreement that the time for healing was at hand. To facilitate freedom of discussion, the council of the clergy withdrew from any collective relationship with the general assembly, and the bishop submitted his resignation to the council. He then delivered an address, published as "Notes on Government of the Church," which one observer described as "especially influential in restoring a state of harmony and confidence."[47] It emphasized "use" as a basic organizing principle, and distinguished between the ecclesiastical functions of the clergy and the civic functions of the laity. "The recognition of a common head," Bishop Pendleton said, "should be a voluntary act of all parts that constitute the common body." He suggested that the choice of primate should originate in the council of the clergy, taking "the form of an *invitation* to some one priest to exercise the office of Bishop over the Church," and that the laity's role involved *"recognition* of the one so invited by the clergy." Members of the Church, Pendleton stressed, could for just cause "withdraw that which they have given," but he counseled against creating in advance of necessity the actual machinery for removal of a disorderly or incompetent primate.[48] One discussant expressed the scorn felt by many for the term "High Priest," as used by Benade; others reviewing the immediate past with the utmost candor, warned that their recent experiences with an unbalanced, tyrannical old man should not impel the framers of the new government to enact precipitate restrictions upon their bishop.[49] Equally fearful of autocracy and anarchy, the assembly voted to place the administration of ecclesiastical affairs in the hands of the council of the clergy until the next meeting, and chose a provincial, executive committee of laymen, under the chairmanship of John Pitcairn, to administer the financial affairs of the Church.[50] Bishop Pendleton withdrew his tendered resignation and was confirmed as head of the ecclesiastical body. In 1899 a permanent executive committee was elected, and the bishop formulated the doctrinal position of the sect on central issues identified through the years as Academy principles.[51] (See Appendix.) His codification represented not so much a statement of faith as an attempt to apply the heavenly doctrines to the life of the Church.

It is primarily, however, "out of the context of concrete acts of religious observance," as Clifford Geertz has said, "that religious conviction emerges on the human plane." As cultural performances, rituals constitute for participants "not only models of what they believe, but also models for the believing of it. In these plastic dramas," the anthropologist notes, "men attain their faith as they portray it."[52] But in reaction against the exaggerated ritualism fostered by Benade, the symbolic activities associated with public worship received scant attention for the first few years following the reorganization of the General Church.

Still, for Bishop Pendleton, they remained a matter of importance, and as early as 1900 he announced that "the need of a Liturgy more suited to the genius of our work seems quite apparent."[53] A man whose forebearers had been associated with the Anglican communion for centuries, he was drawn to High Church ceremony. He did not believe that a liturgy could be created *de novo* any more than a painting, and he noted that while dissenting sects had been inclined "to disregard all previous forms of worship, . . . the Episcopal Church forms were several times sanctioned in the Writings." Swedenborg's theological treatises were "not a new revelation of externals of worship," the bishop observed, "and the Lord leaves us free to choose these." He noted and regretted that in the past the New Church as a whole had been influenced by Protestant models, which he felt were "cold and lacked the elements of devotion and humiliation . . . needed in New Church worship."[54] His dissatisfaction reflected a recognition of the importance of both cognitive and affectional orientations for human growth, and he saw in ritual an arena of convergence for conceptual and dispositional aspects of religion. In the ceremonial he saw an opportunity to reenforce intellectual commitment to a belief system. The internal of worship upon which salvation depended involved "charity, or the shunning of evil, and the honest performance of one's daily use," but in external worship, Pendleton noted, "the internal is strengthened and confirmed."[55]

The *Book of Worship* initially used by the General Church had been prepared by order of the Convention in 1876. It contained a simple order of service for the morning and the evening patterned on the *Book of Common Prayer*. Its most distinctive features were a version of the Lord's Prayer, beginning: "Our father, who are in the heavens," and a hymn, entitled "The Second Coming," which included a stanza saying: "Blessed be he who comes to reign/In Zion's happy land!/Jerusalem is built again,/And shall forever stand." The tone was unmistakably Broad Church, and as a replacement Bishop Pendleton produced in 1908 a comprehensive new *Liturgy for the General Church of the New Jerusalem*. Taking its form from the Anglican service, the focus of the ritual was not, however, on Christ crucified, but on Him glorified. The volume provided twelve general offices for use on Sundays, and the rubric called for three lessons, thereby introducing into the service recognition of the threefold revelation that the General Church believed had been given by God under the form of the Law, the Gospel, and the heavenly doctrine. A section on the latter represented the most detailed public expression then extant of the sect's belief system as derived directly from the Writings. Several credal statements were included for use on various occasions, and in the most frequently repeated, the worshipper declared:

I believe in the Lord Jesus Christ, the almighty and everlasting God, the Maker of heaven and earth, the Redeemer and Savior of the world. I believe in the Sacred Scripture, the Word of God, the Fountain of wisdom, the Source in the Scriptural Sense of the Word, and in the Heavenly Doctrine of the New Jerusalem. I believe in the New Angelic Heaven in the New Christian Church, in the communion of angels and men, in repentance from sin, in the life of charity, in the resurrection of man, in the judgment after death, and in the life everlasting.[56]

Antiphons, which consisted of responsorial readings, were related not only to such general Christian themes as faith, repentance, and thanksgiving, but also to specifically Swedenborgian themes—the Second Coming, the New Church, and the unity of God. Scant emphasis was placed on the sequential events in the earthly life of Jesus, but the adoption by the General Church of the two Christian festivals of Christmas and Easter is reflected in the hymnody included in the *Liturgy*. No special services were prepared, however, either for these holy days or for the nineteenth-of-June celebration, the sect's unique festival. The texts for readings from the Old and New Testaments adhered to the style and language of the King James Bible, as Pendleton believed that the time had not yet come for a new translation of the Word.[57] Music occupied an important place in the liturgy. Great stress was laid on chanting, and an English stockbroker, Charles James Whittington, devoted years of his leisure to preparing a psalmody, which was financed by John Pitcairn.

With the exception of the celebration of the Holy Supper, which closely resembled the Episcopal communion service, the distinctive understanding of the New Church was reflected in the sacraments and rites given in the 1908 worship book. In baptism parents were charged with the responsibility of having their children instructed "in the Word of the Lord, and the Heavenly Doctrine of the New Jerusalem." The voluntary, confessional basis of membership in the sect was emphasized in the confirmation service in which the candidate was asked if, in addition to believing in the "Lord Jesus Christ, the one only God, heaven and earth," he believed in the "Word of the Lord, and in the Heavenly Doctrine of the New Jerusalem." Linked to the central importance of marriage in the world view shared by members of the General Church was the inclusion among their rites of a betrothal service. It was a ceremony celebrated before parents and intimate friends, retaining thereby more a private than a public character, in which engaged couples were asked to declare their "undivided love for each other, and . . . mutual consent to become one in affection and thought, and in all the ends and purposes of life." In the marriage service itself, the bride walked to the altar rail not on her father's arm, but at the right hand of the bridegroom, because the Writings taught that such was the custom in heavenly weddings in which the bridegroom represented wisdom and the bride love. During the ceremony the two were instructed that marriage was "most holy, not only from its origin in heaven from the Lord," but also because it was "seminary of the human race and . . . of the angelic heaven." After the priest pronounced the couple husband and wife, they changed places, representing thus the Church, that is, wisdom and the love of wisdom. In the ordination service, the candidate for the ministry was instructed that "the priesthood was representative of the Lord as to all the work of salvation from Divine Love." Finally, the service of burial of the dead was notable for the absence of any mention of resurrection of the body, and the emphasis throughout the brief ceremony was on death as a "gate of life" after which the "spiritual body is released and lifted up . . . to live in the spiritual world forever."[58] Throughout the *Liturgy* a great deal was left to the discretion of ministers, as the bishop regarded the work as experimental and stressed that only by trial and error could the New Church discover the forms "best suited to express the states and conditions of its worship."[59] Revised liturgies were issued, in fact, in 1939 and again in 1966, but in the original and in later works, the reality intensified by symbolic activities was Swedenborg's dualistic ontology. The public ritual enacted in Bryn Athyn corroborated the belief of participants in the correspondence between the extant realms of nature and of spirit.

The representation of heaven on earth in human art forms was nowhere more magnificently rendered in the New Church than in the architecture of the Bryn Athyn cathedral. (See the frontispiece.) In design and execution, it constituted a stunning achievement, which many of the first generation lived to see as a towering symbol of their faith. The earliest Huntingdon Valley sanctuaries were modest affairs. The main building on the Academy campus contained a chapel, and it was there that the congregation had begun to hold Sunday services in 1904, after having worshipped successively in an evergreen grove, a barn, and a community center. Meanwhile, residents of the colony established a church building fund, and in 1908 John Pitcairn took it over, assuming full financial responsibility for the erection of a house of worship. The site finally chosen was a hill overlooking the creek and the countryside. It was property the philanthropist once had given to his only daughter, Vera, who died in 1910 at the age of twenty-three. Architectural plans were solicited from a Philadelphia firm, and Pitcairn was moving toward acceptance when his eldest son, Raymond, voiced such vehement objections that the plate-glass manufacturer appointed him a committee of one to select an architect and build the church.[60] A young attorney lacking any formal training in architecture, Raymond immersed himself in studies of medieval forms, which had captured his imagination on numerous trips to Europe. Seeking cognitive confirmation of his affection for the period, he wrote that "early Gothic art, which was the glory of the twelfth and thirteenth centuries, was inspired by truths of doctrine of the unperverted Christian Church."[61] Although Bishop William Pendleton, whom Raymond consulted fully about the design of the cathedral, briefly considered a radical departure from traditional forms in terms of a literal "upper room" where worshippers would receive communion, it eventually was decided that in architecture, as in liturgy, to draw upon what the New Churchmen considered the best of the past. They found appropriate models in the great medieval cathedral built 500 years before the Last Judgment, which, Swedenborg taught, was the spiritual event confirming the consummation of the Christian world.

The felicity of the form for a New Church temple is suggested by Otto von Simson's observation that the Gothic "church is, mystically and liturgically, an image of heaven." The vision of the celestial city, as recounted in Revelation, was explicitly related to the earthly edifice in the language of the dedication ritual, and as von Simson further notes, medieval theologians frequently tried "to interpret all important elements of Gothic architecture as almost literal reinterpretations of features of the Heavenly Jerusalem as described by St. John."[62] Augustinian aesthetics demanded the anchoring of beauty in metaphysical reality, and the concept of correspondence, so basic to the Writings, pervaded the masterworks of the builders of Gothic churches. At Chartres and Amiens, luminosity and proportion are the ordering principles, and quite apart from their formal value, it seems quite fitting that Raymond Pitcairn turned to an architectural style wrought of these prime ingredients in seeking to build a house of worship for subscribers to a heavenly doctrine in which God is portrayed as order itself and His love as a sun.

The Boston firm of Cram and Ferguson, perhaps the most respected interpreters of Gothic architecture in America, were engaged in 1912 to design Bryn Athyn's cathedral-church. As plans were discussed, the Pitcairns' conception of a building of flawless design soon led the architects to set aside all question of cost; nor was time to be taken into account as a limiting factor.[63] Ralph Adams Cram made preliminary sketches in response to liturgical considerations outlined by Bishop Pendleton, and while these were received with enthusiam, the design initiative never rested wholly with the architect. Like a medieval patron, Raymond Pitcairn assumed a role in the construction of the church which far surpassed that of a man who merely commissions a building. As time passed, there became less and less room for another person between him and his chief mason, but initially the relationship between owner and architect was a highly creative one. Unable to read drawings with any confidence, the young lawyer requested Cram to prepare a quarter-inch plaster model of the proposed cathedral and ship it to Bryn Athyn for him to study. It arrived in June of 1913, and after several weeks, Raymond sent the architect a seven-page letter suggesting various changes. Cram accepted them with good grace, and ground was broken for the church that autumn.

The use of models was a medieval practice, and as a basis for criticism and design alteration, it contributed immeasurably to the beauty of the finished work. Another practice, dating from the eleventh century, which played a significant part in the final perfection of the cathedral, was direct employment on a time basis of artisans and workers. "I became convinced," Cram said, "that it mattered far less how a building was designed than how it was done."[64] In August 1913 he wrote to the Pitcairns proposing the establishment of a guild on the construction site for the making of stained glass and furniture.[65] Their response was positive, and "in a space of short time," the architect said:

The idea of a sort of cooperative, neo-medieval organization for the building of the church grew into dominance, and every new suggestion along these lines was welcomed, put in force and further developed, until at last, by the time the walls began to rise above the ground, the system had reached a point of development never achieved in any place since the close of the Middle Ages.[66]

General supervision of the growing group of craftsmen, at first stone cutters and joiners, then metal workers and glass makers, and finally stone carvers and cabinetmakers, fell to Edwin T. Asplundh. At Raymond Pitcairn's request, the eldest son of the first treasurer of the General Church, who was graduated in 1912 from Pennsylvania State University and forty-five years later became chairman of the board of the Pittsburgh Plate Glass Company, left his newly established civil engineering practice across the continent in Washington and returned to Bryn Athyn to supervise the more than 100 workmen employed in the shops clustered on the cathedral hill. (See Figure 5.)

The church builders, whose presence in Bryn Athyn increased the total population of the community by about one-fifth each day, constituted a colony within a colony. They were men of various ethnic and religious backgrounds, speaking several different languages. A few established homes in the Huntingdon Valley area, but most tramped up the road from the railway station to the cathedral site each morning and down again each evening to board a train for Philadelphia. No effort was made to proselytize them; their social identities excluded them from participation in community life, but on a professional basis, their

Figure 5. Stone by stone, immigrant masons raise the nave clerestory wall of the Bryn Athyn Cathedral. They came to work each day by train from Philadelphia. The granite used for the exterior of the building was quarried beyond the first hill on the north bank of Pennypack Creek. *Photo courtesy of the Academy of the New Church.*

employers treated them with the utmost respect. "From the start," Cram said:

The policy was followed of arousing their enthusiasm and emulation, giving them the widest leeway in original work, and crediting them publicly with everything done that deserved recognition and praise. At every visit of the architects, the foremen formed a party of inspection, and the new work was examined and criticized, examples of notable achievement, even in the surfacing of a piece of ashlar, being traced back to the individual workman, who then and there was commended to his face.[67]

Integrity of performance and quality in issue were the watchwords of the whole operation. As a Scots carver who cut tracery and capitals for two decades said: "Here with Mr. Pitcairn excellence in the work was everything. He demanded truth and honesty, for these were what the church stood for."[68] No talent, whether for carrying a hod or stoking the forge, was insignificant; no amount of effort was superfluous, and finished sections of the building actually were torn down if reconstruction held out the promise of improvement. Pride in workmanship was encouraged at every level, and the final product of this labor attests to the ability of the craftsmen to work side by side, attuning their individual styles and techniques to a momentarily common vision.

The metamorphosed granite used for the exterior walls of the cathedral was taken from a quarry less than a mile from the church on the north bank of Pennypack Creek. A road was built from the construction site to the excavation, and up this twisting path teams of horses hauled ton after ton of rough-hewn stone. By the nineteenth of June, 1914, the work had progressed sufficiently to lay a boulder, uncut by men, as the cornerstone of the church. On its weather-smoothed surface were carved the Hebrew characters signifying "the Head of the Corner," and before the whole of Bryn Athyn, it was placed at the southeast corner of the sanctuary in a ceremony conducted by a fully vested Bishop Pendleton, a sixty-nine-year-old man with a trim white beard in a flowing white alb draped with a red stole and cinctured with a golden cord. At this point in the building process, Raymond Pitcairn had given up his law practice to devote his time to working on the design of the cathedral with the draughtsmen Cram had assigned to the Huntingdon Valley project. He undertook the search for suitable timber, and found in the great white oaks growing nearby wood for beams large enough to span the nave and chancel. The trees were felled and roughly squared at a sawmill several miles north of Bryn Athyn, then transported by horse-drawn wagon to the cathedral site where they were to lay seasoning until needed for the roof of solid timber. (See Figure 6.) Some of the wood already had been hewn and mortised when a fire, which began in the metal forge, destroyed the hand-worked lumber in April of 1916. The loss represented a major setback, but such was the spirit of the workmen that by mid-June the north aisle roof was in place on the church. The carpentry had been accomplished with new tools, as the men had lost their old kits in the fire and John Pitcairn had supplied each one with a full set of planes and saws and chisels in replacement.

The collaboration, between designers and those who executed designs in stone and wood and glass, was endorsed by Cram in theory, but in practice, the architect soon found the procedure onerous. "The idea of cooperation, begun with such enthusiasm, grew to the point," he said, "where a suggestion from any source . . . meant a fair trial in the shape of sketches, details, scale, and full-size models, all perhaps to be rejected, with a return to the first or second scheme." The architect resented Raymond Pitcairn's insistence that models be constructed not only of the building as a whole, but also of such details as the grape leaves for the chancel columns. In a shop on the cathedral grounds, miniature representations on a scale of an inch and a half to the foot were cast in plaster, and set on a track so they could be more easily drawn from the shed for study in full daylight. These models, Cram felt, contributed to a situation in which the authority of the architect "became only one amongst many authorities, with equal rights of suggestion but bound to submit their recommendations in visible, full-size form, first to a sort of plebiscite, and finally to the official ratification of a single and supreme authority."[69] Cram paid his final visit to Bryn Athyn in the autumn of 1916, and early the following spring, the increasingly troubled association between patron and paid profes-

Figure 6. Horses haul a log along Quarry Road toward the site of the Bryn Athyn Cathedral. Timber for the roof spanning the nave and chancel came from white oaks growing in the borough's woods and fields. *Photo courtesy of the Academy of the New Church.*

sional was severed, formally confirming what had been apparent for some time: the role of supervising architect belonged to Raymond Pitcairn.

In contrast to Cram's admiration for the English perpendicular, the young New Churchman was becoming ever more strongly attracted to earlier Gothic forms.[70] The buildings themselves reflect his changing taste, for while the church proper is based on the style of the thirteenth, fourteenth, and, to a limited degree, the fifteenth century, the later council hall and choir hall groups take their inspiration from twelfth-century Romanesque. As early as 1914, Pitcairn participated in the decision to line the interior walls of the cathedral with stone, not plaster them as originally planned, and working ever with his models, he continued to make a series of significant design alterations. The nave was lengthened and the clerestory walls raised; transepts and a south porch were added, and these changes in proportion engendered other adjustments, such as the deepening of buttresses to lend strength to the height. The design of the cathedral grew, as one observer has noted, "barely ahead of the structure itself—line by line, plane upon plane."[71] Indeed, the entire chancel and sanctuary were redrawn in Bryn Athyn, and in the plan of the latter is found the most significant structural deviation from the traditional Gothic pattern; for it is built to surround the altar upon which rests the open Word. The application of a building technique long lost by even the early Middle Ages was undertaken in the introduction of curves and optical refinements. Aesthetic devices know to the Greeks, those horizontal and vertical departures from the straight line, such as the unequal spacing of the nave arcade and the rising slope of the nave pavement in the direction of the chancel, along with endless variation in such details as the metal door hinges and the stone tracery of the windows, contribute to a charming multiplicity without detracting from the overall harmony of effect. The final result is a subtle beauty, which can only serve as a material reinforcement of the community's sense of spiritual elitism. (See Figure 7.)

A Sunday afternoon ritual for the people of Bryn Athyn during the second decade of the twentieth century was to visit the cathedral site to inspect the workmen's weekly progress. Comparable in size to an English parish church, the great grey struc-

Figure 7. The exquisite detail of the cathedral is suggested in this view from the slope of the vestry stairway. The rail, like all decorative metal used in the building, was handmade in shops on the church grounds. *Photo courtesy of the Academy of the New Church.*

ture rising slowly above their homes and schools "imperceptibly molded," as one resident wrote, "the ways and mores of those living near [it]."[72] Children gathered many of the small quartz and flintlike stones used in the floors. Members of the congregation helped search for suitable oaks to provide the roofing timber. One of the architects involved in the project married a New Church woman, converted to her faith, and settled in the community. A local artist, Winfred Hyatt, who through the interest of John Pitcairn was studying at the Pennsylvania Academy of the Fine Arts, was engaged to design the windows. Recognizing the crowning achievement represented by the stained glass of the twelfth and thirteenth centuries, the philanthropist's son accepted an extraordinary challenge. It involved, as one New Church critic has observed, securing the design of "windows of equal artistic integrity to reflect in symbolic form the doctrines of a New Christianity; and to make glass worthy of its use."[73] Pitcairn sent Hyatt to France to study the great cathedral windows in Chartres and Poiters and Rouen, and when the estate of Henry C. Lawrence, the New York collector of medieval glass, put the broker's collection up for auction, he dispatched the Bryn Athyn artist to bid for it. Besting several formidable international dealers, Hyatt acquired for his employer fifteen panels, among them an exquisite fragment, picturing the head of Christ, from the Jesse Tree which once graced a window in the Cathedral of Soissons. Its use was to serve as an inspiration to artisans seeking to match the unrivaled colors of Gothic glass.

Ceaseless experimentation, together with the close study in translation of accounts of medieval glass making, was the method adopted by the Bryn Athyn craftsmen. In 1916 a master glass blower, the Swedish-born John Larson, agreed to test formulae for various types and tones of glass. Pitcairn, who had met Larson through Louis Tiffany, persuaded the glass blower some six years later to set up a shop at the cathedral site. It had been decided that the only way to even approach the thirteenth-century palette was to revert to the old technique of making the glass from "pot metal," which involved introducing colors by metallic oxides into the molten glass rather than enameling pigments onto the hardened surface. Larson brought one assistant with him, and an apprentice was chosen from the 1922 graduating class of the boys' school. He learned the craft so well that, when the master glass blower left in 1925, he was able to take charge of the glass factory. The New Churchman, Ariel Gunther, was responsible for developing a remarkable striated ruby, and under his direction, glass was produced until the beginning of the Second World War. The design process, the tedious painting of details, glazing, and the leading of the carefully selected and prepared glass into panels went on long after the factory closed, and the last windows in the chapel finally were completed in the early seventies, a half century after the first glass was melted at Bryn Athyn.

In no feature or structure of the cathedral is the theology of the New Church given clearer expression than in the symbolism of the windows. The stained-glass designs in the sanctuary, the most sacred space in the community, are inspired by the Apocalypse, in which John described his vision of the New Jerusalem. In the great east window, filling the wall above the altar, the Lord, looking down as from a throne, is represented in the tracery medallion. Below in twelve panels, four in each of the three lights, are ranged Jesus' earthly disciples whom, Swedenborg taught, He again assembled and dispatched in the spirit world to spread the good news of His Second Coming. The chancel symbols are taken from the Gospels, and the medallion-type clerestory windows there tell the story of Christ's life among men, focusing upon His six visits to Jerusalem. The representative figures pictured in the chancel aisle windows are Moses holding tablets of the Law, at the north, and at the south, John with the book sealed with seven seals. The nave representations are based upon the Old Testament, although there are also grisaille windows lighting the aisles, which are made in geometric patterns outlined by bands of glass in intense hues. The ten clerestory windows depict angels and the Biblical personages to whom they appeared as messengers from God. Major and minor prophets are pictured in the two large lancet windows in the south transept, and below it, in the chapel, there are two unique medallion windows depicting scenes from Swedenborg's description of events he claimed to have witnessed in the world of spirits. The great west window above the narthex contains figures from both testaments symbolizing the periodization of history in five successive dispensations, as detailed in the Writings. In the central light, gazing down upon the congregation, as a representation of the New Church, is the woman clothed with the sun.

The cathedral proper was dedicated in the early autumn of 1919. By then it was far enough completed to be used as a house of worship, and the central tower, reached by a spiral stairway signifying the process of regeneration, had risen to a height of 150 feet above the ground. Dedication of the council building took place early in 1926, and just before Christmas in 1928, the same ceremony was held to bless the uses of the choir hall. In these Romanesque groupings, which include two fine towers, non-Scriptural symbolism has been employed along with canonical representations; the council chamber itself contains corbels carved as portrait heads of Robert Hindmarsh, Richard de Charms, William Henry Benade, John Pitcairn, Walter Childs, and William Frederic Pendleton. In the hall's east window is a full-length representation of Swedenborg, surrounded by female figures representing, in one light, physics, cosmology, and philosophy, and in the other, anatomy, psychology, and theology. On the outside of the building is a granite cornice accented by heads signifying the races of men, and on the south wall, overlooking the original settlement, are the seals in bas relief of the Academy and the General Church.[74] (See Figure 8.)

When Bryn Athyn's cathedral-church will be completed, like how much it has cost, is a question for which there is no answer. Herman Melville wrote that while "small erections may be finished by their first architects; grand ones, true ones, ever leave their copestones for posterity." In 1982, sixty-nine years after ground was first broken for the edifice, the capitals on some columns must still be carved, permanent chancel furniture made, and a mosaic assembled for the council chamber. The original plan, moreover, called for the extension of the nave to the west by three bays, the construction of a banquet hall, and the completion of the cloister. Whether these structural additons will ever be made is doubtful. The generation which laid the cornerstone mostly has passed away, and few remember when the cathedral's shadow did not lie upon the countryside. Not only on Sundays and festival days, but on all momentous occasions, members

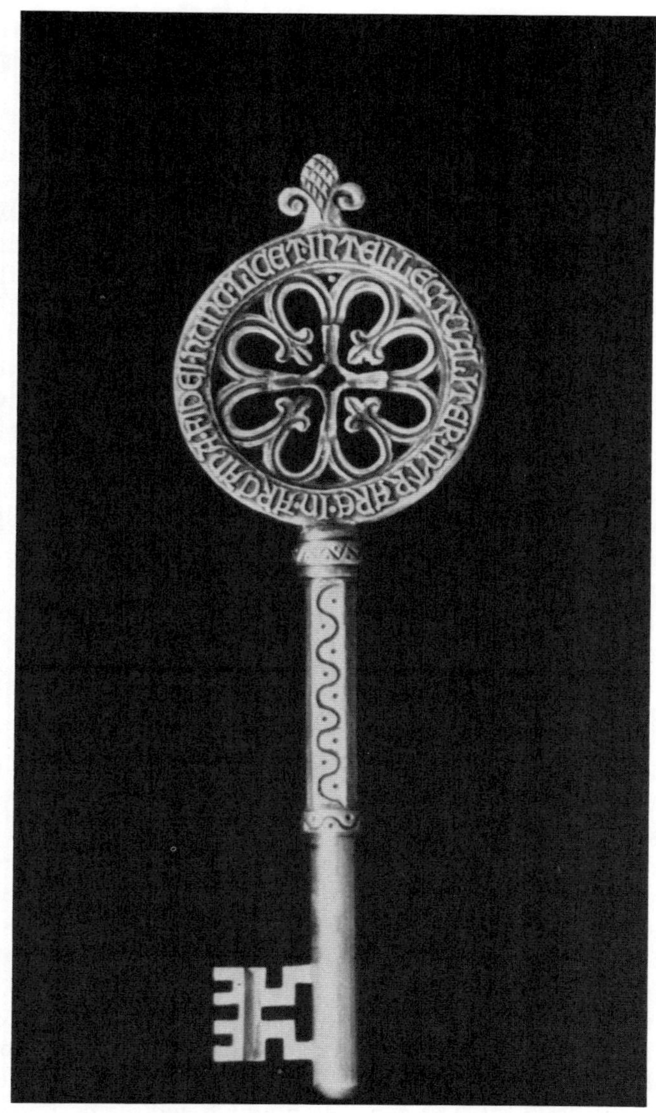

Figure 8. A handwrought key to the Bryn Athyn Cathedral, made of monel metal, is the work of the designer Parke Edwards. It was presented at the service of dedication on October 5, 1919. *Photo courtesy of the Academy of the New Church.*

of the community turn toward the church by common consent. Even before it was dedicated, some four hundred people gathered there in November of 1918 to join in a service of thanksgiving for the Armistice. Absent from this first public act of worship to transpire in the stone temple was John Pitcairn. He had not lived to see the timber roof in place above the nave, but six months before his death on the twenty-second of July in 1916, he had seen Bryn Athyn incorporated as a borough

Seeking the right to raise money for community maintenance and improvement by taxation and assessment, the freeholders of Bryn Athyn petitioned Montgomery County early in 1915 for incorporation of the village.[75] The community had entered the twentieth century burdened by double taxation, that is, an involuntary tax levied by Moreland Township, from which it received little benefit, and a voluntary tax imposed on residents by the Village Association to finance housekeeping necessities, like roads and public utilities. The boundaries of the proposed borough were drawn to include: 398 people residing in sixty-two houses; schools with an assessed property value of $100,000; a public library, maintained as part of the Academy; a railroad station and post office, telegraph, and express office; a stone quarry; and a coal yard. In opposition to Bryn Athyn's application, a petition was filed by Moreland Township, which received not only road tax but also school tax monies from the New Churchmen who sent their children, nevertheless, to the sect's private institutions. The opponents of incorporation argued that Bryn Athyn was not a village, but a religious colony, and that the proposed borough limits were fashioned to exclude all except members of the General Church.

Underlying the obvious civic needs, which would be met by incorporation, was a psychological need for moral recognition by the state. The curious requirement was linked to a legal dispute settled six years earlier, but having its origin in a will drawn by a German tailor in 1854. Frederick Kramph, an immigrant from Heidelberg, had become a prosperous member of the Lancaster New Church Society by the middle of the nineteenth century. Keenly interested in Benade's Cherry Street educational experiment, which he felt was the "seed for a New Church university," he bequeathed his residuary estate to seven specifically designated trustees "for the purpose of endowing a university of the New Jerusalem in the consolidated City of Philadelphia."[76] As Kramph's young wife survived him by more than forty years, his estate did not come up for settlement until 1902. In the meantime, as the original trustees died, those sympathetic to the Academy principles were replaced by others who were not, for the tailor's widow came increasingly under the influence of members of the Convention. At her death, only John Pitcairn represented the theological position of the New Churchmen named in the codicil to Kramph's will. Nevertheless, the other trustees agreed in principle that the Academy was entitled to the estate, and when the Lancaster property was sold in 1907, it amounted to $37,000. The case was heard in the Orphan's Court of the central Pennsylvania city the next year, and the counsel for the Bryn Athyn institution confidently claimed that his client fulfilled the conditions set by the 1854 will as it was a New Church university founded in Philadelphia. Even though physically located fifteen miles outside of the city by 1908, its business office remained there, and no one seriously disputed that the Academy satisfied the geographical requirements of the document. What was at issue, as it turned out, was whether the Academy was a New Church institution, as one of the trustees, a Convention loyalist, now opposed the Bryn Athyn school's claim to the bequest on the grounds that it taught the doctrines of a schismatic body. The specific teaching on which the case turned was that extra-connubial alliances were permitted under certain circumstances, according to the second half of *Conjugial Love,* which the General Church held, equally with the first half and all Swedenborg's other theological treatises, to be the Word of God. When the Convention attorney led an Academy witness to declare that the so-called immoral book was studied in the Bryn Athyn institution, Kramph's heirs seized the issue as a means of denying either New Church faction the tailor's estate, and the Orphan's Court ruled in their favor, declaring the will illegal as the Academy's teachings were contrary to the laws of Pennsylvania.

As newpaper headlines screeched "School Accused of Teaching Free Love,"[77] the Academy at once appealed the decision to the State Supreme Court. At issue was the good name of the community and a far more precious inheritance than Frederick Kramph's bequest. ''The sole purpose, intention, and end of the work on Conjugial Love is to teach . . . the sacredness of marriage,'' declared the brief for the Huntingdon Valley schools.

Swedenborg teaches that fornication and adultery are evils. Swedenborg further teaches that there are degrees of evil; and sexual evil is of a greater or less degree, in proportion to the extent that indulgence in evil operates against the preservation of Conjugial Love in man.''

The Academicians further argued that the General Church was not the only one which had teachings ''in conflict with public policy,'' and noting that ''in the case at bar, there is . . . no charge of ACTS,'' they concluded with a ringing challenge to the court to uphold freedom of religion: ''Matters of *opinion or doctrine* are never amenable to the law.''[78] Unanimously, on June 22, 1909 the judges agreed to reverse the lower court opinion, but because there were some differences as to which of the parties claiming as legates met the requirements imposed by Kramph upon his intended beneficiary, the Supreme Court ordered the case reargued in the fall. When it was, the final decision was a triumph for the General Church, but it did not prevent train passengers peering out of coach windows when the Reading stopped at the Bryn Athyn station. The community had need, then, of the further approbation entailed in county acceptance of its incorporation petition. Indeed, it was precisely because the suspicions raised in the Kramph will case played a part in Moreland Township's opposition to its application for recognition as a borough that the decision, rendered by Judge Aaron Swartz on January 20, 1916, was so sweet a draft. He said:

The Swedenborgian faith of Mr. Pitcairn and of his associates may have been the cause, in part at least, for the development of this village settlement, but if the cause or purpose was not unlawful, then we can not reject or overlook the conditions that followed therefrom and now confront us. If the statutory requirements for incorporation are present, the demand for the borough should prevail. . . . To hold otherwise it would be necessary to refuse the application because of the religious faith of a majority of the petitioners.[79]

The successful battle for incorporation had been led by the second generation of settlers. The petition was prepared by the sons of the Academy founders, Randolph Childs and Raymond Pitcairn, childhood friends and roommates at the University of Pennsylvania Law School from which they had graduated in 1908. With homes built, a school system firmly established which educated New Churchmen from kindergarten through theological school, and the cathedral rising on the hill, the acquisition of borough status symbolized the inauguration of a new era in the life of the community. Its dawn was confirmed six months later by the death of John Pitcairn, "an old gentleman of small stature," as Ralph Adams Cram said, "grave, courtly, keenly intelligent, vigorous beyond his years, an acute businessman, and withal possessed of imagination and intense idealism."[80]

5

The Physical and Social Structure: Contemporary Bryn Athyn

Today Bryn Athyn is the home of nearly a third of the world's members of the General Church of the New Jerusalem, including many of John Pitcairn's descendants. At his death, the plate-glass manufacturer left an estate of some $60 million, and its settlement created, in the place of one man, three whose great wealth made them leading citizens of the Swedenborgian community. The heirs, Raymond (1885-1966), Theodore (1893-1973), and Harold (1897-1960) Pitcairn, shared not only a fortune, but an abiding commitment to the New Church. Their world view shaped their behavior, and Raymond's political forrays, Theodore's ministry, and Harold's pursuit of a safe mode of flight, reflected their individual interpretations of the concept of use. Each married, produced nine children, and raised them in mansions which they built within a few miles of their father's house.

The eldest, lawyer and cathedral builder, served for forty-three years as president of the Pitcairn Company, the investment firm incorporated to unify the management of the assets left to the industrialist's heirs. As a financier and pamphleteer, moreover, Raymond was a figure of note in American politics for two generations. His theological opposition to compulsion as an instrumentality of reform propelled him to the forefront of fights against prohibition, a revenue act requirement that the source and amount of individual earnings be open to public examination, and repeal of the "right to work" provision of the Taft-Hartley law. After initially supporting Roosevelt, he sought his defeat, supporting every Republican candidate from Willkie to Goldwater, though none with such ardor as Ike.

For more than fifty years, Raymond actively participated in affairs of the Academy and of the General Church as a member of the board of directors of both organizations. Having built the cathedral, moreover, he ensured its upkeep by endowing a substantial sustentation fund. Various cultural amenities which the borough residents have enjoyed for half a century are products of his largess, and the plate-glass heir and his wife played a major part in keeping alive the communitarian spirit forged by the first generation. Their castle-like home, Glencairn, is the site of an annual Christmas celebration and spring dance, along with chamber music concerts featuring both talented amateurs and world-renowned performers. All these events are ingredients in the cultural cement which bind the people of Bryn Athyn together. (See Figure 9.)

Ironically, the principal strain in community social relations since the first days of settlement was a product of the beliefs and behavior of John Pitcairn's second son. In 1937, Theodore, a New Church priest and an art collector, led a small number of borough residents in the establishment of a rival Swedenborgian sect called the Lord's New Church. Their essentially existential position was that the Writings contained an internal sense that readers could discover by means of the science of correspondence. But to the General Church such views involved a profane downgrading of the authority of the heavenly doctrines and a blasphemous upgrading of the human power of comprehension. They quickly were deemed heretical, and for thirty-five years the only Pitcairn ordained to the ministry presided over a schismatic church within the boundaries of the borough. Today the forty-five odd members of its Bryn Athyn branch worship in a Romanesque chapel, built as part of Theodore's estate. The Lord's New Church is the owner, moreover, of three El Greco's, which were once hung in the plate-glass heir's Impressionist collection. Through the years, these Monets and Van Goghs were sold for sums totaling more than two million

Figure 9. Glencairn, Raymond Pitcairn's castle-like home, was built with an eye for displaying its owner's fine collection of medieval statuary, rare tapestries, and panels of exquisite stained glass. Begun in 1926, it was completed in 1938, and since Mrs. Pitcairn's death in 1980 has housed the Academy Museum. *Photo by George Faragan. Courtesy of the Academy of the New Church.*

dollars to benefit various charities, but principally his variant Swedenborgian faith.

It was Theodore's younger brother, Harold, who, to a far greater extent than Raymond, challenged him in doctrinal discussions. John Pitcairn's third son studied a year for the priesthood, but left the Academy theological school to manufacture aircraft. His aim was to develop a plane which the average citizen could operate as safely as an automobile. The likeliest possibility seemed to be the rotary-wing autogiro, the creation of a Spanish mathematician for which Harold obtained the U.S. patent rights. But he also produced a biplane which he used in his commercial air transport business, the first to carry mail along a 1,350-mile Eastern seaboard route. Indeed, he made plans to inaugurate a passenger service, then sold his aviation firm to concentrate on perfecting the autogiro. When the United States entered World War II, he turned over his inventions to the government.

The New Churchman's patents covering rotor structures and control systems of rotary wing aircraft were utilized to make the helicopter a viable machine, and after the war the helicopter, less costly and more efficient, superseded the autogiro. But Washington refused to pay any royalties, and in 1951 Harold initiated the largest and, as it turned out, the longest lawsuit ever brought against the government. It took twenty-seven years of legal maneuvering first to establish liability then to determine the amount, but in 1978 his heirs won a record-breaking patent infringement award of nearly $39 million when the Supreme Court left standing a lower court ruling. Two pending parallel claims could cost the government another $90 million. More than half a century, then, after Harold Pitcairn invested in the autogiro, his foresight served to increase dramatically his inheritance. Because a major component of that legacy was an internalized obligation to support the uses of the New Church, however, the pay-out from the Treasury of the United States enriches not only his children and grandchildren, but the inhabitants of Bryn Athyn.

Living in the borough or its immediate environs are some 800 adults who have signed the roll of the local society, as well as another 240 who are members of the international ecclesiastical body but not of the Bryn Athyn Church.[1] As the episcopal seat of the sect, the Huntingdon Valley community is the home of the executive bishop. The prelate's staff, administrators, and teachers bring the total number of General Church priests residing there to twenty-two, or 31 percent, of the sect's seventy clergymen. Total adult membership in the General Church is about 3,660 persons divided among twelve countries. Some 69 percent of the Swedenborgians live in the United States, with another 11 percent in Canada, 4 percent in England, and only 2 percent in Sweden. The membership is organized into fourteen societies with resident pastors and another twenty-nine circles made up of Swedenborgians who meet together for worship services without the benefit of a regular minister. The Bryn Athyn Society is more than three and a half times larger than any other in the General Church, and education is the biggest "business" in the borough.[2] The Academy dominates the community not only economically, but socially to the degree that its cultural offerings, athletics contests, and festivals provide residents with shared experiences. In but four other societies—in Glenview, Illinois, Washington, D.C., Kitchner, Ontario,, and Durban, South Africa—do New Churchmen attempt to live together, and Bryn Athyn is clearly the model for community life throughout the New Church.

The community idea is for members of the sect not so much a human concept as a divine ideal. Commenting upon the innumerable societies in heaven, Swedenborg wrote: "Like are drawn spontaneously . . . to their like; for with their like, they are as if with their own and at home, but with others they are as if with strangers and abroad; also when with their like they are in their freedom, and consequently in every delight of life."[3] From love of the Lord and of the neighbor arises the chief activity of angelic communities which is the sharing of blessings.[4] On earth, New Churchmen, historically skeptical of the value of investments in evangelism, continue to find imitation of the angels easier in association with other receivers of the heavenly doctrines. They tend to interpret the concept of neighbor narrowly, but their construction is eminently functional. Distinctive schools and social life, in practice largely interdependent uses, have accounted for the survival of the sect. Still, the geographic mobility in pursuit of occupational advancement, which is so characteristic of upper-middle-class life in the United States, does not make the religious community a practical model from an economic standpoint; and occasionally, too, a note of uneasiness is heard among New Churchmen about the morality of a distinctiveness which can easily become exclusivity. But for Swedenborgian leaders "the New Church community is the hope of the church." The pastor of the Bryn Athyn Society says: "We must cling desperately to our community form of life. We must encourage the founding of new communities in other parts of the country. . . . With New Church neighbors we can begin to assume a common belief, and work together in seeing how it applies to the activities of life." Pointing to a Bryn Athyn street as a social paradigm, he continues: "This is the solid phalanx that can really serve to build the Lord's Church on earth."[5] The Huntingdon Valley community, then, is as much a psychological phenomenon as it is a social organization and a geographical entity. It is a state of mind, and at its best, the borough is the structural correspondent for its residents of a state of grace.

Less than two miles from the northeastern sprawl of Philadelphia, Bryn Athyn has a higher percentage of undeveloped land than almost any borough in Pennsylvania.[6] With 951 acres out of a total of 1,216 in estates and farmsteads, agriculture, woodlands, or idle, its undeveloped land totals more than three-fourths of its total acreage.[7] Almost all of these verdant pastures are owned by members of the Pitcairn family, and under the commonwealth's Clean and Green Act, those in agriculture are taxed at a lower percent of assessed valuation than other real estate because the owners have agreed not to sell the land for ten years. Indeed, for the foreseeable future, they seem intent upon avoiding intensive development. The aged widows of Raymond and Theodore Pitcairn lived out their last years on their husbands' estates. In 1980 Glencairn was given to the Academy just as twelve years earlier, Cairncrest, Harold's estate, was turned over to the General Church. The dominant form of land use in the borough, representing nearly a third of the total acreage, is agriculture, although it is unimportant in terms of the community's economy, nor is it a significant source of income to the owners of the tenant-run farms. Food products are consumed within the county, and grain crops serve as fodder for local beef. Some prize bulls are sold throughout the country, but most are marketed in Philadelphia. Essentially, devoting land to agriculture is a method of preventing residential development while securing a tax break and making an aesthetic contribution to the borough. Certainly woodlands, the second largest land use in Bryn Athyn, enhance the physical beauty of the area. Representing 29 percent of the total acreage, they extend the entire length of Pennypack Creek, where they help to preserve the soil of the watershed, as well as providing land suitable for passive recreational pursuits. Beyond question the semirural character of the community affords a splendid setting for the cathedral. Retention of the country atmosphere is directly linked, however, to the Pitcairns' ability to withstand increasing pressure to sell their holdings.

Their staunch resistance to date has forced many people, who would like to live in Bryn Athyn, to seek housing in neighboring communities. During the half-century between his father's death in 1916 and his own in 1966, Raymond Pitcairn made extensive real estate purchases, and sold his land selectively and with apparent reluctance. Five tracts originally outside the borough limits were annexed before 1949, but when Lower Moreland became a first-class township, the geographical expansion of the New Church community was brought to an abrupt halt. Today, more than three-quarters of a century after the first settlers built their homes in Bryn Athyn, residential development is concentrated in two small areas. The oldest includes the original lots laid out in the heart of the borough in 1893 by John Pitcairn. A contiguous tract was developed after World War I by a New Church priest who in 1918 purchased thirty-five acres on which he reconstructed officers' houses, acquired from a New Jersey Army installation, and sold them to New Church families. The second concentration of residences is behind the Academy buildings on land developed by John Pitcairn's sons in the early twenties. By the beginning of the Depression, however, few of the eighty-one lots had been sold, so in 1936 the plate-glass manufacturer's heirs cut their asking price by about 25 percent, a move which, with the gradual improvement of economic conditions, greatly facilitated sales.

Today there are 286 housing units in the borough, of which 55 percent were constructed before 1939.[8] Another 33 percent were built between 1940 and 1959, and 12 percent were erected during the sixties. Very little housing has been built in Bryn Athyn in the past decade, and what comes on the market is generally the result of turnover arising from deaths and changes of residence. To a degree, the shortage has been alleviated by the availability of lots in Lower Moreland Township on a tract which Raymond Pitcairn's son, Garthowen, was instrumental in developing through the West Chelten Corporation. The seventy-acre area, know as Pine Run Park, was laid out in 1952, and Garth restored an old farmhouse there as his own residence. He put in streets and curbs, and during the past several decades these properties have been sold to New Church families, as well as to some people who do not share their faith. The initial attempt of the Pitcairn holding company to deny non-Swedenborgians the right to purchase lots resulted in an appeal being brought before the Pennsylvania Human Relations Commission, which ruled that a Quaker had been illegally discriminated against in a specific transaction. To try to prevent the recurrence of similar suits, the Bryn Athyn Society purchased the remaining twenty-five lots for $100,000 from the West Chelten Corporation in 1972. Since then it has made property available to New Churchmen at 50 percent of market value. Deeds require the owner to sell his lot back to the society if he does not build on it within two years, and gives the church organization first right of refusal in case of resale. The Academy itself occasionally is bequeathed property, which is then made available to New Churchmen on easy terms. Within the borough limits, however, just over 10 percent of the total acreage is used for residential purposes.

The value of houses in Bryn Athyn is high even excluding estates on ten or more acres of land. In 1970 nearly a fifth were worth more than $50,000, and 35 percent were valued at more than $35,000. Two years earlier, the Montgomery County Planning Commission had designated the borough an ''upper-middle to lower-upper class community,''[9] and at present the market value of residential property in the borough ranges from $45,000 to more than a million dollars.[10] Institutional uses occupy thirty-seven acres, or 3 percent, of the land, and another 3 percent is devoted to recreational purposes. There is no industry in the community, and the amount of land in commercial use is negligible. Bryn Athyn did have one small grocery until 1973, but now all that is left are the business office and storage facility for a local construction firm. Yet, according to a survey conducted in the late sixties, residents are not distressed by a lack of drug stores and supermarkets.[11] They simply drive to nearby Bethayres or Southampton for daily consumption goods, and a few minutes longer on the road takes them to Jenkintown, Abington, and Willow Grove for large-scale shopping. By automobile or train, Philadelphia is easily accessible. The inconvenience of not having local merchants is more than offset in the minds of New Churchmen by having neither local storefronts nor creditors, and there is relatively little grumbling about taxes. A few years ago, however, an item in the *Bryn Athyn Post* reminded readers that a proposed decrease could be wiped out if property were sold to someone who would send their children to public schools.[12] It was an example of the kind of pressure brought on residents to maintain the religious homogeneity of the borough, often subtle but always intense.

Like other suburban communities, Bryn Athyn also is racially homogenous. Only thirteen persons, or a little over 1 percent of the population, are black. All employed as domestics, the borough's nonwhites represent but one-tenth of 1 percent of the nonwhite population of Montgomery County.[13] About a quarter of the residents, however, are either foreign born or native born of foreign or mixed parentage. Of these, 82 percent are of Anglo-Saxon stock, and, indeed, the character of the community is preeminently Waspish, except, of course, that the Swedenborgians are not Protestants. In 1970 Bryn Athyn's total population stood at 970 persons, which was a loss of 87 persons, or more than 8 percent, since the 1960 census. The borough's greatest growth rate occurred during the twenties when the population increased more than 95 percent, and while that rate was never again even approached, the community never suffered a population loss until the sixties.[14]

People obviously cannot live where there is no available housing, so young adults who wish to remain in the borough must often seek residences outside. It is significant that nearly a third of the population is over forty-five years of age, and only 29 percent is in the twenty-five-to-fifty-four-year age range. With 12 percent of the population over sixty-five and, according to one estimate,[15] some 12 percent of the households in the borough composed of persons living alone, care of the elderly has been a problem in the New Church community. But as the result of the work of a committee of concerned individuals who attempted to generate interest in building such a facility,[16] an apartment complex for retired New Churchmen was constructed on property bequeathed to the General Church upon the death of Raymond Pitcairn's widow. It is anticipated that eventually many older people will be induced to give up large homes they no longer have the energy to maintain, which in turn will alleviate in a small measure the housing shortage. Still, even given an attractive alternative, the wealthiest members of the community will probably continue to hire, as they have in the past, paid companions for their elderly family members.

Bryn Athyn easily ranks among the higher income communities in the Philadelphia metropolitan area.[17] The 1970 census indicated that 7 percent of the family units in the borough had incomes of greater than $50,000 a year, while 14 percent had annual incomes in excess of $25,000. The mean income then was $18,720, and inflation, of course, has driven the figure considerably higher in the course of the decade. As a matter of fact, Academy teaching personnel are paid on a relatively modest scale, with salaries in the college and theological school ranging from $11,500 a year to $24,500. Under terms of a unique investment savings plan, however, the institution invests the equivalent of 5 percent of the employee's annual base salary in a fund managed by the Pitcairn Company, upon which teachers can draw after a specified period of time. There is virtually no unemployment in Bryn Athyn. Nearly half the labor force falls in the census categories of professional, technical, and managerial workers, and more than 70 percent are engaged in white-collar occupations. There are six physicians, all with substantial New Church practices, and seven lawyers residing in the borough. Related to the social structure of the community is the fact that a relatively high 14 percent of the residents are employed as private household workers or laborers. These people work for the well-to-do, and a significant number of the borough's white-collar workers, of course, are employed by the General Church and the sect's schools.[18] The educational level of the Bryn Athyn New Churchmen is high, with 87 percent of the population over twenty-five years of age having at least a secondary school education. Only 2 percent failed to complete elementary school, while 26 percent have had some college training and another 26 percent are college graduates. The borough population is also extraordinarily stable. The 1970 census indicated that 72 percent of the residents had lived in the same house for the past five years and that another 24 percent had resided in the same metropolitan area. Of John Pitcairn's eighteen surviving grandchildren, fourteen still live in Bryn Athyn.

The Huntingdon Valley New Churchmen are linked in an intricate web of kinship. Through the years, most of the original families have intermarried, and until about a generation ago, children were taught to refer, in direct address and conversation, to every older relative more distant than an uncle and aunt as "cousin." It was an appellation accepted in the community as striking the right balance between familiarity and respect and possibly reflected the influence of the southern Pendletons. Undoubtedly, inbreeding has produced social cohesion in Bryn Athyn. Because Academy students come into contact with age mates from a wide geographic area and many students transfer to other institutions for their final collegiate years, there appears, however, to be a sufficient amount of outbreeding to preserve a degree of vigor. Continuity is preserved, but individuality is not entirely repressed by marriage patterns. Nor indeed is humor. With a nod to Gilbert and Sullivan, a Bryn Athyn editor and filmmaker wrote an operetta, locally performed to great applause, in which he noted:

> I think it providential . . .
> That this entire community . . .
> Is tied into a family tree
> (Including those of the Starkey key)
> That's either supported by A.T.E.
> Or else dependent on P.P.G.

> Genetic links or marriage ties,
> Link Actons, Bostocks, Sonesons,
> The Synnestvedts and Odhner tribes,
> The Crofts, Coles, Childs and Pendletons.
> Each infant, child, teen-age, adult
> Resigns his fate to grow and live
> In family clans—It's not his fault—
> That everyone is a relative.[19]

The initials A.T.E. and P.P.G. refer to Asplundh Tree Experts and Pittsburgh Plate Glass, and both Asplundhs and Pitcairns took part in the show, willingly poking gentle fun at themselves.

Kinship ties notably affect social as well as economic life in the community. The proximity of close relatives is conducive to frequent family gatherings. Beyond these, it is possible for an individual to be part of a dozen different social groups without ever leaving the borough. Although older people look back with nostalgia on the days when everyone "knew" everyone else, even today most people in Bryn Athyn are at least acquainted with one another. The oldest, largest social phenomenon in the New Church community is Friday supper. Held nearly every week during the school year, the shared meal attracts an average of 300 adults and college students to the Academy assembly hall, where they dine well at modest cost. In 1975 a new custom was inaugurated when a reception for the General Church ministers residing in the borough was held before one supper; among the oldest community traditions is the doctrinal class which follows most of the Friday meals.

If Bryn Athyn's weekly supper provides individual New Churchmen an opportunity to associate with a wide assortment of their co-religionists, representing a range of income levels, occupations, and social statuses albeit most identifiable "church goers," special interests are met in a variety of civic, social, and service organizations. The Friday meal is prepared and served by members of the Women's Guild who have chosen community domestic chores as their particular use. The sect's "Marthas," they have taken on responsibility for local hospitality and such typical volunteer tasks as aiding homeroom teachers in the elementary school and operating the borough blood bank. Theta Alphia, the Academy alumnae organization, provides auxiliary support for the educational aims of the Church. Members supervise the distribution of age-graded religion lessons to New Church children living in isolated areas, provide Academy scholarships, and serve as liaisons between the community and boarding students in the college and secondary schools. An alumni society, Sons of the Academy, also makes a substantial contribution to the Academy scholarship fund, sponsors seminars on religion which bring faculty and college students together on an informal basis, arranges special trips to sporting events, finances Sunday dinners which boarding students share with Bryn Athyn families, and organizes a special program each year to acquaint students with the possibilities for an adult life in various New Church communities. The Epsilon Society is the sect's heretofore stunted evangelical arm. Members find their principal use in the distribution of copies of the Writings and collateral literature, and they also operate a cathedral guide service.

The well-developed social limb of the Church is the Civic and Social Club. Open to adult members of the sect residing in or near the borough, as well as certain other categories of persons such as spouses of club members who, although not members of the General Church, are in sympathy with it, the organization was spawned during the initial settlement of the community. Over the years it has assumed many of the social responsibilities, which in smaller societies would fall to the pastor; and in a community lacking commercial establishments, it serves as the borough barroom. More than simply a place to stop for a drink, however, the C&S Club offers its nearly 400 members a special program or party each month, as well as sponsoring community Fourth of July and Memorial Day celebrations and providing Friday suppers during the summertime. It sometimes organizes a Bryn Athyn Society New Year's Eve party, and traditional events include a clambake and golf tournament.

Bryn Athyn's several community organizations range from a garden club to an association which maintains a playground in Pine Run Park. The latter is a kind of ''bridge'' group because it includes not only New Churchmen, but a few other families living in the development adjacent to the borough who are not members of the sect. A potentially more significant link connecting the Swedenborgian community to the outside world is the Pennypack Watershed Association. It consists of people whose concern about the environmental future unites them despite the fact that they occupy different present positions on the tme line of salvation history. Formed in 1970, the private conservation organization supports a staff of eight paid professionals who have turned a twenty-five acre estate, located just outside the borough, into a thriving nature center. Theodore Pitcairn's son, Feodor, serves as president of Pennypack Watershed, and the center's naturalist is also a Bryn Athyn New Churchman. The association was inaugurated when a group of concerned citizens organized to attack the problem of creek pollution. Members subsequently assumed responsibility for flood-plain management and initiated an educational program which brings hundreds of school children to the center each year. In 1976 the conservation organization received a gift of nearly 200 acres from the West Chelten Corporation. The undeveloped land will form the core of a planned 800-acre wilderness park, which will not only run through Bryn Athyn but extend into parts of Lower Moreland and Upper Moreland townships. It is the first project of its kind, supported largely by New Churchmen, which will benefit the region as a whole.

Youngsters in the community, of course, are protected from precisely the sort of mixing with people from other religious, or nonreligious, traditions represented by Pennypack Watershed, although the local boys' and girls' clubs do emphasize wilderness experience in their camping programs. They serve generally the same functions as scout organizations elsewhere, but the sect's historic stress upon sheltering its children from what the General Church regards as ideological contamination precludes the presence of any national or international youth organizations in Bryn Athyn.

Private entertaining in the borough is not wholly restricted to Swedenborgians; nevertheless, unless individual residents share the love of a specific use with persons outside the sect, they are likely to invite mainly New Church people to their parties. Their religious affiliation is their predominant social identity, and a common faith is far more significant in residents' interpersonal relationships than incidentally shared interests, whether for music or golf or environmental protection. Like everyone else, they tend to avoid situations in which they suspect they might be offended or made to feel uncomfortable. Although two-thirds of Bryn Athyn's labor force works outside the borough,[20] wives are more apt than husbands to draw up guest lists in middle-class American society, and the contact of New Church women with the world outside of Bryn Athyn is considerably more restricted than that of male members of the community. Even if she were so inclined, therefore, a borough resident planning a cocktail party or a dinner is not likely to know many non-Swedenborgians well enough to invite them. But quite apart from friendship pools is the General Church's still strong theological emphasis upon the importance of its members maintaining a distinctive social life. An animated doctrinal discussion generally is taken as a sure sign of a party's success, and while it is true that many residents of Bryn Athyn speak English with the broad ''a'' of the wellborn, all of them, rich or of modest means, speak the same peculiarly Swedenborgian language. ''Use,'' as a synonym for ''vocation'' and ''responsibility'' are among the most common words in their vocabulary; ''ultimate'' is employed as a verb meaning ''manifest''; ''influx'' is an inflow not from foreign treasuries but from the spirit world; ''remains'' are not dead bodies but divine imprints stamped on young minds which shield older ones against the assaults and temptations of the world; ''permission'' is an evil allowed by the Lord; and ''proprium'' is the treacherous ego whose assertions are held responsible for so much of the world's misery. In a sense, Bryn Athyn is a distinctive speech community, and a New Church vernacular is heard at the Friday afternoon salons held by a local artist who serves her friends homemade soup and bread and cheese, at the informal gatherings of older borough residents for cocktails preceding Friday supper, at Saturday night dinner parties, and at the brunches often given by the Huntingdon Valley New Churchmen after Sunday worship services. In the presence of familiar speech patterns, as well as the theological concepts responsible for them, members of the General Church of the New Jerusalem feel at home.

Affiliation with secular organizations is not unknown, however, among the borough residents. In addition to maintaining professional ties with regional and national societies, New Churchmen hold memberships in a variety of groups from the Philadelphia Union League to the Huntingdon Valley Country Club to the Jenkintown Kiwanis. A small number are socially prominent in the wider metropolitan area. A Bryn Athyn Asplundh is president of the African Safari Club, whose fashionable dos regularly attract the attention of Philadelphia society editors, and other members of the tree company clan are active in the social affairs of Abington Hospital. Theodore Pitcairn's daughter, Diene, and her New Church husband, the jeweler Douglas Cooper, maintain an elegant international lifestyle. At their posh homes on Philadelphia's Rittenhouse Square, in New York, and near Montego Bay, they entertain a wide circle of glamorous friends at lavish parties duly covered by the press. Garth Pitcairn still owns Glen Tonche, the house his father built on a mountainside in New York State, and Raymond's other children have their own places further down the slope in the Catskill summer colony. Less affluent members of the community maintain vacation homes around Lake Wallenpaupac in the Poconos, and for those unable to get away, the borough swim club makes July and August bearable despite the heat.

Daily toil is made more palatable, and kept in perspective as not the end of existence but one element contributing to human fulfillment, by feast days and festivals during which Bryn Athyn residents lay work aside. New Churchmen are a celebrative people, and on their holy days and holidays the adherents of an essentially cerebral religion are able to relate affectionally to the past. Drawing upon common memories, they incorporate the experiences of previous generations into their lives through what theologian Harvey Cox identifies as a very central element in religion—festive observance.[21] The rituals, both calendrical and nocalendrical, in which borough residents participate are rationalized by their system of beliefs. Those occuring on fixed occasions are communal, but even those performed in connection with critical individual events generally constitute congregational experiences. Merry or solemn, these rituals have as their aim what anthropologist Anthony F. C. Wallace has described as ''social control in a cybernetic sense.''[22] They serve to keep the Swedenborgian ship afloat and on course, shoring up weaker elements and providing directions for the crew each time members enter upon new duties. Sunday worship services at the Bryn Athyn cathedral provide the opportunity for a shared experience seized each week by an average of 68 percent of the members of the local society.[23] A morning family service followed by an adult liturgy and, during the academic year, an evening service attract an average total attendance of some 675 adults and about 165 children, of whom a considerable number come to more than one of the services. Essentially restorative, the weekly liturgies function to maintain what Wallace calls the "general value-tonus of the community" by symbols and exhortation.[24] Their implicit goal is religious intensification, and it becomes explicit on the six Sundays a year when communicants share in the Holy Supper. As Bishop W. F. Pendleton long ago pointed out to his fellow Swedenborgians, in communion, as in no other sacrament or rite of the church, "all the senses come into active play. There is sight and hearing as in ordinary worship, and in addition, touch, taste, and smell."[25] Leaving their pews in the nave of the cathedral, proceeding forward and upward to the communion rail, which separates chancel and sanctuary, New Churchmen kneel side by side to receive from the hands of priests broken pieces of unleavened bread and red, slightly sweet wine. They are meant to signify the divine good of the Lord's love and the divine truth of His wisdom, and for borough residents the elements of the common meal effect conjunction with heaven for those who partake of them.

Rites of passage are provided in the liturgy of the General Church to correspond to the predictably significant role changes in the lives of individual members. These alterations of state involve attendant changes in a person's relationship to the community, and for the most part the group is called to witness the ceremonies of the church connected with a member's assumption of new rights and duties. Baptisms sometimes are held in private homes in the presence of friends and relatives, but more often they are scheduled to follow regular Sunday services. By way of an announcement on the hymn board, the congregation is invited to observe the simultaneous introduction of a person into the New Church on earth and in heaven. Effected by a sprinkling of water, the sacrament is representative of the initiation of the work of regeneration. Infants usually are baptized during the first few months of life, and even today they are likely to be attired in "Pitcairn gowns." These are delicate wool, ecru-colored garments which were part of the layette Raymond Pitcairn's wife once had made for every new baby in Bryn Athyn. A continuation and completion of the sacrament of baptism, which reflects the Swedenborgian concept that no one can compel another in matters of religion, is the rite of confession of faith. In the Academy ritual it was called the rite of the "Coming of Age," and while the General Church eventually rejected the designation as lacking specificity, the ceremony does signify a gaining of maturity permitting the indivdual to voluntarily declare his acknowledgment of the heavenly doctrines. Women present themselves for the confirmation of baptismal vows at eighteen, men at twenty-one; and the always individual ceremony may be either a private family affair or a semi-public one following a cathedral worship service. Symbolized by a laying on of hands, the rite marks the young adult's organic incorporation into the community of saints with which he now may share the Holy Supper. Upon application to the executive bishop, he becomes a member of the General Church, and afterward is free to sign the roll of his local society.

Betrothal is the solemnization of consent to marriage, and in the past it was usually a private ceremony, often with no witnesses. In recent years, however, the unique Swedenborgian rite has begun to be held earlier in the engagement period than was once the custom, and sometimes it is performed in the presence of friends and relatives. Betrothal is representative of an internal state; it is marriage which establishes an external one, and except in cases where the officiating minister feels a public ceremony would appear to give church sanction to a disorderly lifestyle or in some cases of second marriage following the death of the first partner, New Church weddings are community affairs. A general invitation to borough residents is issued through the *Post,* and while receptions in private homes or rented quarters may be restricted to invited guests, these parties always are preceded by postnuptial festivities in the choir hall or on the cathedral lawn. Everyone in Bryn Athyn is thereby given an opportunity to extend congratulations to the couple and join in toasts—first to the church, then to wife and husband. Ordinations usually constitute part of the adult service on the Nineteenth of June, and even if scheduled at a different time, they always are public ceremonies. Garbed in a white surplice, the candidate for the ministry, whether of the first, second, or third degree, presents himself to a bishop who, by the laying on of hands, inaugurates the ordinand into the special uses of the Lord's representative on earth. Investiture into a priestly office generally is followed by an open reception.

Funerals also are community events, and the spirit which informs them marks these memorial services as the most distinctive of all the sect's familiar rites of passage. Affirmed for members of the General Church by Swedenborg's meticulously detailed reports of his own experience and observations in the spirit world, the reality of life after death is a core belief uniting everyone in Bryn Athyn. Possessed of a chart, as it were, of the soul's expected progress once it is separated from the body, death loses for them the quality of mystery. Heaven and hell are as real localities in their behavioral environment as Pine Run Park and Philadelphia. The seer describes the topography and the climate of the spirit world and the dwellings and garments of its inhabitants. The distinctions among angelic societies are as clear to borough residents as those among various occupational groupings on earth. A realm characterized by infinite variety and constant activity, the other world is a kingdom of uses, where good spirits increase in perfection forever and dwell in innocence and peace. True marriages are preserved there, and true friendships. Sadness at the removal of a loved person from the earthly company of New Churchmen is mitigated, therefore, by a collective sense of joy that he is even then awakening in the spiritual world for which his previous life was but a preparation. Seizing the model presented by the Psalmist of the third dispensation, the Huntingdon Valley Swedenborgians turn mourning into dancing.[26] The definition of death they traditionally have accepted is cessation of heart action. The Writings teach, however, that a subtle motion may continue for some time after a heartbeat can no longer be detected, and consequently, New Churchmen try to avoid an autopsy, embalming, or cremation for at least three days in order to interfere as little as possible with the process of the soul's separation from the body. They believe that through the good offices of angels, whose special use it is, the gradually released spirit is led into an awareness of his new circumstances. It remains for those left behind in the natural world to dispose of his discarded body in an orderly fashion. Artificial preservation of the corpse is regarded as inappropriate, and a public exhibition of the remains is thought distateful if not obscene. Usually the body simply is removed from the home or hospital to an undertaker's establishment where it is placed in a plain coffin, sealed when the family feels ready, then either committed to the earth or to fire. In the case of cremation, the ashes are scattered; in the case of burial, it is customary for the closest male relatives or friends of the deceased to attend a brief service of interment, though no rule proscribes the presence of women. The memorial service, which follows the committal ceremony, is open to the entire community. Designed to aid the bereaved in their reorientation to the uses required of the living, its focus is upon the resurrection of the spirit. A reception follows at a New Church home, giving everyone an opportunity to share food and wine, and it is by no means a dolorous occasion. The annual report of the Bryn Athyn Church, in cataloging events, lists not funerals but "resurrections." Grave markers in the borough cemetery are the simplest of granite stones or, occasionally, just brass plates level with the ground.

Calendrical rituals observed in Bryn Athyn are a further method for fostering and cementing common bonds, which, in addition, give children access to their parents' memories. A baker's dozen of thirteen are marked on the borough's annual calendar, and for at least some segments of the community, they are each one festival days on which attention is turned from ordinary work to the work of celebration. In the past the New Year always was welcomed by a society party. While now such festivities are not necessarily an annual occurrence, a worship service on the morning of the first day in January traditionally is presented as an opportunity to take stock and consider one's personal future. Later in the month a Founder's Day banquet marks the anniversary of the establishment of the Academy. Good Friday was observed for many years simply by the sharing of Holy Supper, but in the early seventies a service was inaugurated in which passages from the New Testament and the Writings are read to commemorate the events through which, the Swedenborgians believe, the Lord effected the glorification of His Human. The union of the Lord's nature from Mary with the Divine from the Father is symbolized by His rising on the third day, according to the Writings, and Easter is a major festival in the New Church as in the churches of Christendom. Memorial Day is marked by a civic ritual, which includes patriotic speeches in the borough park and a community picnic. The Academy commencement is attended by residents anxious to learn who among their young relatives and friends will graduate with honors. Observance of the Nineteenth of June, the New Church's birthday festival, takes all day and begins with a children's service, after which beautiful handmade gifts, red yarn balls, wooly white lambs, dolls, boats, blocks, and velvet Word covers, are distributed to the youngsters. An adult service, held late in the afternoon, is followed by a candlelit banquet in the Academy fieldhouse. Afterward the diners walk back to the cathedral to sit and meditate as the unique feast day draws to an end. On the Sunday nearest the nineteenth a pageant is presented on the sweeping lawns of the Gothic edifice. Usually involving some 300 youngsters, it portrays the history of the five churches, and regularly attracts the relatives of all the participants. Bryn Athyn celebrates Independence Day with an old-fashioned parade around the Academy grounds, featuring the school band, elaborately decorated floats, and bicycles festive with crepe paper. Until just before World War II, the local patriots were led by a genuine Kentucky Colonel astride his white horse, but in more recent years the borough has had to make do with speeches by a less colorful military person. The remainder of the Fourth is devoted to foot and swimming races, softball games, and a community picnic, after which residents watch the distant fireworks set off in a neighboring township. Labor Day is the occasion of go-cart races, and sometime in October, Charter Day, a moveable feast determined by the Academy football schedule, inaugurates homecoming weekend. Always held on a Friday, it begins witn a procession of Academy directors and faculty in academic gowns and of scrubbed and shining students carrying class banners. The marchers wind their way from the campus to the cathedral for a worship service, then recross Huntingdon Pike for a song fest outside the Academy buildings. Luncheons, football, a dance, and on Saturday, meetings and a banquet, complete the festivities. In Bryn Athyn, as elsewhere, Halloween is a ritual of rebellion for children, although in the New Church community, the costumed youngsters are permitted to seek sweets only at homes with lighted candles burning in the windows. On Thanksgiving, a worship service is held in the Academy's fieldhouse, as the only place large enough to hold the congregation swelled by visiting friends and relatives who come with their borough hosts to watch a procession of children carrying harvest offerings. Christmas in Bryn Athyn is marked not only by caroling at Glencairn, but by an annual nativity tableaux presented in the assembly hall, and on the holy day itself, cathedral services which stress that the babe born in Bethlehem was Jehovah God.

In any year there are more events even than rituals to draw the Huntingdon Valley New Churchmen together. For a borough with under a thousand inhabitants, Bryn Athyn has remarkable cultural offerings. Academy plays and musicals attract residents of all ages. Three times a year, community concerts are presented by the local orchestra, which includes among its regular members a cellist who plays with the Philadelphia Orchestra and a violist from the Metropolitan Opera Orchestra in New York. Bryn Athyn is the headquarters of the Swedenborg Scientist Association, and its annual meeting, open to the public and regularly attended by about ninety borough residents, features a paper on some aspect of the seer's philosophical work. The Academy Museum, beneficiary of a Nile expedition made by John Pitcairn and William Henry Benade, as well as the European travels of the plate-glass manufacturer's sons and the wanderings of other New Churchmen, has an eclectic collection which is now housed in Glencairn. It includes such Egyptian antiquities as a predynastic vase; the spirit door of Tet-Emankh, high priest of Cheops; the head of Sehket from the temple of Mut at Karnak; pottery; amulets; bronze figures; scarabaei; and papyrus scrolls inscribed in hieroglyphics. A Babylonian collection contains cunieform tablets, and other treasures range from a Cretan libation cup to Greek vases; Roman sculpture; Romanesque and Gothic statuary, columns, capitals, and corbels; two sculptured groups by the English New Churchman John Flaxman; Chinese porcelain, friezes, a writing box, and Han Dynasty pillar; North American Indian relics; and Zulu and Bantu artifacts. The museum sponsors courses, open and free to the community, on hieroglyphics and New Testament Greek, as well as shorter lecture series on such topics as the correspondences of gardens and medieval art. French stained glass and sculpture from the twelfth and thirteenth centuries fill Glencairn itself. The rare and beautiful fragments were acquired by Raymond Pitcairn to inspire the cathedral workmen, and during 1982 more than one hundred pieces from his collection were exhibted by the Metropolitan Museum of Art at the Cloisters.

Various opportunities for continuing education are provided borough residents through the college. The weekly doctrinal class, which follows Friday supper, attracts an average of more than 320 New Churchmen, and in addition, special classes devoted to specific religious topics are held for smaller groups throughout the year. A Theta Alpha discussion class meets biweekly to pursue such subjects as child development in the light of the Writings. Twice a year the laymen of the community have an opportunity to make a retreat at Glen Tonche, and generally several dozen, accompanied by members of the clergy, drive to the the Pitcairns' Catskill colony for a weekend of spiritual reflection.

For those residents for whom age, infirmities, inclination, or lack of leisure prove impediments to active participation in the General Church's ongoing religious education program, the sect's publications offer a plethora of reading material to peruse at home. Its official organ, *New Church Life,* is a monthly devoted to discussions of theology, ethics, sectarian history, and the annual reports of the organizational affairs of the Swedenborgian body. *New Philosophy,* the quarterly published by the Swedenborg Scientific Association, is a scholarly journal which serves as an outlet for some of the most creative minds in the New Church. The *Academy Journal*'s annual literary number provides a forum for discussion of the sect's distinctive educational philosophy and psychology. The periodicals published by the Sons of the Academy and Theta Alpha report on the activities of the two alumni societies, as well as printing a wide variety of short articles bearing on the interface of the New Church and the world. Bryn Athyn's weekly newspaper is the *Post*. Published under the aegis of the local society, it contains an occasional series of articles on the borough's past and a record of current events. The *Post* serves as a psychologically critical channel of communications between church institutions and members. It is a kind of "letter from home" for Swedenborgians living outside the Huntingdon Valley, and as they consider their immediate obligations and pleasures, residents always consult the eight-page sheet.

There are other voices in Bryn Athyn, however than those heard in the establishment press. Well-polished mechanisms of cultural reinforcement and transmission have not precluded questions about the appropriateness of community values, especially on the part of the generation which came of age in the sixties. Electronically linked to the world beyond the New Church borough from childhood, they are nearer, in a significant sense, to their great-grandparents' generation than that of their parents. As Margaret Mead has pointed out, immigrants and pioneers "have no certain models of behavior except their peers."[27] Crossing oceans and mountains necessitates the replacement of cultural paradigms, but so too do spiritual journeys. The initial settlers of Bryn Athyn had to try to raise their children with values which, for the most part, they had embraced as adults. These New Church adventurers could not turn, therefore, to their own parents for guidance, but had to rely on their contemporaries as together they constructed civic, educational, and ecclesiastical institutions. The first birthright members of the General Church finished cutting the pattern for life in the borough, and their children could look, then, for precedents in their own experience for bringing up the great-grandchildren of John Pitcairn and Robert Glenn. But while middle-aged New Churchmen can take their culture for granted, many young adults have not been able to accept uncritically models derived from their forebearers. Catalytic agents in their dissent are the experiences they have shared via television with their age cohorts everywhere—the Vietnam War and an awareness of the availability of drugs and of the crumbling of sexual taboos in highly visible and attractive segments of American society. Because their parents had faced neither the same temptations nor the same opportunities, Bryn Athyn's fourth generation, like its first, could turn only to their New Church peers for clues to appropriate behavior. As some of them began to wonder what, if anything, in their own past was communicable, however, they discovered that if their inheritance was inadequate in terms of formulas, they had acquired in their homes and at the Academy certain research skills of value. The Writings themselves emerged as a priceless legacy. What had come down to them through three generations was the freedom, indeed the obligation, to consult the Swedish seer's theological treatises directly, and some ability to search them profitably for guidance in a world where a border skirmish could threaten nuclear annihilation and continued pollution might make the planet uninhabitable.

A young woman who had marched on Washington, a young man who smoked marijuana, a couple who with no immediate plans for marriage shared a bed—they represented a small segment of Bryn Athyn youth who were experimenting with alternative lifestyles. Leaving the General Church was a possibility, but most wanted to try to find a place within it. Nor was the ecclesiastical institution anxious to lose either members or potential ones. As early as 1966, Erik Sandstrom, then pastor of the Cleveland Circle and later dean of the theological school, had urged his fellow clergymen to consider the idea of a young people's assembly, and in 1968 he took the initiative for arranging one which was held over Labor Day weekend in western Pennsylvania's Laurel Hill State Park. The sect's executive bishop came and fielded questions from the gathering of nearly 100 met to consider the possibility of an "accommodation without compromise." On the one hand, the young Swedenborgians shared their generation's distrust of organized authority; on the other, they felt the need of improved communication with their elders in the New Church. The possibility of a periodical was raised, and with Sandstrom's encouragement but no guarantee of financial support, a nucleus from Bryn Athyn decided to start one.

The first issue of *The Publication* appeared in October of 1968. Its declared purpose was "to provide a place for current interaction and not simply to set up a pulpit for juvenile clericalism. We don't want this to become a Radio Free Old People enterprise," the editors asserted, and they expressed the hope that the journal reflected "a dream within reach."[28] In subsequent issues questions were raised about Academy governance and the institution's choice of sanctions. Articles were published dealing passionately with war and frankly with human sexuality. The General Church was criticized for ignoring issues the young editors considered its proper concern and for intruding into areas they felt were beyond the scope of its legitimate interests. For a time community response was lively, and *The Publication* printed unhesitating letters and articles which both commended and condemned stands taken in its pages. "Many of us are listening," one Bryn Athyn couple wrote. "Few publicatons in the Church have evoked so much discussion. The spirit of open-minded searches for answers is what we obviously need. . . . We need your active, thoughtful participation in this exciting and important era in the Church."[29] The journal had hoped to be self-supporting, but subscriptions did not always cover printing and distribution costs, and once the Cairncrest Foundation made a small grant to help balance the books. The subvention relfected the view of some members of the New Church community that *The Publication* was a sign of the sect's good health. The journal was not, however, free of cavilling, and other coupled its negativism and occasional lapses of taste to prove that the editors had failed in their effort to serve a genuine use. To yet another segment of the borough population, of course, the nascent publishing venture represented an unalloyed threat, and they were relieved when, after several years, the monthly began to appear less and less regularly due to a waning of the editors' initial enthusiasm and to increasingly troubled finances.

If *The Publication* proved an outlet for youthful frustration, it also prodded the General Church to respond to some of its young peoples' real concerns. The Laurel Hill weekend evolved into an annual week-long retreat for those of college age or older, and a similar religious camp experience was instituted for secondary school students. Eventually, personnel shifts in the administration of Bryn Athyn Church and the Academy held out the promise of continued responsiveness. As an organized group, *The Publication* staff dissolved; one member severed connections with the sect, but for most of the others, an indication of some institutional changes together with an awareness that other changes had to be personal, combined to keep them within the sphere of the General Church. To the extent that a dialog was maintained, the monthly journal had served as a forum for the exchange of ideas, but then the tradition which spawned it was proudly intellectual. The sect had not expended much energy in dealing with man's affectional nature, and a journalistic venture was not an appropriate mechanism for even beginning to restore the balance. The initial effort of a minister to introduce encounter-group techniques at the summer camps was a well-aimed effort to address emotional problems, but it provoked sufficient opposition among his superiors to bring the methodological experiment to an abrupt halt. The need on the part of the New Church young people to confront feelings as well as thoughts remained, however, engendering at length experiments in ritual and briefly raising a prophet.

''Anti-cathedralism'' is the summary description Bryn Athyn's counterculture sometimes uses to convey its attitude toward formal worship and pedigrees in the Huntingdon Valley community. Generally well connected themselves, a core group of young men and women were eager to try to live lives oriented toward the Writings outside inherited liturgical and social structures when a fairhaired boy came out of the West with a name which did not bring instant recognition, respect for subjective as well as objective determinants of human behavior, and religious ideas the General Church would not immediately identify with the literal sense of Swedenborg's theological treatises. Cliff Barry was a young man from Glenview, Illinois, who had graduated with honors from the Academy boys' school in 1967 and during the next year attended the borough college. After a year away at a secular institution, he returned to Bryn Athyn to study for the ministry of the Lord's New Church under its resident bishop. His interest in the splinter group had been stirred by a Hemelsche Leer priest who became his father-in-law. Convinced that people recognize and can evaluate their own states of regeneration, Barry also disputed the concept of the eternity of the hells for any given individual as inconsistent with divine mercy. After completing nearly the full course of study for the priesthood, however, he broke with the Lord's New Church in the spring of 1974 because of the unacceptability of his interpretation of portions of the Writings to the ecclesiastical organization founded on the principle that each man is to apply to Swedenborg's treatises the tools the seer applied to the Old and New Testaments, and derive for himself their spiritual sense. Cut off from his former source of support, the ex-theolog sold ice cream to support his wife and children. About this time, several young adults, recently returned from a Laurel Hill camp session, initiated their own outdoor worship services, and in the autumn of 1974 Barry led them in a discussion of baptism on the shore of Pennypack Creek. Described by his peers as "personable," "infectiously enthusiastic," and again and again "charismatic," the former Academy student became their "minister." Although some among the original two dozen young people continued to attend morning worship at the cathedral, they regularly met with Barry, minus coats and ties and prayer-books, for religious discussions and experimental liturgies. Several meetings, initiated by the dean of the Bryn Athyn Church, to discuss with him their dissatisfaction with cathedral services, resulted in strengthening the bonds among the dissidents as they sensed formal opposition, and "Sunday Circle" became "Cliff's Church."

The subsociety never numbered more than thirty individuals, but its determination was strong enough to prompt Barry to give up other part-time employment and seek the members' financial support. Several had substantial inheritances, the rest were relatively poor, but each gave what he or she could, and the un-licensed cleric managed to house and feed and clothe his family on their voluntary offerings. Gathering either in the woods or in someone's home for worship on Sunday afternoons and at least one evening during the week for discussion sessions, the group experimented with various liturgical forms. Readings from the Word invariably occupied a central place in these rituals, but the young people also stressed group prayer and the sharing of personal experiences and feelings. They found meaning in something like the "testimony" historically associated with revivalism, and more recently incorporated into the ritualistic formulas adopted by the spiritually awakened among America's former flower children. Members of Cliff's Church also shared with some of their "old church" contemporaries an interest in establishing a one-to-one relationship with Jesus Christ. The General Church, in the opinion of many, emphasized the Lord's Divine at the expense of His Human, and for them the historical Jesus was curiously inaccessible. A distinctive New Church cast was given to the movement, however, by Barry's particular method of periodizing history. He suggested that the General Convention corresponded to the Most Ancient Church, the Lord's New Church to the Israelitish Church, and his own congregation to the Christian Church. The New Church of the New Church was yet to come, and the idea contemplated with considerable sympathy by his followers was that it would be not an ecclesiastical organization, but a body of kindred spirits.

Speculation about the dissenting group's activities naturally was widespread in Bryn Athyn, but the fact is that far from advocating "free love," as suggested by some residents whose own parents and grandparents had been the victims of the same vicious rumors as a result of the Kramph will case, Cliff Barry simply had no appetite for hurling either the first or any subsequent stone. He accepted as full members of his congregation individuals involved in what the General Church termed disorderly relationships, as well as those who scrupulously observed the sexual precepts of the sect. What the group did, in addition to talking and meditating, was to share a Holy Supper of bread and wine once a month, then dine on a fare of more material substance, which was contributed to by every member. As the months passed, the issue of ordination arose. It was essentially a question of legitimizing Barry's authority on a basis other than his own charisma, and in the late summer of 1975 some fifteen young people made a retreat to Lake Wallenpaupac in the Poconos to consider the matter. The ex-theolog wanted to be consecrated in his use, and the reluctant among his followers eventually agreed on the appropriateness of ordaining him. They built a stone altar, placed wildflowers on it, and as their minister knelt, they placed their hands on his head in a ritual of consecration. Earlier each had read a passage from the Word or a personal contribution especially prepared for the ceremony, and now they held a feast of thanksgiving. Shortly after this episode, Barry conducted a betrothal service, but despite the ostensible regularization of the relationship between priest and people, his financial support began to erode as some followers moved away and the others failed to reach an agreement on the desirability of attempting a more formal ecclesiastical organization. Dissension among the members of his congregation, together with bureaucratic harassments, finally prompted him to take his wife and his children into the West from which he had come, and they have not returned to Bryn Athyn.

The borough Establishment finds the situation, if predictable, also comforting. The erstwhile members of Cliff's Church suggest, however, that it would be an error to conclude their experiment was a failure. A few are convinced that the "final" dispensation about which their pastor preached is even now emerging as a spiritual church. They avow that their group experiences led them into a more intimate relationship with the Lord. While some members of the group never completely stopped attending cathedral services, the return of others has been made easier by the willingness of the clergy to hold a series of simpler services in addition to the regular Sunday liturgy. The General Church, the young people readily acknowledge, ultimately left them in freedom, and they are reluctant, in the last analysis, to remove themselves from its sphere, having no guarantee that another atmosphere will be more conducive to personal growth. For nearly forty years, after all, two Swedenborgian sects have coexisted peacefully in a borough of little more than two square miles. Traces of bitterness remain on the part of members of the older generation, especially among General Church people who are offended by the perceived connotations of the name Lord's New Church. Nevertheless, time has healed many wounds, and the fourth generation of Bryn Athyn settlers rarely distinguish between contemporaries who are "Hemies" and "General Church." Several members of the splinter group teach at the Academy, and children from the Lord's New Church frequently attend the local parochial schools. The first and present Hemelesche Leer bishop, ordained in 1947 by Theodore Pitcairn who himself never sought inauguration into the third degree, is married to a granddaughter of the first bishop of the

General Church. The kinship ties between members of the two New Church bodies ultimately have served to blunt theological differences, especially when one group is too small to consider endogomy.

If a tolerance of mildly divergent world views exists in Bryn Athyn, however, it is also true that Cliff's Church represented a Swedenborgian manifestation of what Peter Berger has identified as a general effort among the religiously oriented young "to cope with the discontents of modernity that they associate with functional rationality." Openess is the ultimate virtue from their standpoint, and as the sociologist has observed, "staying by oneself, keeping apart, 'holding back' in any sense are negatively defined qualities." In the ideal community envisioned by these youths, all others would be, in George Herbert Meade's phrase, "significant others," and as Berger himself further notes, they yearn for "small groupings within which relationships will be profound."[30] For a time, Cliff Barry led a group of dissident New Churchmen in a search for a more effective ritual of salvation and a more satisfying culture, but the disillusionment they experienced was never sufficiently widespread to engender a genuine revitalization movement in Wallace's sense of the phenomenon.[31]

There have been other youthful residents of the borough, nevertheless, who have considered Bryn Athyn too urban and too institutionalized. In the summer of 1974 two New Church families moved some sixty-five miles to Kempton, Pennsylvania, a village in the foothills of the Poconos. The families of two Academy professors, married to John Pitcairn's granddaughters, had brought property in the area as a holiday retreat, but after long consideration, the family of one of the plate-glass manufacturer's great-granddaughters and the family of Yorvar Synnestvedt, the grandson of another prominent first generation settler, decided to permanently abandon the Huntingdon Valley in search of a more rural environment. A contributing factor was their feeling that "too much is done for you in the Bryn Athyn Society" and a desire to assume more responsibility for planning their own worship services. Within the past several years, eighteen other Swedenborgian couples and two single people have made their homes in Kempton. Most of the men are self-employed or work in the area. At first their children attended the district public school, but in 1979 a New Church elementary school was established in the village. The minister who visited once a month was replaced by a resident pastor, and the Pocono outpost was granted society status. Yovar Synnestvedt observes that the Kempton tribe misses Bryn Athyn's cultural advantages, but pleasures of country life, he insists, vastly outweigh the burdens.[32]

Bryn Athyn, as the parent community, continues in most respects as the model for the Pocono New Churchmen. The borough, for its part, recently has fought and won another skirmish in the frequently quiescent but neverending battle to maintain its identity. The United States Post Office briefly contemplated the possibility of eliminating the Huntingdon Valley community as a postal entity, but a petition with 600 signatures plus the threat of a court battle caused the government agency to think better of the plan. Among other things, instituitional bulk mailing, most of it pre-sorted, assures the local Post Office of an annual profit. For residents, however, the clapboard building by the railroad track is more than a convenience. It is a social institution inasmuch as there are no local household deliveries in the borough, and every day many members of the New Church community make a ritual visit to the Post Office not only to pick up their mail, but to visit with their neighbors and check the bulletin board for announcements of births, betrothals, marriages, and deaths. Residents are reluctant to see even a single thread snapped in the web uniting them, but even more important is their determination to keep their name. Bryn Athyn stands for a way of life, which in many ways is an anomaly in twentieth-century America. An enclave of leisure and comfort and privilege, it is distinguished by vast open spaces and religious cohesion. "Cushy" is the word some scions of its first settlers have used to describe life in the borough, and concern occasionally is voiced that residents remain more for love of the colony's material than its spiritual advantages. A high level of religious intensity, nevertheless, is evident, and if a degree of unanalyzed consensus bodes ill for the community's capacity to respond to the needs of new generations of Swedenborgians, a belief in freedom as a precondition of salvation signifies to those who would inform anew the vision of the General Church that it is useful for them to tarry along the Pennypack.

6

The Authority Structure

Apart from schism, change in a religious community depends upon the cooperation of persons in power with those who would effect an altered state. But unlike modern political dissidents, who seek evolutionary rather than revolutionary transformation, spiritual rebels of every age have had to mount their challenge against a polity claiming to represent not the people but the Lord. Discovery of a method for the historical expression of divine sovereignty is a fundamental problem in all ecclesiastical bodies. Theism characteristically attributes to God not only supreme, universal, and infinite power to do His will, but also the absolute and perfect right to act without control, confinement, subjection, or consultation. The question confronting men who would act in His name is how best to mediate His authority in society. Should they rely on the spontaneous inspiration of special individuals, or on the legislative ability of believers acting in consort, or on an official class delegated to preserve and transmit oral and written tradition? In every instance ecclesiastical authority is derivative, but its origin neither dictates the form nor removes the necessity of its social manifestation in a given collectivity.

Location of ultimate authority in the theological works of Emanuel Swedenborg, as not only the inspired Word of God but the vehicle of the Second Coming, was the question upon which turned the Academicians' break with the General Convention in 1890. Determination of a mode of expressing the authority of the Writings was essential, nevertheless, to the establishment of social order in Bryn Athyn, and on popular consent to the method of conveyance has hinged the continued existence of the community. Written in Latin more than two centuries ago, the treatises accepted as a third canon by New Churchmen require interpretation for modern receivers, and inextricably linked to the survival of the sect is the necessity of teaching doctrine derived from the Writings to succeeding generations. To this end the General Church sets apart from other men priests, who are solemnly charged with the responsibility of instructing the people and leading them "by truths to the good life."[1] Clerical authority is validated in the Writings themselves, and on the basis of the nature of its claim to legitimacy, the authority structure of the sect can be classified in Weberian terms as rational-legal.[2] The right of the General Church priest to make decisions and command actions, if necessary under the threat of negative sanction, does not rest in any special attributes of his person, but flows from his occupation of a legally established office. The system of rules which defines the powers of the ministerial office is confirmed, in turn, by having been "enacted or imposed," to use Talcott Parson's words, "by an agency which has legitimate authority to do so,"[3] that is, in the view of the Bryn Athyn Swedenborgians, by God Himself. They believe that divine authority is rationally channeled through a priesthood which was instituted by the Lord in His Second Coming. Reporting on what he saw and heard in the realm of spirits, Swedenborg had proclaimed that in heaven "all preachers are appointed by the Lord. . . . No others are permitted to preach in the churches."[4] As for earth, the Writings say: Order cannot be maintained in the world without *praefecti.* . . . Those in authority who are placed over ecclesiastical things, are called priests."[5] The seer taught, moreover, that "good can be insinuated into another by anyone in the country, but not truth, except by those who are teaching ministers. If others do this, heresies arise, and the church is disturbed and rent asunder."[6]

The qualitative differentiation between classes of individuals in the General Church is derived specifically from the Swedenborgians' concept of use. From the Writings, the generic idea is of a function ordained by the Lord. "When man was first created," *The True Christian Religion* declares, "he was initiated into wisdom and its love, not for his own sake but that he might impart it to others from himself. . . . To live for others is to perform uses: uses are the bonds of society, and these are as many as there are good uses, and their number is infinite.[7]" Swedenborg's map of the spirit world revealed heavenly divisions to be wholly functional. Adhering to the doctrine of correspondences, New Churchmen arrived at the dignity-bestowing notion that on earth each individual has his particular uses, and they believe, moreover, that groups have distinctive uses. No one presumes to know precisely what any given person's use may be at any one time; that is between him and God. The General Church does seek, however, to explicate collective uses, and this explication is the basis for social roles in the sect.

The authority of its priesthood comes from the Swedenborgians' belief that their ministers represent the Lord. Ordination confers a special character on a man which is described in the rite itself as "the promise of the Holy Spirit."[8] According to the Writings, "the clergy in particular receive enlightenment and instruction because these relate to their office, and inauguration into the ministry brings them with it."[9] Status in the New Church is grounded in the concept of vocation or of a "calling" to particular uses, each of which is characterized by a particular combination of rights and duties. The "laying on of hands" signifies the transference of grace necessary to carry out a divine appointment, given for the administration of God's laws and the conduct of worship "with a view to the salvation of souls."[10] Ordination is a holy act, and New Churchmen believe it sets a man permanently apart from his fellow men. Gifts of the Spirit cannot, in their view, be retrieved by the Church. A priest whose teachings or whose life gives scandal can be separated from the Church, but he can still validly administer its sacraments and officiate at its rites. He may be deprived of the licit use of his powers, but not the powers themselves.

The priesthood is instituted to provide for a three-fold ministry of instruction, of worship, and of government, as called for in the Writings, which say that "in the church, there must be a filleted primate, parish priests, and curates under them."[11] By ordination into the first degree, a candidate for priestly office becomes a minister and enters fully into the uses of instruction. He is authorized to teach the Word of God according to the doctrine of the General Church, to administer the sacrament of baptism, to hear and receive confession of faith, which is a Swedenborgian rite corresponding to confirmation, and to lead in public worship. The sign of this degree is a white stole, and a minister customarily serves a year as an assistant to a pastor or as an instructor of religion before being ordained into the second degree which is the ministry of worship. In addition to the duties prescribed in the first degree, a minister who becomes a pastor is authorized to administer the sacrament of the Holy Supper, to solemnize betrothals, to consecrate marriages, and to dedicate homes. The sign of the second degree is a blue stole, and a man ordained into it usually serves as a pastor of a society and a superintendent of its school. The ministry of government is provided for in the third degree of the priesthood. When becoming a bishop, a pastor, in addition to his other duties, receives the authority to ordain priests, to dedicate places of worship, and to preside over a general body of the Church. The sign of the episcopacy is a red stole, and in the eighty-five-year history of the General Church of the New Jerusalem it has been worn by nine men, including the five executive bishops of the sect.

The executive bishop is the first among equals. He is in no sense regarded as Christ's vicar, but as chief governor, the primacy of his office being set forth in the Writings as necessary to order in the New Church. Chosen from among priests of the third degree, the executive bishop is nominated by the council of clergy, a deliberative body made up of General Church priests. The council must submit its candidate to the Church's board of directors, a lay body which administers the financial affairs of the sect. In theory, the board could ask the council to reconsider its nomination, but in practice the lay group has approved without question the priests' candidate who always has been an obvious choice groomed for the preeminent position in the secondary post of assistant bishop. In agreement, then, the council and the board place the name of the nominee for executive bishop before all the members of the Church meeting in a general assembly. They are empowered to accept or reject the candidate guided by majority rule. No name presented to an assembly ever has failed of approval, but always there have been dissenting votes.

Once elected an executive bishop continues in office until he resigns, which is compulsory at age seventy-two, or dies, or is separated from his office by the same procedure by which he was selected, that is, by a decision of the council ratified by the board and approved by the assembly. As judiciary functions are vested in the primatial office, the power exercised by the chief executive of the General Church is unchecked save by the threat of removal. At no time since 1897, however, has such drastic action been taken or even contemplated, and the brilliant but afflicted Benade seems to have been the only tyrant in the history of the sect. None since him have been charismatic leaders, nor altered in any way the uses of the New Church.

In the view of the Swedenborgian community, their chief pastor's great power is commensurate with his responsibility. His principal duty is to provide for the government of the General Church. He appoints all pastors, though a local society has the option of rejecting his choice. Decisions about inaugurating men into the priesthood and thereafter moving them into successive degrees of the ministry are made by him on the basis of the needs of the sect. Although by virtue of their ordination into the third degree of the priesthood, all bishops have ordaining power, they do not exercise it without the consent of the executive bishop. There is but one diocese in the General Church, and in practice the chief pastor ordains men into the third degree for the purpose of assisting him and training a successor. The office of assistant bishop is filled in the same manner as that of executive bishop; other bishops, and there have never been more than two at one time, are appointed by the executive bishop himself.

The second duty of the chief pastor is to preserve order on the grounds that the General Church cannot fulfill its uses in the absence of order. He has the power to remove from membership anyone who causes a persistent disturbance. If contention arises between a society and a pastor, moreover, it is his duty, as former executive bishop Willard D. Pendleton has said, "either to put the fire out or get rid of the priest."[12] In most cases the latter option would involve finding another place for the minister, but if circumstances warranted, the executive bishop could remove an offending priest from the council of clergy, thus denying him any voice in the ecclesiastical affairs of the sect.

A final duty peculiar to the office of executive bishop is the provision of doctrinal leadership. It is a somewhat vague responsibility which the chief pastor seeks to fulfill through preaching, writing, and, less obviously, policy decisions affecting the Academy schools. He customarily gives either the Easter or the Christmas sermon at the Bryn Athyn cathedral, preaches there and elsewhere at other times during the year, and addresses church assemblies. These are general meetings which the executive bishop convenes at the local, district, national, or general level for the purpose of speaking to members on matters of doctrine or the uses of the Church and, in stated cases, holding elections. The Swedenborgian primate also discusses principles of faith in articles published in *New Church Life* and in longer studies published by the Academy Book Room. As chancellor of the Academy itself, the executive bishop is responsible for the religious aspects of the New Church secondary, collegiate, and theological schools, though this is a duty which, in recent years, executive bishops have delegated to other clergymen who have served as presidents of the Academy. The president functions, in the words Anthony Wallace used to describe staff people generally, as "an extension and externalization of the cognitive operations which the executive is expected to perform."[13] Nevertheless, the chief pastor continues to preside at meetings of the theological faculty and of the joint faculties of the Academy and the Bryn Athyn elementary school. He appoints the dean of the theological school and nominates the president for board approval after consulation with a committee of directors. He provides doctrinal leadership directly or by delegation through the action he takes on academic or social matters referred to him for policy decisions. The *ex cathedra* pronouncements of the executive bishop on matters of faith and morals are not considered immune from error, but given his responsibility for the government of the Church, the primate can expect attention and deference from all its members.

In the last analysis, the chief pastor's authority is confirmed only by the willingness of his flock to accept it. The extent to which his decisions are morally binding on New Churchmen resides entirely with them.[14] Swedenborgians may agree that the executive bishop's power is derived from the Writings, in which they believe not only that God speaks but that Christ made His Second Coming; nevertheless, the origin of the primate's authority does not confer *carte blanche* upon him. "To be continuously effective," as Robert Merton has observed, "authority must be exercised within the constraining limits provided by the norms of the group; therefore, leaders must have substantial knowledge about the collective values of their followers.[15] As a direct result of their comprehensive system of parochial education, the normative orientation of prelate and people in the New Church is similar if not identical, but this does not reduce the importance of the executive bishop's obtaining information about attitudes of the priesthood and laity on given issues. "Let us take no step in advance," said the first leader of the General Church, "until its use is seen, and it can be maintained with the intelligent co-operation of the worshippers."[16] Bishop William F. Pendleton was speaking in this instance about liturgical matters, but he expressed a key concept of New Church leadership which is, as a former dean of the Theological School, Erik Sandstrom, defines it, the "idea that no decision is taken without counsel."[17]

The principal mechanisms in the social structure of the General Church for providing the executive bishop with needed information about group norms are the consistory and the council of clergy. The consistory is an advisory council of priests appointed by the chief pastor, which meets weekly with him. Generally, it includes the other bishops of the sect and ministers who reside in or near Bryn Athyn. The consistory considers a broad range of ecclesiastical questions from clerical appointments to liturgical changes to doctrinal issues, and while its membership changes at the will of the executive bishop, its influence remains steady and strong. Indeed, as a practical matter, the impact of this group on episcopal decisions is far greater that that of the council of the clergy. The deliberative body meets annually in Bryn Athyn, and the General Church provides the financial means for the eligible participants, wherever they live, to attend the week-long council sessions. Traditionally considered ineligible are the black ministers serving under the aegis of the sect's South African Mission, although all were trained in theology in the mission school and ordained into the same priesthood as their white colleagues. The agenda of council meetings includes papers on doctrinal and ethical issues, as well as discussions on a wide range of topics from rites of the Church to parochial education to translation of the Writings. A primary function of the minsterial sessions, however, is reinforcement of group solidarity. Wives accompany husbands, the social calendar is full, and while a substantial portion of the clergymen's deliberations are printed in *New Church Life,* they do not have the same immediate effect on the executive bishop's decisions as the weekly discussions of his consistory.

Quite apart from these formal channels of communication between primate and priests, the chief pastor of the General Church has important informal means of informing himself about popular attitudes and opinions. Lay leaders are encouraged to consult with him. He likes to know what is going on in various organizations because of his sense of responsibility for the New Church community as a whole; officers of these groups are motivated to seek his assent to contemplated new forms of action because to act without such support is to jeopardize their position and perhaps risk censure. Even less structured are the social contacts between prelate and people in a small borough. The executive bishop's multiple social identities are significant because as brother, cousin, husband, son-in-law, and father, he has access to information unavailable to him as chief executive, as well as obligations which may not be altogether consistent with his episcopal status.

The overwhelming majority of priests in the New Church are ordained into the second degree of the ministry. A minority of these are teachers in the Academy schools; most are pastors of Swedenborgian societies. When the oldest and largest, the Bryn Athyn Society, was established concurrently with the

General Church in 1897, a reaction against the extraordinary centralization of powers which had occurred under Bishop Benade resulted in the Society's election of not the executive bishop but another priest as pastor. Members came to feel, however, that it was not in the best interests of the sect to divide authority in this manner, so from 1902 to 1980 the executive bishop also served as the nominal head of the Bryn Athyn Society. But as the church grew in size and complexity, pastoral duties were performed to an increasing extent by an assistant pastor or, after 1962, by a priest designated as dean of the cathedral. Then, in 1980, Bishop Louis B. King called for a return to the early model of a nonepiscopal pastor for the largest Swedenborgian society, as for the rest. His proposal met with community approval, and the Bryn Athyn Church chose the Rev. Kurt H. Asplundh, who as dean had already served the local society for six years.

The usual method of electing a pastor of a society is for the executive bishop to submit the names of several willing candidates to an ad hoc committee of laymen. The committee then meets with the prelate and agrees upon one name to be presented to the whole society for ratification. On the grounds that a priest of the New Church, whomever he may be, represents the Lord and in an effort to preclude a society from orienting itself around one man, a pastorship customarily is held only from five to seven years before a priest is moved on to another society or another position within the Church. Where there are Swedenborgian elementary schools, the pastor generally serves as headmaster, although in Bryn Athyn, a priest with no pastoral duties holds this post.

The pastor of the Bryn Athyn Church has four major areas of responsibility. In the first place, he is responsible for the liturgical life of the society. He must arrange for three Sunday worship services, a 9:30 A.M. family service, an 11:00 A.M. service, and an 8:00 P.M. service, as well as for special services on feast days. Four times a year, a special Holy Supper liturgy replaces the adult morning and evening services on Sunday, and four other times a year, a communion service follows morning worship. For all of these occasions, the pastor, in consultation with an assistant, must schedule preachers, drawing on other clerical personnel attached to the General Church administration or Academy as he needs help. In addition to regularly scheduled services, moreover, the pastor must arrange, upon request, for baptisms, confirmations, the solemnization of betrothals, marriages, and memorial services. He responds to individual requests for communion, encourages and gives advice on the form of home worship services, and conducts worship services for various organizations, which range from simple invocation and benedictions to longer liturgies. A second area of the pastor's responsibility is instruction. In addition to teaching religion in the Bryn Athyn elementary school, he conducts doctrinal classes every Friday night throughout the academic year for adult members of the society. Special classes meet on Wednesday to explore particular doctrinal issues in more depth, and for both these and the regular classes, the dean is able to draw upon the assistance of other priests residing in Bryn Athyn. The pastor also holds "inquirer classes" for persons of other or no religious faith and for new members who have become affiliated with the sect in adult life. To a limited extent, moreover, he is involved in private instruction, usually in connection with a sacrament or rite of the Church, but often too in connection with his administrative responsibilities, such as in school disciplinary cases or when a society group seeks his opinion on the appropriateness of using a given piece of music. Although more characteristically a duty of pastors of smaller societies, a final area of his responsibility involves the social uses of the Church. Structurally located under his office are the Boys' Club, the Girls' Club, and the Women's Guild, as well as the Civic and Social Club on whose board of directors he serves as an ex officio member.

Just as the executive bishop benefits from the information and advice provided by the clergymen he appoints to his consistory, the pastor of the Bryn Athyn Church profits from the deliberations of a council made up of sixteen laymen and, since 1979, women in addition to priests on the pastoral staff who serve ex officio. Appointed to three-year terms, the council members discuss any matters their pastor may present to them, ranging from proposed changes in the order of a worship service to summer recreation programs. The fiscal affairs of the Bryn

Athyn Society, like those of the General Church and the Academy, are the responsibility of an elected board of trustees.

The concept that financial administration is the particular use of the laity is grounded in Swedenborgian doctrine only negatively, that is, in the sense that the Writings nowhere mention it as a clerical use. Historically, lay control of fiscal matters is rooted in John Pitcairn's initial support of the New Church community which made possible the exodus to Bryn Athyn, or at least cushioned the move, and the continuing and exceptional generosity of the Pitcairn family whose members contribute a substantial portion of their incomes to the Church. In Bryn Athyn, lay leadership is exercised through the governing boards of the General Church, the Academy, and the Bryn Athyn Society, and to a lesser degree, through administrative posts in the secondary schools and colleges and through offices in various service organizations. Continuously since 1900, a Pitcairn has served on at least two of the boards; for the past sixty-four years at least two members of the family have served on them. And while the Pitcairns have not wholly dominated community affairs, in the course of the past eighty years, fiscal authority has been vested to a great extent in the hands of five families, with three others playing a significant part in church government. In addition to the heirs of the plate-glass manufacturer, the Asplundhs, Synnestvedts, Gyllenhaals, Childses, Pendletons, Actons, and Bostocks have regularly held directorships. But recent rule changes limiting an individual's opportunity to succeed himself on the various governing boards already is democraticizing Swedenborgian polity.

The board of directors of the General Church is elected from and by the corporation of that body, which is composed of some 400 men. When male adults have been members of the Church for a minimum of five years, they become eligible to apply for membership in the corporation, and their applications are accepted upon reception. Formerly, directors were elected annually and could be reelected until they died. In 1950, however, new rules were adopted whereby terms were set at three years and a third of the membership was elected or reelected each year. In 1969 a resolution was passed limiting membership to two consecutive terms, after which a member would have to step down for a year before reelection was possible, unless his absence from the board would harm a use of the Church. A principal criterion for membership is active interest in the work of the sect, demonstrated by financial support, and members, usually successful business and professional men, are drawn from the major New Church societies in the United States and Canada. Geographical representation plays some part in decisions made by the corporation nominating committee, and there is an effort made to seek out people who have particular talents or insights into New Church affairs. The executive bishop, who serves as president of the corporation, is perpetually reelected to the board.

The General Church directors meet quarterly, but much of the group's work is carried on between meetings by committees open since 1961 to all corporation members. Although it is responsible for all the financial operations of the General Church, the board's major areas of concern are salaries, pensions, and investments. The treasurer of the Church serves on all its committees, and perhaps the most important of these is the five-member finance and development fund committee which he chairs. It is concerned with the long-range financial planning for the General Church and advises the board on the allocation of funds. The budget committee takes responsibility for how income is to be spent. A diversified $100-million investment fund is the sole concern of the investment committee. The salary committee is responsible for the administration, review, and adjustment of salaries of New Church priests and elementary school teachers. Administration of the General Church's noncontributory pension plan is the responsibility of the pension committee, and an orphanage committee arranges financial assistance to Church members unable to obtain help from their local societies.

The seventh and last board committee is the unique joint financial planning committee, which is made up of representatives of the General Church, the Academy, and the Bryn Athyn Society. These directors meet once a year with a representative of the Pitcairn family to divide between the three bodies the family's annual contribution to the New Church. The gift often amounts to 30 percent of the adult members' annual income.

It is received in the form of stock, which is sold upon receipt, and the cash is invested immediately in the Church's own fund. During the past decade this annual multimillion dollar transaction has been the most important single factor in preserving the New Church from deficit financing. Even in the present period of inflation, it has been able to continue various social services and, indeed, has undertaken new initiatives.

Structurally parallel to the General Church's board of directors is the board of directors of the Academy. It is, however, a smaller and less representative body drawn from a pool of candidates limited to the fifty men who serve on the Academy corporation. Antedating the formation of the General Church by twenty years, the Academy corporation is a self-perpetuating body which in 1876 included seven ministers and five laymen.[18] When the Swedenborgian sect was reorganized under Bishop Pendleton in 1897, and the role of the Academy was established as that of an educational arm of the New Church but in no sense that of an ecclesiastical rival, service on the coporation bcame a lay use. Membership was increased over the years to thirty, then forty, and now fifty men, including the executive bishop of the General Church, who serves as chancellor, and a priest who serves as president. When vacancies are created by resignation, retirement, or death, they are filled by vote of the remaining members who choose among candidates proposed to them by a nominating committee appointed by the executive bishop. The corporation's only function is to elect the Academy board of directors. The qualifications for membership in the parent body, and thus in the governing board itself, are explicated in the bylaws of the corporation. They state that a candidate "should be imbued with the purposes and traditions of the Academy; deeply interested in the work of New Church education," displaying that interest "either by personal effort or by way of financial contributions in keeping with his ability to give, and preferably by both," and a "man of established ability in his business or profession."[19] An informal but long-standing opposition exists to electing Academy teachers to membership in the corporation. To New Churchmen, these criteria mean, then, that lay leaders in Academy affairs are sought among the doctrinally sound, the dedicated, and the relatively rich.

The Academy's board of trustees is composed of fifteen men elected to three-year terms. A third of the membership is elected or reelected each year, and according to a resolution adopted in 1971, no member may serve more than four consecutive terms unless his absence would harm a use of the institution. As in the case of the General Church directors, the loophole permits the continual reelection of the chancellor and president of the Academy, who serve, by tradition, as the only priests on the board. Prior to 1960, elections were held every year, and the corporation usually reelected the entire board by acclamation. Customarily, the Academy trustees meet quarterly, and now, unlike in the past, when they were involved in academic matters, their sole concern is the institution's fiscal affairs. Working through standing committees, they take responsibility for determining the budget, soliciting contributions from alumni and friends, recommending student fees, adjusting faculty salaries, approving land acquisition, building construction, the purchase of major equipment, and supervising investments. Members concerned with this last board use meet every three months with the investment committee of the General Church to offer criticism and suggestions related to the directors' administration of the New Church investment fund.

Of the three principal lay governing boards meeting in Bryn Athyn, that of the General Church, the Academy, and the Bryn Athyn Church, only the latter is chosen by a group which includes women. While elected by the members, both male and female, of the Bryn Athyn Society, however, the board of trustees of the Bryn Athyn Church, like its counterparts, is composed only of men. A third of the twelve trustees are elected or reelected annually for three-year terms, and in accord with recent changes in the bylaws of the board, no member is to serve more than two consecutive terms unless absence would harm the uses of the organization. By virtue of his office, the pastor of the Bryn Athyn Society serves as president of the trustees. Meeting with the board by invitation are the secretary and treasurer of the society, who are appointed by the president, and the business manager, who is a full-time employee.

Until the mid 1970s the fiscal affairs of the Bryn Athyn Church and its elementary school were attended to primarily by the priest (or priests) who served as dean and headmaster, the treasurer, and serveral prominent trustees who submitted their decisions to the rest of the board for almost automatic approval. The economy and a growing dissatisfaction with this type of paternalism led to a reorganization in 1973, and now the work of the trustees is accomplished through fifteen standing committees. The most important is the financial planning committee, which is responsible for recommending changes in fiscal policy. Although headed by the treasurer of the Bryn Athyn Society, who has no vote at board meeings, the remaining members of this committee are all trustees. Membership on other committees, however, is not confined to board members or those who meet with the board, and in fact, the women of the church are represented on two committees concerned with providing assistance to disadvantaged New Church families.[20]

Other areas of trustee involvement represented by committee structure include budget determination, cathedral operations and security, cemetery care, contributions, editorial review, investments, real estate, salaries, school needs, and use and maintenance of buildings and grounds. Obviously the scope of the authority of some of these groups extends beyond finances. The committee on school needs, for example, must approve new textbooks and changes in classroom sturcture. An editorial revision board exercises prior censorship over each issue of the *Bryn Athyn Post.* Finally, the Bryn Athyn real estate committee is involved in maintaining the religious homogeneity of the community. To date no legal action challenging its buying and selling operations has been initiated, and the board continues to include the role of realtor in its collective identity.

As important as trustee positions are in the life of the New Church, an accounting of these does not exhaust the catalog of lay leadership in the community. Given the Swedenborgians' view of their parochial school system as essential to sectarian survivial, the heads of the boys' and girls' schools and, more especially, the dean of the college are persons of considerable consequence in Bryn Athyn. They enjoy the respect of the villagers, and although their educational attainments are hardly unique in the middle-class borough, they exert a combination of moral and intellectual authority which is linked to the inestimable value placed by New Churchmen upon distinctive education. Their academic authority is peculiarly limited by the fact that the priest who serves as president of the academy actually functions as chief hiring officer. As a matter of practice, he would make no decisions about personnel without the concurrence of the dean and department head involved, and all three interview prospective candidates. Decisions related to curriculum and degree requirements are left to the dean, and those in the area of student life also are his by delegation. When a situation arises in the college not covered by an existing policy, the normal procedure would be for the dean to bring the matter to the attention of the president. After discussion, the Academy's executive officer would render an opinion on the uses to be served by particular courses of action and the spiritual principles he believed should govern their implementation. The dean, with his faculty, then would develop a policy and a method for instituting it, returning once again to the president at the end of the decision-making process to seek his consent. A veto would send the college staff back to the drawing board, as final authority in academic affairs rests with the Academy president and, on appeal, the executive bishop of the General Church. "The dual processes of counsel and assembly" have been described as "the most effective representation of the Lord's leading from use."[21]

Apart from institutional trustees and Academy administrators, lay leadership in Bryn Athyn also is reflected in the dozen organizations which lie outside the main structure of authority in the community. One of the largest, with some 300 members, is the local chapter of the Sons of the Academy, and leadership in the alumni society at the international level has traditionally served as a kind of training ground for potential members of the Academy corporation. What motivates lay leaders to participate in New Church affairs? The traditional explanation for status achievement within sectarian organizations, that it serves as a compensation for relatively low status in the wider society, is not applicable to the Swedenborgian.[22] By and large, lay leaders are successful business and professional men, in a few cases spectacularly so, and their position in the Church can only confirm their leadership qualities already acknowledged by the world. Is it, then, a matter of *noblesse oblige?* In no traditional sense, clearly; for however mixed the motivations for significant involvement in individual cases, in general it comes down to the question of use. Ecclesiastical, liturgical, and doctrinal leadership are clerical uses; fiscal leadership is a lay use, and the Writings teach that "charity consists in the performing of uses for the sake of uses."[23] Participation is, from this point of view, valuable in itself, although New Churchmen also attach importance to the organizational effectiveness which results from a continuing supply of able, willing workers. A less obvious product of involvement is a strengthening of the commitment of individual leaders to the values of the collectivity, including the doctrine of a distinctive priesthood. As a result of a lifelong process of socialization, then, New Churchmen share a culturally produced normative orientation which makes possible self-appraisal. The negative sanctions available to the clergy, chastisement and even excommunication, are employed rarely precisely because members of the community *know* their place.

For women, it is on the periphery of the authority structure of the New Church. Barred from the sect's three principal governing boards, they do not have the right to vote for directors of the General Church nor the trustees of the Academy. Enfranchisement stops at the society level. Women cannot aspire, moreover, to the position of greatest prestige in the borough. By reason of their sex alone, they are exluded from the priesthood. No personal qualities of intelligence, virtue, or leadership can overcome the handicap of gender. Although now a potential threat to the Church's male-dominated polity has appeared as a cloud on the cognitive horizon, historically members of the sect have viewed the position of women in Bryn Athyn as fixed by the Lord Himself in the revelation made to Emanuel Swedenborg.

The Writings present not the individual but the couple as the fundamental unity of society. The emphasis throughout the Swedish seer's theological treatises is on the complementary nature of the sexes, and, paradoxically, their essential equality arises from their inequality. Neither man nor woman is complete without the other, and the highest achievement of which the human person is capable as a creature made in God's image depends upon a sharing of gender-linked gifts. Swedenborg posited the existence of distinct and unchanging masculine and feminine essences. Physical differences between men and women reflect, according to his doctrine of correspondences, psychological differences as profound as those revealed to the eye and ear. "The male is born intellectual," the Writings state, "the female voluntary; or, what is the same thing, the male is born into the affection of knowing, understanding, and being wise, and the female into the love of conjoining herself with that affection in the male. And as the interiors form the exteriors into their own likeness, . . . therefore, it is that the male is different in face, in tone of voice, and in the body from the female."[24] No qualities of mind, however, are the exclusive possessions of either sex. "Everyone," Swedenborg observed, "possesses understanding and will; but with the man the understanding predominates, and with the woman the will predominates; and the character [of each] is determined by that which predominates."[25]

Human talents are all derivative in the world view of the General Church. It is just that members believe that whereas love of wisdom flows from the Lord directly into the male, women must draw rational truths from male minds; likewise, love of molding these truths for the common good is an affection characteristically inflowing into the female, and for bringing wisdom forth in uses, men must rely on women. Individual escape from the ravaging frustration attendant upon everlasting potentiality and the possibility of collective progress depends upon the conjunction of male talent for acquisition of knowledge and female talent for its application. In heaven, the Writings teach, marriage consists of the union of two elements, understanding and will, into one mind, and there "a married pair is spoken of, not as two, but as one angel."[26]

On earth, the General Church maintains that innate psychological differences between the sexes are more directly responsible for social roles than any culture-bound conditions. From Swedenborg's theological works, members of the sect traditionally have concluded that woman's use is mainly domestic and man's forensic, that is, the one is based in the sphere of the home, the other in the public domain. In essential respects, moreover, performances in these realms are portrayed as mutually exclusive. "A wife cannot enter into the duties proper to the man," the Writings assert, "nor on the other hand a man into the duties proper to a wife. . . . In the duties proper to men, understanding, thought, and wisdom act the leading part; but in the duties proper to wives, will, affection, and love act the leading part. . . . Their duties are therefore of their own nature different, and yet are conjunctive."[27] The seer dismissed as deficient in observation environmental theories which suggested apparent differences in the aptitude of men and women were grounded in disparities of expectation and opportunity. Suggesting that some people may have been led into the fallacy of cultural conditioning by "learned authoresses," he disclosed that "in the spiritual world, when these writings were explored in the presence of those authoresses, they were found to be works, not of judgment and wisdom, but of genius and eloquence; and works which proceed from these two," Swedenborg said, "by reason of the elegance and fine style of the verbal composition, appear as thought sublime and erudite—but only before those who call ingenuity wisdom."[28] The social identity of woman had been established, it seemed, at the creation. The Writings themselves do not portray her as man's inferior. This is a status assumption unavoidable, however, in cultures raising the cognitive above the affectional, which is the value system the New Church inherited from the Reformation and the Enlightenment and has never renounced.

But while heretofore New Churchmen were able to count on the abiding satisfaction of their wives and daughters and mothers and sisters in the performance of only domestic uses because, for most women, governance fell within what Chester Bernard has called a "zone of indifference,"[29] today there is evidence that female members of the sect have an interest in playing a formal part in decision making.

Discussion of the question of women serving on the governing boards of the General Church, the Academy, and local societies has been prompted by the action taken by the doctrinally allied and organizationally affiliated General Church in Canada. A separate legal body from the General Church of the New

Jerusalem, the Canadian corporation accepts women as members, and in 1975 its nominating committee presented the names of two women for election to the board of directors of the Canadian church. After considerable discussion a motion to alter the bylaws of the corporation to explicitly enjoin female members from serving on the board was defeated, but the women candidates later failed of election.

A Canadian priest had written in the *Life*, prior to the time that the issue was raised in the context of specific nominations, that uses of the board, which had an inspirational and developmental as well as a business and legal side, "could, with great benefit, involve the genius of women."[30] After the Canadian corporation addressed itself to the question, a prominent Bryn Athyn layman sent a letter to the editor saying he found the nominations "disturbing." Asserting that in a good marriage "the wife is represented . . . through her husband," he said that the "presence of women in a council of men tends to inhibit the freedom of debate" and labeled the Canadian action "a concession to the new liberal thinking expressed by the National Council of Churches, and the modern trend."[31] The dean of the college responded that "marriage in the church on earth is between two minds that are uniquely different," and he expressed doubt that one could fully represent the other. The dean further suggested that Academy faculty discussions refuted the assertion that the presence of women inhibits discussion, and he advocated the inclusion of women, not on boards of directors responsible for forensic uses, but on the pastors' councils of New Church societies, which he differentiated as concerned with moral and spiritual issues.[32] Women writing to Swedenborgian publications also expressed a desire to see women serve on these essentially advisory bodies,[33] and in 1979 they finally won a place on them.

The most eloquent argument in favor of female members on governing boards was made by an elderly Academy teacher who once served as the college's dean of women. Speaking as the first woman to address the executive committee of the Sons of the Academy, Margit Boyeson declared that the marriage relationship is intended by Swedenborg as a paradigm for the relationships of the sexes in other social institutions. She then went on to note that:

Men who develop their rational faculties and who cultivate their form of intelligence, which is robust and not easily swayed by emotions, are particularly suited to make judgments, but since the intelligence of man is also apt to be harsh, and since truth which is his immediate concern condemns if not tempered with mercy, men would do well to consult women who from their concern, which is primarily from what is good, may be able to temper man's judgment so that by joint efforts justice might more easily be served.[34]

Fear that opening boards to women might displace men looms, however, as an ultimate practical argument in some minds against their inclusion. The priest who serves as Academy president has suggested that the "enthusiastic support" of Swedenborgian men in church affairs is tied to the fact that the bylaws of the corporation prevent them from abdicating their responsibilities. "For every woman on the board there is one less man present," he asserted, and pointed to the example of old churches, which he saw as bereft of masculine leadership.[35] Echoing the minister's sentiments, a New Church woman wrote to the *Life:* "Let us not invade their domain."[36] But a 1975 survey of the views of a model sample of 100 residents of Bryn Athyn eligible for membership in the General Church, that is, men twenty-one or over and women eighteen or over, indicates a majority doubt the appropriateness of the sect's male-dominated polity.[37] The specific action taken by the Canadian Church and the more general influence of the women's liberation movement have combined to create a sphere receptive to a change in the lay authority structure of the New Church. In the larger society beyond Pennypack Creek, of course, the issue in relation to women and religion is not the franchise or board membership, but women priests. In the Convention, the Swedenborgian body from which the General Church separated in 1890, three women have been ordained since 1975 and two others are studying for the ministry. But Swedenborg's explicit observation in his *Spiritual Diary* (5936) that "women who . . . preach in assemblies destroy their feminine nature" has served to exclude the question from even much discussion in Bryn Athyn.

Whether in a distant future gender will continue to be a determining factor in a person's qualification for holy orders depends upon whether succeeding generations of doctrinal exegetes consider Swedenborg's insights into the psychological differences between men and women as bearing on the sacerdotal function. That the decision will reside with the priesthood is certain for a hierarchical structure is sanctioned by the Writings as the paradigmatic expression of divine sovereignty. No new models for the mediation of ecclesiastical authority can be conceived by members of the General Church who believe the Swedish seer's works constitute the final revelation. Whether women can ever aspire to the positions of greatest prestige in the New Church community, then, lies entirely with men.

7

Threats to Structure

The function of Bryn Athyn's carefully constructed educational and social institutions over more than three-quarters of a century has been to protect members of the sect from the contagions of what in their world view is a moribund Christianity. In a psychological and geophysical enclave fifteen miles from the center of Philadelphia, they have sought to avoid the insidious miasma emanating from a decaying church. In an era when increasing numbers of Swedenborgian young people are continuing their college educations on secular campuses, when the pill has become widely accepted and virtually fail-safe form of birth control, when abortion is available on demand, when divorce is nearly as common as marriage, when drugs are readily available, when pornography affronts the passerby on each marquee and newsstand, and when the changing mores of the larger society are conveyed via television into every home, vicinal separation has become a decreasingly comprehensive means of preserving innocence. "All evils are contagious," Swedenborg wrote, "and may be compared to a pestilence." Some two centuries later a clerical receiver of the heavenly doctrines noted that "the problem of disorder is pressing on us from all sides."[1] By continuing to adhere to a definition of reality generated by their religious tradition, New Churchmen find themselves, more than ever before, in the position of a cognitive minority. Bereft of even ostensible support from the societal norms operative beyond the Pennypack, New Churchmen continue to look to the Writings as justification for what in the world's terms are rigorous behavioral expectations. At the very time, moreover, when environmental conditions might tempt the General Church to convolve like a morning glory at dusk, a barely perceptible counterforce is pushing it toward the world on the grounds that the sect can no longer evade the moral imperative of a more aggressive missionary effort.

New Church ethics are inextricably linked to the concept of use, and, in particular, the notion that conjugial love excels all the other uses of creation. "Neither with the male alone nor with the female alone," according to Swedenborg, "is there full conjunction with the Lord; but with both together."[2] A perception of the salvific role of a good marriage underlies the sect's attitude toward an array of contemporary issues. The views of members on divorce, premarital sex, birth control, abortion, and homosexuality are shaped by their conviction that family life is a cell of unsurpassed potency in the body politic. It is to marriage, moreover, that the Church looks for growth on earth and in heaven, and assaults upon it call forth a powerful arsenal of theological weapons. A certain air of tolerance prevails in Bryn Athyn, nevertheless, as the result of the sophisticated theodicy manifested in the doctrine of permissions and the idea that guilt is ultimately tied not so much to actions as motives. Evil deeds stand condemned, but Swedenborgians deny the possibility that the interior causes of human choices are discernible by men. The Last Judgment occurred in 1757, according to the Swedish seer; therefore, those passing into the spirit world subsequently face not a divine tribunal, but self-ordained destinies—the pleasures and pains of which Swedenborg observed and recorded in detail in the memorabilia interwoven in his theological treatises.

Marriage within the New Church is perceived as critically important, and it is one of the key foci of the sect's whole process of socialization. The extensive system of parietal rules maintained by the Academy is designed, in large measure, to preclude dating outside the Church. The subject arose at the very first young people's assembly at Laurel State Park in 1968, and an adult lay leader told the gathering that it simply was not "sensible to date outside the established social life."[3] Except through organized athletic contests when, for example, a visiting football or hockey team comes to the Academy, secondary school students have virtually no opportunity to meet non-Swedenborgians of their own age group, but contact chances increase, of course, with advancing age and social mobility. A more liberal attitude toward dating outside the sect discernable among the largely college-educated younger generation can be tied to the social predicament of New Church students on a secular campus.[4] Women are more apt than men to welcome such friendships, and it is significant that according to the 1970 census there are 16 percent more women than men over twenty in Bryn Athyn. In a strictly numerical sense, therefore, religious compatibility is a luxury more easily afforded by men than women in the borough.

But whatever the attitudinal differences between the sexes and the generations about the acceptability of making personal social engagements across sectarian borders, members of the General Church appear to draw the line at marriage, and they support the sect's traditional emphasis upon endogamy.[5] Swedenborg taught that a common faith was essential to real marriage. Conjugial love cannot exist "between two partners belonging to different religions," he said, "because the truth of the one does not agree with the good of the other; and two unlike and discordant kinds of good and truth cannot make two minds one; and in consequence . . . [their] love . . . does not have its origin in anything spiritual. If they live together in harmony, it is solely on natural grounds."[6]

The primary use of marriage within the sect, in the view of Swedenborgians, is that it increases a couple's chances of experiencing truly conjugial love. A secondary function is genetic, and according to the General Church's theory of spiritual mutation, a consequence of achieving conjugial love is an "improvement in the hereditary inclinations of the offspring of those marriages." By such unions, it is suggested, New Churchmen have an opportunity "to rectify perverse and twisted inclinations that have been handed down through the ages."[7] What is held out to Bryn Athyn's young people as a potential result of endogamy is no less than the possibility of creating a new spiritual species. Conversely, exogamy is presented as fraught with potential hazards for the individual and the sect. "At best," a Bryn Athyn priest has written, "there is a lack of sharing in the inmost things. . . . and this can make the heart ache. At the worst, there are disagreements, resentments, and even a striving for dominion. Moreover, the risk that the children will be lost to the church and the Lord's kingdom is increased."[8]

The belief that the survival of the sect is tied to its ability to retain the newborn of each generation has not wavered in eight decades, but a degree of flexibility characterizes the definition of a suitable marriage partner. "Sojourners" in the old church make acceptable husbands and wives so long as they are willing to receive instruction in the doctrines of the New Church. No vows are elicited from non-Swedenborgians, but it is the responsibility and prerogative of any minister approached by a couple to determine if he can in good conscience officiate at the proposed marriage service. He must be satisfied as to the willingness of the pair to look to the Writings as a source of divine instruction. To contract a marriage without the blessing of the Church is, for a Swedenborgian, to cut himself off from the sect. The duty of members would be to shun him as a participant in an evil heinous in the sight of God.

Marriage within the General Church of the New Jerusalem is not a two-part contract between human partners, but a three-way convenant involving a man and a woman and the Lord. The normative expectation is that it will continue until the end of life on earth, if it is a truly conjugial alliance, throughout eternity. The Writings teach that even when internal accord is absent, external harmony is to be simulated for the sake of domestic uses. "With good men this is not a matter of hypocrisy but of spiritual honor," according to a New Church theologian.[9] It proclaims to the world the sanctity of marriage, and stands in direct opposition to a substantial segment of public opinion in American society, if the divorce rate of nearly one failed marriage for every two contracted reflects societal attitudes toward the nature of nuptial vows.[10]

Abolition of the conjugial covenant, with the attendant right to marry again for the innocent partner, is permitted in the General Church only on the grounds of adultery. Swedenborg presents sexual infidelity as the sole basis of divorce, and even then, it is given as a permission, that is, a divine accommodation to human frailty, and by no means the necessary outcome of an adulterous situation. If the breach cannot be healed by repentance and forgiveness, however, the Writings permit the termination of marriage in such cases for the reason that spiritual union and physical perfidity are opposites precluding coexistence. In a subtle distinction, which has been a source of debate in the New Church for two centuries, the Swedish seer included under the definition of adultery profanations of marriage he described as "manifest obscenities" and "malicious desertion." Without claiming to understand precisely what the revelator had in mind, a former executive bishop of the General Church has suggested that sexual "perversions" and the act of a spouse in divorcing his partner so he may marry another are aspects of infidelity which free the innocent person to seek a truly conjugial alliance.[12]

True marriages, however, are not made by men but by God, for only the Creator of souls can effect their conjunction, according to Swedenborg. Human beings are enjoined, save under explicit circumstances, from making a judgment about the absence of internal union on the basis of external behavior. Condemning as a pernicious aberration the notion that people have a "right" to marital happiness, the New Church teaches that it is a blessing "granted to those who are willing to strive for it, and who realize that the striving will certainly involve temptation."[13] The willingness of Bryn Athyn residents to work at making marriage work is suggested, moreover, by 1970 census figures which showed that less than 1 percent of the borough population was divorced, and while the government's statistics do not take into account divorced persons who have remarried, there is firm support in the community for the sect's stand against the easy termination of cunnubial alliances.[14] It is highly unlikely that a basis other than adultery would be accepted by a New Church priest in consenting to officiate at a second marriage when either partner had been a party to a previous alliance. The seriousness with which the community views the dissolution of marriage is reflected further in the fact that a divorce on the *curriculum vitae* of an applicant for an Academy teaching post is regarded as a proper subject for discussion in evaluating his or her qualifications and constitutes an aspect of social identity warranting the most careful scrutiny. The Writings present human unions as corresponding to the relationship between the Lord and His Church; therefore, Swedenborgians admit the dissolution of marriage only in the gravest circumstances lest, they believe, men and women destroy the possibility of receiving from the spiritual world influxes of good and truth.

The Swedish seer's theological treatises reflect, nevertheless, a shrewd assessment of human limitations, and apart from divorce, the Writings five three grounds for separation from bed and/or board. Under the general headings of blemishes of the mind, blemishes of the body, and impotence before marriage, Swedenborg presents an array of psychological reasons from insanity to habitual wastefulness and an outdated list of "incurable" diseases, as well as concealed sterility and inability to copulate, as examples of conditions which, when they preclude sexual intercourse, may justify husband and wife living apart with the attendant right of concubinage.[15] In certain cases, the Writings teach that the cohabitation of a man with a woman not his wife is legitimate though it appears to the world as adultery. The mistress, however, must be neither a virgin nor a married woman, and entrance into a concubinal relationship is permissable only for a man who cannot otherwise restrain his sexual desires from manifesting themselves in fornication. The question of whether a wife legitimately separated from her husband is allowed to take a lover is nowhere addressed in the Writings, and New Church priests have had to field queries on its propriety since the women's movement approached its first swell in the late nineteenth century. As early as 1888 a *Life* reader posed the issue, and the editor replied:

A woman who has separated from her husband from lawful causes, is not in the liberty of choosing another man in his place, although, if the separation be a total one, and if it become necessary for her, it would seem that she would be at liberty to enter into such a relation if she be addressed on the subject.[16]

In 1974, however, a Bryn Athyn minister writing in the same journal declined to make even his predecessor's guarded allowances for feminine frustrations, holding instead that concubinage seemed to be "an accommodation to the peculiarly masculine nature."[17] In any case, it is not presented in the Writings as a desirable life-style for either sex, but rather as a recognition of human weakness. Implicit in the doctrine is a hope that separation, even when involving another physical alliance, may effect an eventual reconciliation between partners, and in addition, a recognition of the sacred nature of marriage vows, which are made with the expectation that they bind for life those who plight them.

Remarriage after the death of the first spouse is not uncommon in the General Church, but given Swedenborg's teachings about the persistence of conjugial love to eternity, it is not entered into quite so readily as it might be in other communions. The Writings declare that if a widow or widower has not enjoyed a "love truely conjugial" with his first spouse, there is no obstacle to remarriage.[18] When a spiritual union has been effected, however, it is said that the partners "are not separated by the death of the one, since the spirit of the deceased . . . dwells continually with the spirit of the one not yet deceased . . . until the death of the other, when they meet again and reunite and love each other more tenderly than before in the spiritual world."[19] The problem is that men and women cannot know with certainty during their life on earth whether they were united in a true conjugial alliance. Swedenborg gives a number of reasons, moreover, why even a surviving partner who feels his first marriage was of a spiritual character may wish to take another spouse, such as mutual comfort and assistance in the rearing of children. The General Church emphasizes that it is not for others to judge anyone's motivation for entering into a second union. But an editorial in the *Life* asserted that the sect "should not entertain or foster a climate of opinion which takes for granted that widows and widowers will marry again, and thus comes to expect and accept second marriages as the normal practice."[20] Bishop Emeritus George de Charms has suggested, moreover, that remarriages should be solemnized by a different ritual than first unions,[21] but the Church has yet to make any official change in its liturgy.

The fundamental principle governing Swedenborgian rites is that some correspondence should exist between internal states and external ceremonies. For this reason, most Bryn Athyn priests would refuse to officiate at a public marriage service involving a pregnant bride, insisting instead upon a private exchange of vows. But at a time when it is estimated that 80 percent of American women lose their virginity before marriage,[22] the premarital physical relationships characteristic of the larger society are not unknown in the Huntingdon Valley community. The ripple effect deeply concerns parents as the Writings are explicit in the condemnation of sexual alliances prior to marriage. "During the time of betrothal it is not lawful to be conjoined corporeally," Swedenborg declared, "for thus the order which is inscribed on conjugial love perishes."[23] The danger lies in the spiritual damage precipitated by a corporeal act, and the General Church teaches that premarital sex is to be shunned as an evil odious to the Lord. When considered in terms of the Swedenborgian concept of the existence of degrees in all things, however, a late bishop of the sect has observed that physical "union during the engagement is not as serious a disorder . . . as promiscuity."Responsibility for the latter as a reflection of what he considered the prevailing permissiveness of the age, the New Church leader attributed to Christianity whose "doctrine that marriage is only for this world has removed from it [the nuptial relationship] the very essence that makes it holy." It is taught in Bryn Athyn that one product of a consummated religion is a "laxity in sexual relations in and out of marriage," and a disregard for the significance of "bringing virginity to the wedding ceremony" as a crown.[24]

There may be no secular trend that has accounted for more soul searching in the New Church community along the Pennypack than the widespread acceptance of birth control as a parental right, indeed, obligation, and the improvement in contraceptive methods which make it easy and effective. The General Church has never repudiated the teaching of its first bishop that interference with the procreation of offspring is an abomination, but in counseling, priests instruct couples that the question of the propriety of limiting births is one that, guided by the Writings, they must answer for themselves. The sect's hierarchy in recent times has not put itself in the position of condemning in general a practice their people have come to consider justified in specific cases. Signaled out as a key teaching on the subject, however, is Swedenborg's statement that "the first end of conjugial love is the procreation of offspring and the ultimate end, which is the effect, is the offspring procreated."[25] What the seer presents as indispensable to a true marriage is the love of bearing and raising children; he does not say that conjugial love is impossible where there are no progeny. The point is that it cannot exist where the responsibility of parenthood is avoided from love of the self or the world. A decision to interfere with the procreation of offspring "is wrong and indefensible," the Church teaches, "if it springs from materialistic considerations such as an undue concern for standards of living or for worldly ambitions for our children or ourselves."[26] Indeed, the Academy's tuition policy of progressively lower fees for each additional student from the same family is designed explicitly to avoid penalizing couples for prolificacy.

Families of a dozen or more children are not unheard of in Bryn Athyn even today, but there is no question that the fertility rate is declining in the New Church community as everywhere else in the nation. In 1960 the borough ranked first out of sixty-two municipalities in Montgomery County with an average of 3.95 persons per household. A decade later, with an average of 3.53 persons per household, it had dropped to tenth place, although still remaining considerably above the county average of 3.22, which represented a decline from the 3.40 county average of 1960.[27] Changing attitudes toward birth control are reflected, moreover, in the dramatic drop in kindergarten enrollments in the Bryn Athyn elementary school, from a high of fifty children in 1966 to twenty-nine in 1980. Still, at a time when the national fertility rate is 1.8 children per woman over a lifetime,[28] families of four and five children are common in the borough. The issue today is not whether couples should practice contraception, but for what reasons in the light of the heavenly doctrines given to Baron Swedenborg two centuries ago.[29]

In 1960 a granddaughter of John Pitcairn wrote to the editor of the *Theta Alpha Journal* suggesting a number of possible bases for justifying birth control. Her letter was a query seeking guidance in determining in which circumstances contraception might be considered legitimate. In reply, Bishop de Charms said:

It would be a grave error for the priesthood to formulate a doctrine concerning the application of those principles [given in the Writings for the protection of conjugial love], based on some fallible human interpretation, and to make it binding upon the conscience of the church.[30]

In the subsequent two decades, nevertheless, the question has received considerable attention in Swedenborgian journals. Arguments in favor of a young couple's having a few years alone together before the assumption of parental responsibilities are generally dismissed as pleas "for prolonging the honeymoon beyond what is useful." New Churchmen concerned about their ability to properly support and educate their children are warned of the "dangers inherent in mere human prudence taking upon itself . . . to decide what constitutes a satisfactory standard of living or to foretell what kind and amount of education will be needed and how much it will cost, what the family's circumstances will be—all without taking the Divine Providence into its calculations."[31] When the natural caution of men is made subservient to an acquired trust in God's guidance, then, it is said "the number of . . . offspring will reflect the will of the Lord."[32] Debate over actual methods of birth control, quite apart from that related to reasons for practicing it, focuses upon Swedenborg's teaching that in marriage "the life of the husband adds itself through the seed to the life of the wife; and from this there is inmost conjunction, by which they become not two, but one flesh."[33] The critical point, according to a contemporary New Church theologian, is "that the seed of the husband may be appropriated by the wife and so serve her and their marriage in ways inscrutable but very real."[34] For this reason, he cautions against vasectomy as a literal elimination of the marital contribution to the conjugial relationship, and contraceptive techniques deflecting the sperm also invite explicit doctrinal censure. A Bryn Athyn minister writes that the counsel he gives to married couples and young people preparing for marriage is to the effect that "they should recognize that birth control is a disorder and if they decide to practice it, the reason why they so decide determines whether it is a permission or an evil.'' Insofar as their reasons are selfish, he observes, ''it is an evil hurtful to the development of the couple's conjugial union. But insofar as their reasons generally look away from self towards use it is a permission which in some way will be turned in the Lord's mercy to contribute'' to their relationship.[35] In the best of all possible worlds, the General Church holds that there need occur no contemplation of contraception. It always has striven, however, to grapple with the realities of a flawed social order, and given the limitations of human beings and their resources, the sect teaches that couples are obliged to exercise their own judgment in regard to procreation, keeping the preservation of the conjugial relationship ever in view.

The 1973 decision by the United States Supreme Court invalidating all restrictive state antiabortion laws drew the attention of the General Church to a moral issue to which it had thitherto not addressed itself. Early the next year, the executive bishop of the sect gave a doctrinal class dealing directly with pregnancy termination. Observing that the Writings do not treat the subject of abortion specifically, he emphasized that all revelation proclaims that life is from the Lord. ''The embryo in the womb,'' the prelate said, ''is not, as many at this day believe, merely a part of the mother; it is, in its own right, a potential human being.'' Combating, thus, head-on, the contemporaneous theory that a fetus is a woman's property which, until birth, she can destroy as an artist can his painting, Bishop Pendleton declared that what is involved in the act of abortion is ''a direct intervention on the part of man with the Lord's work of creation.'' Swedenborg taught that the soul is infused into the zygote at conception, and that what is lacking in the unborn child is not life, but awareness of it. Keeping in mind that the embryo is ''a being who, when the days of its creation are accomplished, may enter into a reciprocal relationship with his Creator,'' the prelate said to the New Church audience:

We can appreciate the serious nature of the decision . . . to be made when one is confronted by circumstances which require a judgment in regard to the continuation of life. One thing is certain, however, the act of abortion is contrary to Divine order, and what is contrary to

Divine order is evil. . . . But an evil . . . is not necessarily a sin. Although a man may do what is evil, it is not imputed to him as a sin unless he refuses to acknowledge it as evil and thereby justifies what he has done.

Pendleton defined pregnancy termination, therefore, as a permission, and he went on to take up the question of when it is allowable to abort life. His conclusion was that there seemed to be specific situations in which other human values take precedence over the rights of the conceptus. In the first place, the emphasis in Swedenborg's theological treatises upon the conjugial relationship suggested to the prelate that when a pregnancy threatened a woman's life, her life should be a couple's primary consideration. In cases of rape and of the seduction of a young girl, moreover, he felt the seer's teaching that all conjunction requires consent justified the termination of a resulting pregnancy.[36]

Just as the Swedenborgians have confronted the question of abortion, they also have endeavored to explore the problem of homosexuality in the light of the Word. The Swedish seer spoke of it as "the most abominable adultery" and as "a filthy abomination that is contrary to the order of nature."[37] The severity of his judgment is related to the salvific role he assigned to the institution of heterosexual marriage. Homosexual behavior perverts, in the world view of the General Church, the holiest use to which men and women are called on earth, and the sect regards it as the rotten fruit of a decadent civilization. Expressing the hope that his co-religionists were "still relatively free from the evil of homosexuality," a Swedenborgian priest wrote to his clerical colleagues that he knew the Church was not "entirely untroubled by it," and, therefore, he shared with them a preliminary study of the subject, which was formally presented at the 1975 meeting of the council of the clergy in Bryn Athyn.[38] In his paper, Willard Heinrichs observed that the people of Sodom were the last remnants of the Ancient Church, and its "morally bankrupt character" was represented by the actions in which they indulged prior to the city's destruction. In explicating the internal sense of the Old Testament, the priest noted that Swedenborg portrayed Sodom as representative of "all interior evil from the love of self."[39] The seer placed, moreover, the eternal habitats of homosexuals in the very depths of hell, and he described the nature of their postmortal existence as excruciating torment. One of their punishments, he said, "consisted in the burning of their lascivious members," and the revelator further observed that "in the other life [those] who have committed the sin of Sodom . . . are dung and dwell in privies"[40] Given the fact that the regions of the spiritual world constitute a part of the behavioral environment of every New Churchman, it is hardly surprising that members of the sect do not view homosexuality as an acceptable life-style. It is regarded as a disorder or a sin depending upon the degree of the individual's complicity in his own deviant behavior. As in all transgressions of moral law, the Bryn Athyn Swedenborgians believe the assessment of guilt is a prerogative of the Lord in His omniscience.

Removal to the Huntingdon Valley no more guaranteed that New Churchmen could escape crime than any other social ailment. Even as it twists through the lushly wooded borough, the Pennypack has become infested with pollutants, and in a like manner vandalism and thievery have penetrated the Swedenborgian enclave along its banks. Bryn Athyn has had a full-time police chief since 1933, and the current chief is assisted by other officers and part-time policemen. Property crimes have ever threatened the rich, and security guards partol portions of the Pitcairns' estates while others are employed to protect the cathedral and the local schools. Violations of the criminal code occurring in the borough often are perpetrated by outsiders who in recent years have been arrested for offenses ranging from dumping trash to burglary to homicide. But local residents, usually young people in their late teens or early twenties, have also contributed to the crime rate, which in 1974 placed Bryn Athyn tenth out of eighteen political subdivisons in suburban Montgomery County in the frequency of both property and violent crimes.[41] One of the most publicized cases occurred in 1969 when one of John Pitcairn's great-granddaughters was turned over to the borough police chief by her own parents after they discovered her smoking marijuana. Later the heiress experimented with harder drugs, and was admitted to a rehabilitation institution where she met and married a black youth from North Philadelphia. It was not a New Church wedding, and the couple made their home in the husband's old neighborhood, where they groomed dogs for a living until the plate-glass manufacturer's great-grandson-in-law slipped back into his addiction. He entered an experimental treatment program at Hahnemann Hospital, and in two days he was dead. His wife later remarried, but her tragic experiences were not the last, as they had not been the first, misfortunes to involve the philanthropist's descendants with the law. In 1959 one of the Scottish immigrant's grandsons was charged with arson when he admitted setting a fire which destroyed an old hotel near the family's summer place on Lake George. Fourteen years later, another grandson, out for a late evening drive, struck and killed a sixteen-year-old motorcyclist who was stopped for a red light at an intersection in Lower Moreland Township. The accident occurred close to midnight, and the plate-glass heir, who later acknowledged he had been drinking that day, went home to bed after the ambulance arrived but before the police reached the scene. A witness gave them Nathan Pitcairn's license plate numbers, and although the investigating officers reached his estate by two o'clock in the morning, they were not able to interview the New Churchman until much later in the day. Waiving his right to a trial at a preliminary examination, Pitcairn pleaded guilty to the technical charge of failing to identify himself and render assistance at the scene of an accident. The Commonwealth called no witnesses, and on the understanding that he receive psychiatric treatment, the defendant was given a suspended sentence and placed on two year's probation. Before it was up, he died of cancer.

Fallible human beings, well-educated and in a number of cases rich, the residents of Bryn Athyn have been as vulnerable to the outrages of fortune as any old church people. Their religious faith, little understood by the world, their endeavor to isolate themselves geographically and socially, their collective and individual legal encounters, occasional political excursions, the magnificent cathedral and castle-like homes which wealth built—all these factors have combined to make the Huntingdon Valley Swedenborgians objects of curiosity to members of a larger society beyond the Pennypack. For more than eighty years, however, New Churchmen have striven to preserve and protect their distinctive way of life. Convinced that their survival depended upon retention of the loyalty of their numerous children, they seldom have been tempted by the prospects of increase through evangelism. The Writings themselves contain no commands comparable to the New Testament injunction to go forth and teach all nations, and, indeed, they offer slight hope for the conversion of Christendom. Implicit, nevertheless, in the conviction that one possesses a new truth is the obligation to share it. The very success of their social experiment has given borough residents a psychological confidence which serves to bolster their spiritual certitude, and in recent years subtle evidence has emerged of a willingness to use, rather than deflect, the world's idle interest. Indeed, some even have become persuaded that the General Church should reach out beyond the pale in a genuine missionary effort.

The initial receivers of the heavenly doctrines were, of course, all converts. For more than a hundred years, no members of the sect had the benefit of a regular New Church education, and as a result, few possessed Swedenborgian parents. Beginning with the Swedish seer himself, however, literary evangelism was much stressed, and up until the Academy's break with the Convention, the sectarians' ranks were swelled largely through conversions initiated by widespread distribution of the Writings. The Linotype was the New Church's plow, and from minds opened to spiritual influx by the printed Word sprang some of finest flowers of early Swedenborgianism. The sect's principal theological and organizational achievements during the course of the nineteenth century were the works of such converts as Richard de Charms, William Henry Benade, William Frederic Pendleton, and John Pitcairn. (See Figure 10.) With the increasing differentiation between clerical and lay uses, which left to the unordained responsibility only for financial affairs, no laymen emerged to put on the evangel's mantle once worn by Francis Baily and Jonathan Condy, and the ablest priests became wholly absorbed in the work of education. Removal to the Huntingdon Valley was characterized by a great turning inward. All the considerable resources to which the General Church had access were concentrated upon building a community dominated by an exquisite cathedral and offering the only comprehensive Swedenborgian educational system in the world. Principally by natural increase, including the conversion of spouses as well as the retaining of children, the

Figure 10. Founding fathers of the Swedenborgian community, Bishop W. F. Pendleton (standing) and lay leader John Pitcairn, pose during a stroll in the woods near Bryn Athyn. They were instrumental in fashioning the distinctive way of life led today by New Church men and women. *Photo courtesy of the Academy of the New Church.*

congregation beside the Pennypack grew from 61 men and women in 1897 to 800 in 1980 while membership in the General Church at large also climbed steadily with each passing year. A few individuals made evangelical forays into the world without notable success, and in 1953 a New Church minister accurately assessed the situation when he observed:

As an organization we are not active in consciously preparing ourselves or our centers for any real influx of new members, for carrying on any organized missionary work, or in developing a philosophy and technique to guide our workers. There seems to be the general feeling that this is the Lord's work, and that He will do it in His time.[42]

The priest, Harold Cranch of Toronto, preceded to issue through the pages of *New Church Life* a call for a new evangelical effort. Numerous Swedenborgians, he acknowledged, "have become discouraged about missionary work before it is begun because of many quotations in the Writings which show that when a new church is raised up by the Lord to replace a consummated church it is transferred to the Gentiles. . . . But . . . the New Church . . . cannot be transferred unless it has first been formed among the remnant [of good Christians]."[43] In explicating the description in Revelation of the fate of the woman clothed with the sun, Swedenborg wrote that her flight into the wilderness, where God had prepared a place, signified "that the church that is called the New Jerusalem is to tarry among those who are in the doctrine of faith separate while it grown to fulness."[44] But in the same passage, the seer added, "while provision is made for it among many," and Cranch hurled the quotation at New Churchmen as a challenge to consider "evangelizing the Christian world a valid, even a vital use." Calling for doctrinal studies on the subject, the development of principles and methods of applying them, the minister declared that instead of simply waiting for missionaries to appear in their midst, Swedenborgians ought to train them and provide tools and support.[45] In response to his plea, the council of the clergy formed an extension committee in 1956. The next year a candidate for the priesthood undertook a survey in which he explored the basis and manner of conversions and the initial attitudes of those who had received the heavenly doctrines in adult life toward the New Church community. Through interviews with fifty converts, the theolog, Douglas Taylor, found that 90 percent had been introduced to Swedenborgianism through personal contact with a New Churchman and, of these, 22 percent joined the sect as the result of a proposed marriage. Fear of death was the most frequently mentioned "problem" to which the converts felt the General Church satisfactorily addressed itself. Eighty percent said they were favorably impressed with the Swedenborgian ecclesiastical organization and community life, but 20 percent complained they had found members of the sect cold and distrustful of newcomers.[46]

Taylor remembered what he had learned, and when he went to his native Australia as a priest, he attempted to reach out to the world through a radio program broadcast from Sydney. Meanwhile, back in Bryn Athyn, a Swedish-born minister, Erik Sandstrom, introduced a course on evangelization in the college in 1969, which the Academy catalog described as involving a "search for a clear understanding of the place and calling of the New Church in our present day spiritual environment."[47] In 1971 Sandstrom addressed the council of the clergy on what he perceived as a nascent evangelistic movement within the sect reflected in an "awakening and apparently widening interest, even eagerness, to reach out to the world." Asserting that the earth's salvation "depends on the New Church," the theologian said:

The Lord alone is Savior. But in His first advent He established His church by means of His twelve apostles and by means of all other disciples, or followers, in the first generation while there was still life and unity in the church. He will do so again.

Sandstrom differentiated between the Church Universal, which embraces all men who love God and neighbor, and the Church Specific, or receivers of the heavenly doctrines, and suggested that the latter "will come into maturity and into full health insofar as she will also reach outside herself." Posing, then, a critical question, he asked: "Is the time at hand when the Church Specific must come out of her isolation?"[48]

Growing numbers of Swedenborgians apparently thought so. The next year, five women sent a communication to *Theta Alpha Journal* forthrightly declaring: "Since we have the truth it is our responsibility to spread it." All members of the Epsilon Society, a General Church organization which since 1950 has been distributing copies of the Writings and collateral material in response to requests from interested readers, the writers suggested that a "slow, non-shocking" approach was the most appropriate missionary technique for dealing with old church people. "Don't tell them their church is dead," the women cautioned.

Unless their interest centers around the Second Coming, it might be wise to introduce this new and startling idea after groundwork is laid. . . . Let them become impressed with the logic and rational approach of the Writings before mentioning that Paul's works are not part of the revealed Word.

Urging that "warmth, friendliness and courtesy" be extended to recent converts, the women observed that when Bryn Athyn was established, its residents had so strong a sense of distinctiveness that they "had to be very careful that distinctiveness didn't turn into snobbishness. . . . Some of that feeling did prevail," the writers admitted, "and sometimes newcomers to the Writings . . . were made to feel like outsiders. . . . Now it is important to make a special effort to consider the *affectional* as well as the intellectual needs of others."[49]

In 1973 the executive bishop moved to reconstitute the extension committee as a small, working group directly responsible to the primacy, and including laymen as well as ministers. His action marked a genuine effort on the part of the General Church to organize the use of evangelization. The priest put in charge of the committee appealed to his fellow Swedenborgians to seek out those who could accept the heavenly doctrines. "Each of us is chosen and called to the work of the establishment of the New Church upon earth," he said. "Upon our fulfillment depends the future of mankind."[50] Members of the sect were asked to contribute time and money to the extension committee. At the end of its first full year of operation donations amounted to some $1,500 and many hours of volunteer labor. By 1980 the committee had a budget of $48,000 and was run by a full-time director of evangelization whose appointment reflects a growing consensus in the community that it is time for the General Church to increase its missionary activity in the United States.[51] Bishop King stresses that Swedenborgians have an "obligation to share with their fellowmen the things they value most insofar as they preserve the freedom of others," and he has made the very practical point that unless the sect witnesses a dramatic success in its evangelical efforts, the Academy faces an enrollment decline until the children of its present student body are ready for secondary school.[52]

If many New Churchmen are agreed about the appropriateness of undertaking missionary work, they are uncertain as to the means. Fiddling on a street corner in South Philadelphia has not appeared promising to anyone since the evangelical escapades of young Theo Pitcairn, but tentative verbal explorations of proselytizing techniques have bred a far more radical proposal. Writing in the *Life*, a layman from New York State laid down a sharp challenge to the traditional New Church concept of distinctiveness. "If we are serious about evangelization," he said:

There seems a question about whether, far from enclave-building, we should not now be doing just the reverse. If we want to get real missionary mileage out of our tiny numbers, real exposure of our example to this world that so desperately needs it, perhaps the time has come to adopt what might be termed a "cluster" approach to community building.

The writer suggested that New Churchmen consider living close enough together to maintain their educational system and social life, but rather than buying houses next door to one another, they disperse themselves throughout a larger area. "Allowing homes in Bryn Athyn, Glenview, Caryndale [Kitchener, Ontario, Canada], and Acton Park [Maryland] to be sold on the open market will appear a painful decision to some," he noted, then observed that "the discriminatory selling practices necessary to maintain such enclaves are already legally questionable and seem likely, sooner or later, to be either strictly outlawed or challenged in court."[53] Beyond preparing for such eventualities, however, the New Churchman presented the concept of cluster communities to his co-religionists as a means of making "the fundamental use of evangelization" intrinsic to their social organization. In reply another layman, whose grandfather had helped settle Bryn Athyn, argued that Swedenborgians needed the "continuing mutual strength" provided by traditional settlement patterns, and urged "a stronger and more deliberate effort to separate distinctiveness from exclusiveness" by introducing outsiders into New Chuch communities on a regular and frequent, but selective basis governed by personal friendship.[54]

The extension committee itself has begun "tooling up," as one member said, for "the big push."[55] In 1974 it introduced the *Missionary Memo* as a vehicle for communicating with Swedenborgians interested in evangelical activity. "Our basic marketing problem," the editors asserted, is that while "we have a vast resource of individuals, trained in doctrine," they are not trained "in adaptation or communication. . . . They do not need motivation; they do need tools and techniques." Without a "trained sales force," the *Memo* said, promotion was futile on any scale.[56] So far the New Church evangels have relied primarily on newspaper and radio advertisements, promotional literature, including a series of graded pamphlets, public lectures, and, when they can be arranged, appearances on radio and television information programs. In an effort to isolate the most effective appeals and to train missionaries in the most effective techniques, "test pieces" are sent out to readers, who are asked to submit them to non-Swedenborgian friends for reactions. The results are analyzed in what amounts to a nascent attempt at market research, and it is alive with possibilities for developing a powerful evangelical program and fraught with the danger of what Peter Berger identifies as a process of turning spiritual traditions into "consumer commodities."[57]

Removal to the Huntingdon Valley constituted for New Churchmen a withdrawal from the pluralistic situation in which most religious groups operate in America. Vicinal separation precluded the necessity of the General Church having to compete with other reality-defining agencies for the allegiance of its clientele. *Ipso facto,* the faith which defines a sectarian community enjoys monopoly status. Stepping back into the world with evangelical goals will involve a return to a competitive environment where the General Church will have to confront religious rivals and, to a far greater degree than in Bryn Athyn, such secular rivals as movements for sexual emancipation and women's liberation. Setting up a stall in America's ideological fairgrounds is bound to have far-reaching consequences for the sect in terms of both form and content. As Berger has observed in an incisive theoretical discussion of pluralism, when the question of "results" becomes important, however subtle the pressure to achieve them, a different sociopsychological type of leader is called for than when a church can take for granted the fealty of a given population. Activists are of more use than academicians; pragmatically oriented men more effective than philosophers. It is also true that a market situation introduces the possibility of changes being made in a group's product to the extent that consumer preferences are taken into consideration.[58] The General Church is not apt to disavow the core concepts on which it has taken its stand for more than three-quarters of a century, but an emerging awareness of the sales value of selective deemphasis is evident in the appeal of the Epsilon women to potential evangels to underplay the Swedenborgian belief in the Second Coming in introducing the New Church to wholly secularized minds. The characteristics of the world, which now compel some members of the sect to try to save it, were the very characteristics, of course, which impelled their grandparents and great-grandparents to leave it, and they offer a profound challenge to the spiritual and social resources of the General Church.

8

Patterns of Adjustment

The line between accommodation and acclimation is as thin as spring ice on the Pennypack. I have viewed the General Church as an established sect precisely because of its ability to avoid compromising its values through three generations. But Swedenborgianism has not imposed on its adherents any test of commitment which requires them to alter significantly the life-style made possible by their wealth. The pattern of adjustment emerging after nearly ninety years is one of rigidity on matters perceived as central to the retention of Swedenborgian children in the embrace of faith and flexibility on matters deemed ancillary to that goal.

From the beginning the isolation of Bryn Athyn's residents has been incomplete. Because economic separation was never intended, New Church men and women who broke with Convention in 1890 at no time contemplated a distant Zion. After removal to the rural community fifteen miles from the center of Philadelphia, those with jobs in the city continued to work there. The international headquarters of John Pitcairn's plate-glass firm was in Pittsburgh, and until the end of his life, the Scots industrialist traveled widely on business and for pleasure. At one time as many as nine trains a day ran between Bryn Athyn and Philadelphia, providing easy access to the world beyond the Pennypack. In 1898, just three years after the establishment of the new community, residents took over from their benefactor responsibility for maintenance of the roads. New Churchmen never hesitated to use whatever they needed of the world's goods or talent, and not only did they shop outside of exclusively residential Bryn Athyn, but they imported a labor force to build their cathedral. Today their economic relationship with the city is similar to that of other suburbanites. Two-thirds of those who are employed work outside the borough, and it is outside Bryn Athyn where much of their income is spent.

Social interaction with the world is another matter. In this realm, in contrast to the realm of economics, the adjustment to their environment differs from that of other well-to-do Americans, but not in gratuitous ways. A New Church education for their children, for example, is a key element in the Swedenborgians' plan for group survival. Their emphasis, however, is on primary and secondary schooling as the stages in human development critical to value formation. Linked as much to their socioeconomic status as to their religious conviction is the expectation of New Church parents that their children will go on to college, and they have always permitted their daughters and sons to attend institutions of higher learning other than the Academy. The Swedenborgian college has offered the baccalaureate since 1879; still such have been its limitations in terms of intellectual breadth and depth that numerous young people have taken their degrees elsewhere. Academically the collegiate division of the New Church has not met the needs of the most gifted of Bryn Athyn's youth, but this does not mean they have been lost to the church. The president of the Academy is a graduate of Quaker Haverford, the pastor of the Bryn Athyn Society tooke his undergraduate degree at Amherst, and the executive bishop of the General Church attended the University of Pennsylvania. A common pattern has been to spend two years at the Academy then transfer to other private or to public institutions. For graduate or professional training in any field save theology, young people have no choice but to study outside the borough. An indication of the sect's viability is that a high percentage of those who go away to school eventually make their homes in Bryn Athyn or other New Church communities—not just the priests and teachers, but doctors, lawyers, and people in business and finance.

Once settled, Swedenborgians take part in at least a few of the same activities that engage their Huntingdon Valley neighbors. A handful hold memberships in suburban golf clubs. The Pennypack Watershed Association is what I have called a bridge group that brings together New Churchmen and others concerned with environmental protection. Raymond Pitcairn was a behind-the-scenes force in the Replublican Party for forty years, and others of his co-religionists have shared his enthusiasm for politics. Still there is an undeniable superficiality characterisitic of these ties when compared to the life-shaping ties the Swedenborgians have to their church. Not only does most social activity revolve around it, but their faith determines their attitude toward a range of moral issues; and their attitude sets them apart but not adrift. Unlike the Shakers, the only other enduring sect to hold that the Second Coming is a past event, the Swedenborgians are not doomed by their own inadaptability. Yet neither do they, like the Mormons—the most successful of the millenial churches—serve only the present, losing all transcendence as they continuously revise their beliefs.[1]

The behavioral expectations flowing from the Swedenborgians' view of marriage are critical elements in the sect's distinctiveness. By comparing them to Shaker and Mormon expectations, moreover, it becomes apparent where and with what deftness the Swedenborgians have drawn the line between worldliness and sainthood.

In relation to Christianity, all three groups view themselves as a reform and a consumation. But it is the Shakers alone who steadfastly refused to compromise with the world. They were determined to remake society on the basis of a new type of human relationship.[2] In their communities natural families of husbands and wives were replaced by spiritual families of brothers and sisters. Mother Ann had taught that those who would take part in Christ's resurrection would be neither married nor given in marriage, but like angels.[3] Inconveniently for the Shakers, however, the practice of holy celibacy in imitation of heavenly creatures did not guarantee the immortality associated with celestial beings, and their stand against sexual union precluded natural growth.

Lacking any systematic scheme for recruitment, the Believers found fewer and fewer people knocking at the gates of their isolated communities after the Civil War. The young left, the old died, and there were no replacements. From an apogee of some 6,000 members in the 1850s, the movement declined to 1,000 in 1900; there were fewer than fifty at mid-century, and today the-Millenial Church is all but extinct. Neither fear nor moral suasion proved a successful counterforce to the lure of the world. As their admiring and learned chronicler Edward Deming Andrews wrote, "such principles as submission to authority, the abnegation of self, and communal ownership had diminishing appeal in a country glorifying liberty and the individual or corporate acquisition of property."[4] The energies of the young are essential to the vitality of any society, and without them, the Shakers could not break the rhythm of decay.

If the followers of Ann Lee were doomed by their inadaptability, the Mormons, according to a recent interpretation, are in some measure victims of their capacity for change. It accounts, according to Mark Leone, for their transformation from "a nineteenth century socialist commonwealth predicated on a radical critique of the American economy and class structure to a twentieth century church endorsing an ideology of acceptance of American society."[5] He argues that Mormonism in this century has failed to maintain its original and fundamental opposition to the world. Joseph Smith's insights about the dynamic quality of truth led to an emphasis on continuing and even private revelation, a useful vehicle, it turned out, for facilitating accommodation, although often at the expense of internal coherence. "Instead of producing a population which knows what it stands for and thus knows how to use modern society's characteristics for its own special ends," Leone believes that "Mormonism has produced a population which directs itself according to society's ends while hiding that fact from itself."[6]

The Latter Day Saints, who under intense federal preseure gave up polygamy in 1890, presently share many Swedenborgian attitudes toward marriage. Both groups view it as necessary, if insufficient, for the attainment of heavenly bliss. They forbid extramarital sex, disapprove and discourage divorce, and officially proscribe birth control. Abortion is an anthema. But unlike official Mormondom, the New Church does not lump all such behavior together as equally inimical to family life. The doctrine of degrees allows for distinctions. Contraception is a disorder; whether it is an evil is determined by a couple's motivation, and the clergy emphasize individual responsibility for determining the propriety of family planning. Abortion, the New Church says, is an evil but not a sin when pregnancy is the result of felonious intercourse or when its continuation threatens the life of the mother. The Swedenborgians' attitude toward divorce has always been tempered by a willingness to recognize adultery as the one legitimate ground for dissolving a marriage and a willingness to permit the remarriage of the faithful partner. But Swedenborgians insist on marriage within the church. In their world view, endogamy holds no less a promise than the possibility of creating a superior spiritual species, while exogomy is fraught with danger for the individual and the sect. Non-Swedenborgians make acceptable marriage partners only if they are willing to be instructed in Swedenborgian doctrine. A New Church priest will bless such unions if he is convinced the couple will look to the Writings as their spiritual guide. He must believe, moreover, that they will raise their children in the sphere of the Lord's Word.

Since first establishing schools more than a century ago, Swedenborgians have held fast to the belief that the most fruitful form of evangelism is educating their sons and daughters in the ways and doctrines of the New Church. Lacking an intellectual tradition, Mormons, in sharp contrast to New Churchmen, have always stressed an aggressive missionary effort as an important secondary means of increasing their flock. In the nineteenth century they populated Utah and much of the desert West with immigrants from Europe. Today half of Mormonism's annual growth is provided by converts. Worldwide membership is approaching five million and each year some 25,000 missionaries, young men on two-year assignment, fan out around the globe. The 1979 revelation opening the priesthood to blacks of African descent holds out the possibility that Mormonism could become a truly universal church.

If the Swedenborgians' current and growing interest in evangelism continues, its potential for achieving the status of *ecclesia* depends on how broadly members define their market. Exploration of the roots and historical development of the General Church reveal that in contradistinction to traditional theory about the nature of sects, it was in origin, as it remains today, primarily a middle- and upper-middle-class movement. Wealth has made Bryn Athyn an extremely comfortable place to live, preserving its rural character while providing an array of cultural amenities, and there is no conclusive evidence that its residents are inclined to make room for people who do not share their social as well as their religious identities. The irony, of course, is that the Jerusalem about which John dreamed on Patmos was not a borough, but a "holy *city.*" By definition, a city is inclusive rather than exclusive. It enfolds all sorts and conditions of men, values human diversity, and tolerates opposition. To date, however, the heavenly doctrines have appealed to a narrow stratum of society, interesting mainly people with an intellectual turn of mind or those provided with a highly specialized type of education. The English renderings of Swedenborg's theological treatises are laced with Latinisms,[7] and, even in the original, tend toward abstrusity. The necessity of New Churchmen looking to the seer's works as a guide in all aspects of living is implicit, however, in their belief that the Second Coming was accomplished in the Writings. Whether the heavenly doctrines are marketable to a broad spectrum of mankind remains, therefore, highly questionable. In the contemporaneous interest in near-death experience there is a potential bridge between old and New Church thought. But how widely the residents of Bryn Athyn wish to cast their nets remains unclear. It is far from certain that they would welcome blacks and blue-collar workers as co-religionists. Non-Christians present another problem. Given the New Church's evolutionary view of moral history, it is difficult for Swedenborgians to imagine Jews leap-froging discrete stages in the religious development of the world. At once universalistic and particularistic, members of the sect cherish the conviction that the spread and growth of their system of belief is inevitable. But as much for sociopsychological as for theological reasons, their inclination has been to wait with patience for an improvement in the capacity of the masses to receive the heavenly doctrines. The Gothic from adopted by the Swedenborgians in fashioning their cathedral is narrow and soaring. The same dimensions characterize the world they constructed on the banks of Pennypack Creek.

The Principles of the Academy

BISHOP WILLIAM F. PENDLETON

The body which is known under the name of the General Church of the New Jerusalem is founded upon the principles of the Academy of the New Church, and is an outgrowth of the Academy movement. It would seem useful and important, therefore, to set before the members of the church, at this time, a brief general statement of the doctrine and faith of the Academy. This doctrine and faith is substantially as follows:

1. The Lord has made His second coming in the Writings of the New Church, revealing Himself therein, in His own Divine Human, as the only God of heaven and earth. In those Writings, therefore, is contained the very essential Word, which is the Lord. From them the Lord speaks to His church, and the church acknowledges no other authority and no other law.

2. The old or former Christian Church is consummated and dead, with no hope of a resurrection; nor can there be a genuine church except with those who separate themselves from it and come to the Lord in His New Church. The New Church is to be distinct from the old, in faith and practice, in form and organization, in religious and social life.

3. The priesthood is the appointed means for the establishment of the church; it is not to be placed under external bond in the exercise of its function in the church.

This appendix is taken from the *Journal of the Third Assembly of the General Church of the New Jerusalem,* 1899, pp. 7-9.

4. Baptism is the door of introduction into the New Church on earth, and establishes consociation with those in the other world who are in the faith of the church.

5. The Holy Supper is the most holy act of the worship of the church; and the wine of the Holy Supper is the pure, fermented juice of the grape.

6. The marriage of conjugial love is between those who are of one mind, in the true faith and the true religion. A marriage of one in the faith of the church with one in a false faith, or in no faith, is heinous in the sight of heaven.

7. Any interference on the part of man with the law of offspring in marriage is an abomination.

8. The laws in the latter part of the work *Conjugial Love*, extending from no. 444 to 476, inclusive, are laws of order, given for the preservation of the conjugial.

9. The doctrine of the New Church is revealed from God out of the inmost heaven; the doctrine is, therefore, in itself a celestial doctrine, and the New Church in itself a celestial church, but the doctrine is accommodated to every state of reception from first to last, and the church consists of all who receive, from the wise even to the simple. Celestial perception is the perception of the truth that is within doctrine; there is no perception outside of doctrine.

10. Unanimity is a law inscribed upon the life of heaven, and ought to be inscribed upon the life of the church. Important action should not be taken without essential unanimity. A doubt gives occasion for delay, that there may be further time for consideration and reflection, in order to reach a common understanding.

11. A law is a use taking form, and uses are indicated by needs. Legislation is the giving of a proper form to present needs and uses; legislation other than this is unnecessary and hurtful.

12. The most fruitful field of evangelization is with the children of New Church parents. In order to occupy this fruitful field of work New Church schools are needed, that children may be kept in the sphere and environment of the church until they are able to think and act for themselves.

Notes

ABBREVIATIONS

AC   *Arcana Coelestia*
AE   *Apocalypse Explained*
CL   *Conjugial Love*
HD   *The New Jerusalem and Its Heavenly Doctrines*
HH   *Heaven and Hell*
TCR   *True Christian Religion*

PREFACE

1. See E. Digby Baltzell, *Philadelphia Gentlemen,* 1958 (Phildelphia: University of Pennsylvania Press, 1979), p. 197.

CHAPTER 1

1. The Shakers, who came to believe that the Second Coming had occurred in the person of Ann Lee, have all but disappeared as a religious sect. In 1981 there were fewer than a dozen left anywhere.

2. A transliteration from the Greek word meaning "presence," Parousia has become a technical term for ideas associated with the Second Coming, which is not itself a Biblical expression, but first occurs in theological writing toward the end of the second century. See John A.T. Robinson, *Jesus and His Coming* (New York: Abington Press, 1957), p. 17.

3. Ibid., p. 142. Cf. Shirley Jackson Case, *The Millennial Hope* (Chicago: University of Chicago Press, 1918), p. 138f.

4. See Norman Cohn, *The Pursuit of the Millennium* (Fairlawn, N. J.: Essential Books, Inc., 1957). Quotation p. 14.

5. Ibid., p. 31.

6. H. Richard Niebuhr, *The Social Sources of Denominationalism,* 1927 (New York: The World Publishing Company, 1957), p. 19.

7. See A. Leland Jamison, "Religions on the Christian Perimeter," in *The Shaping of American Religion,* ed. James Ward Smith and Jamison, vol. 1 in *Religion In American Life* (Princeton, N. J.: Princeton University Press, 1961), p. 172; Werner Stark, *Sectarian Religion* (New York: Fordham University Press, 1967), p. 5; and Sydney E. Ahlstrom, *A Religious History of the American People* (New Haven, Conn.: Yale University Press, 1972), p. 473.

8. Thomas F. O'Dea, "Sects and Cults," *International Encyclopedia of Social Science,* vol. 14, p. 132.

9. *Convention Journal,* 1817, p. 2f..

10. See *Macon Daily Telegraph,* May 7, 1911. Available in the Academy Archives.

11. See Constance Pendleton, ed., *Confederate Memoirs: Capt. W. F. Pendleton* (Bryn Athyn: n.p., 1958) for an account of William F. Pendleton's early years.

12. Letter from W. F. Pendleton to his mother, June 7, 1870. Text in Constance Pendleton, *Confederate Memoirs,* p. 118f.

13. Letter from W. H. Benade to Walter Childs, April 28, 1884. Availa- in the Academy Archives.

14. John Pitcairn left thirty-six notebooks and diaries covering various aspects of his life for the years 1855 to 1914, although the last two decades are recorded only by intermittent notations. These are preserved in the Academy Archives, and it is to them as well as to Carl Th. Odhner's uncompleted work, "John Pitcairn: A Biography," *New Church Life,* vol. 37 (1917), pp. 1-21, 79-94, 151-161, 229-234, 280-301, 414-428, 515-546, and 595-601, and vol. 38 (1918), pp. 19-21, that I am indebted for much of my information about the manufacturer-philanthropist.

15. Letter from W. H. Benade to J. P. Stuart, March 14, 1870. Available in the Academy Archives.

16. *Oil City Derrick,* February 21, 1872. Quoted by Odhner in *New Church Life,* vol. 37 (1917), p. 157.

17. John Pitcairn Diary, February 26, 1872.

18. Jesper Swedberg was in charge of Swedish congregations abroad, and he dispatched a son and three nephews to settlements along the Delaware. Swedenborg's youngest brother, Jesper, taught Swedish children in a log cabin school on the New Jersey side of the river. "Old

Swedes' Church" in Wilmington was served by his cousin Andreas Hesselius, and his cousin Samuel Hessilius was pastor of Gloria Dei Church in Philadelphia. Another cousin, Gustaf Hesselius, was sent to the New World to make maps, and stayed to found the American tradition in narrative painting.

19. See Emanual Swedenborg, *The Way to a Knowledge of the Soul,* in *Psychological Transactions,* p. 46.

20. See Marguerite Beck Block, *The New Church in the New World* (New York: Henry Holt and Company, 1932), p. 14f.

21. Niebuhr, followed by Linston Pope in *Millhands and Preachers* (New Haven: Yale University Press, 1942), saw the sect as a one-generation phenomenon inevitably transformed into a denomination by progeny and prosperity. O'Dea points out that more recent empirical studies suggest the category of established sect as a term for describing religious groups who successfully maintain their opposition to worldly values beyond the lifetimes of their first members. See *International Enclyclopedia of Social Sciences,* vol. 14, p. 131.

22. The first reference to "Swedenborgianism" in a sociological study of sects is found in Elmer T. Clark's 1937 book, *The Small Sects in America.* Clark devotes six lines in an appendix to New Churchmen under the heading of "esoteric" sects, which he defines as "mystical groups that claim to be in possession or have access to truth that is unknown to ordinary mortals." I do not agree that members of the General Church, much less members of its more liberal parent body, the General Convention of the New Jerusalem, can be described as mystics in the sense of people who believe in the possibility of intuitive acquisition of spiritual truth. As I have indicated, however, they consider themselves possessors of a new reality, and using Peter Berger's typology of sectarian movements, I would classify the New Church as a "Gnostic" sect with "a secret to be divulged." The "secret," in this case, is the dualistic ontology contained in the Writings of Emanuel Swedenborg. Members' acknowledgment of the divine authority of the Swedish seer's works places them, moreover, in a cluster of sectarians which Jamison describes as groups which add to the Bible a supplementary source of revelation. For New Churchmen there is no doubt that the Writings constitute a third canon. In terms of typologies which differentiate movements in relation to their conception of the ingredients of salvation, Wilson's category of "introversionist" sects is applicable to the General Church. The British sociologist defines introversionists as "highly segregated sects that have established very effective means of insulating themselves," and thereby "narrow the prospect of choice for their young people." In his phrase, Bryn Athyn is a "gathered community" with "a strong scene of its own sacredness." See

Clark, *Small Sects* (New York: Abington-Cokesbury Press, 1949), p. 234f; Peter Berger, "The Sociological Study of Sectarianism," *Social Research,* vol. 21 (1954), p. 478; Jamison, "Religions," p. 181, and Bryn Wilson, *Religious Sects,* 1970 (New York: World University Library, 1973). pp. 28 and 11.

23. George de Charms, "The Distinctiveness of the New Church," *New Church Life,* vol. 64 (1944), p. 99.

24. The only account of New Church activity in the United States by a non-Swedenborgian scholar is Marguerite Beck Block's carefully researched *The New Church in the New World.* Published in 1932, it is a general history of American Swedenborgianism with but one chapter devoted to the General Church.

25. De Charms, "Distinctiveness," p. 103.

26. Clifford Geertz, *The Interpretation of Culture* (New York: Basic Books, Inc., 1973), p. 123.

27. Ibid., p. 124.

28. Clifford Geertz, "The Impact of the Concept of Culture on the Concept of Man," in *Man In Adaptation: The Cultural Present,* ed. Yehudi A. Cohen (Chicago: Aldine Publishing Company, 1968), p. 24.

CHAPTER 2

1. Kant's *Natural History of the Heavens* was published in 1755, and Laplace's *Systeme du Monde* appeared in 1796. It is now generally acknowledged that Swedenborg arrived at the nebular hypothesis before either philosopher.

2. See A. H. Stroh's translation of Swedenborg's *Summary of the Principia,* p. 10. The *Summary* does not contain a synopsis of the first chapter of the Latin work, but Stroh, in turn, summarizes it.

3. See Emanuel Swedenborg, *The Way to a Knowledge of the Soul,* in *Psychological Transactions,* p. 46.

4. Emanuel Swedenborg, *Invitation to the New Church,* no. 52 in *Posthumous Theological Works,* vol. 1.

5. See Emanuel Swedenborg, *The True Christian Religion,* no. 470. (Reference hereafter *TCR.)*

6. Swedenborg is not saying that there was a time when free will did not exist; only that at first, men instinctively chose good.

7. *TCR,* no. 490.

8. Emanuel Swedenborg, *Divine Providence,* no. 275.

9. *TCR,* no. 247.

10. *TCR,* no. 119

11. *TCR,* no. 94.

12. *TCR*, no. 102.

13. *TCR*, no. 132.

14. *TCR*, no. 355.

15. *TCR*, no. 410.

16. *TCR*, no. 425.

17. Emanuel Swedenborg, *Divine Love and Wisdom*, section 13 in *The Apocalypse Explained*, vol. 6

18. Emanuel Swedenborg, *Arcana Coelestia*, no. 5. (Reference hereafter *AC.*)

19. Emmanuel Swedenborg, *Heaven and Hell*, no. 461. (Reference hereafter *HH.*)

20. *HH*, no. 65.

21. *HH*, no. 47.

22. *HH*, no. 387.

23. *HH*, no. 329.

24. Emanuel Swedenborg, *Conjugial Love*, no. 47. The word "conjugial" as opposed to the usual "conjugal" is peculiar to Swedenborg and the New Church. (Reference hereafter CL.)

25. Cf. *HH*, no. 382 and *CL*, no. 44.

26. *AC*, no. 2335.

27. *HH*, no. 509.

28. *HH*, no. 553.

29. Emanuel Swedenborg, *Last Judgment*, no. 45 in *Miscellaneous Theological Works*.

30. Emanuel Swedenborg, *The New Jerusalem and Its Heavenly Doctrine*, no. 5 and passim in *Miscellaneous Theological Works*.

31. See Emanuel Swedenborg, Preface to *The Doctrine of the New Jerusalem Concerning the Lord* in *The Four Doctrines*.

32. See Emanuel Swedenborg, Introduction to *The Apocalypse Revealed*.

33. Rudolph L. Tafel, *Documents Concerning the Life and Character of Emanuel Swedenborg* (London: Swedenborg Society, 1875-1877), vol. 2, p. 757. The inscription was found on a single manuscript folio page entitled "An Ecclesiastical History of the New Church." The page is contained in Codex 47 of the Swedenborg manuscripts in the Academy of Sciences in Stockholm.

34. *TCR*, no. 791.

35. *TCR*, no. 777.

36. *TCR*, no. 779 beginning with heading.

37. *TCR*, no. 721.

38. *TCR*, no. 728 and the heading of no. 725.

39. *TCR*, no. 508.

CHAPTER 3

1. Emanuel Swedenborg, *The True Christian Religion*, nos. 787 and 758. (Reference hereafter *TCR.)*

2. Letter from Emanuel Swedenborg to G. A. Beyer, 1767. See Tafel, *Documents Concerning the Life and Character of Emanuel Swedenborg* (London: Swedenborg Society, 1875-1877), vol. 2, p. 261.

3. *The Philadelphia Gazette*, August 12, 1801. Quoted in *New Church Life*, vol. 34, p. 48.

4. See Tafel, *Documents*, vol. 2, pp. 1170ff, 996, 514, and 500.

5. See Robert Hindmarsh, *The Rise and Progress of the New Church* (London: Hobson and Sons, 1861) for the most comprehensive account of the establishment of the New Church in England. Cf. Block, *The New Church in New World* (New York: Henry Holt and Company, 1932), pp. 61-72.

6. Hindmarsh, p

7. Ormond de Charms Odhner, "The Origins of the New Church Priesthood," unpublished manuscript, 1975, p. 6. Available in the Academy Library.

8. Letter from Daniel Lammot to Samuel Worcester, March 27, 1822. Quoted in *The Kramph Will Case* (Bryn Athyn: Academy of the New Church, 1910), p. 80.

9. Letter from Samuel Worcester to Daniel Lammot, February 25, 1822. Quoted in *Kramph Will Case*, p. 80.

10. *The Precursor*, vol. 1 (1837), p. 61.

11. See Carl Th. Odhner, "William Henry Benade" *New Church Life*, vol. 25 (1905), pp. 449-618 and 721-731, and vol. 26 (1906), pp. 65-77, for an uncompleted sketch of Benade's life. The chancellor himself left no record of his early years, and, indeed, when he entered the New Church, appeared to close the door on his past.

12. Letter from W. H. Benade to J. P. Stuart, May 5, 1862. Available in the Academy Archives.

13. Letter from J. P. Stuart to W. H. Benade, December 28, 1863. Available in the Academy Archives.

14. Letter from W. H. Benade to J. P. Stuart, March 8, 1864. Available in the Academy Archives.

15. Letter from W. H. Benade to J. P. Stuart, January 5, 1866. Available in the Academy Archives.

16. Letter from W. H. Stuart to J. P. Benade, January 31, 1866. Available in the Academy Archives.

17. John Pitcairn, "Diary," January 12, 1874. Available in the Academy Archives.

18. Letter from J. P. Stuart to W. H. Benade, February 16, 1874. Available in the Academy Archives.

19. William H. Benade, "Declaration of the Principles of the Academy," June 19, 1876. Available in the Academy Archives. The signers of the delaration were: the Revs. William H. Benade of Pittsburgh, James P. Stuart of Vineland, N. J., John Randolph Hibbard of Chicago, Nathan C. Burnham of Lancaster, Pa., Samuel M. Warren of Boston, Rudolph L. Tafel of London, and Louis H. Tafel of Philadelphia; Dr. Francis E. Boericke of Philadelphia; and Messrs. David McCandless of Pittsburgh, John Pitcairn of Pittsburgh, Walter C. Childs of Pittsburgh, and Franklin Ballou of Pittsburgh. When Warren resigned soon thereafter, the Rev. William F. Pendleton of Philadelphia was elected to the council in his place. Rudolph Tafel returned to London directly following the meeting, later broke with the Academy, and never returned to the United States. McCandless died in 1879.

20. The incident of the overheard prayer was recounted by Dr. Boericke's daughter, Malvina, to Maria Hogan, who much later described it in a letter to Harold F. Pitcairn. See Jennie Gaskill, *Biography of Raymond Pitcairn* (Bryn Athyn: Academy Book Room, 1973), p. 6.

21. In the charter granted November 3, 1877, the name of the organization appears as The Academy of the New Church. The word "church" apparently was substituted for "Jerusalem," by the incorporators when they met in June. See Academy of the New Church Council Minutes, June 3, 1877, in the Academy Archives. On January 18, 1879, the Court of Common Pleas No. 2 in Philadelphia approved an amendment to the charter, which was sought to remove any doubt about the institution's right to grant degrees. A copy of the amendment is in the Academy Archives.

22. See *The Academy of the New Church* (Bryn Athyn: Academy Book Room, 1926), pp. 30-34; Richard R. Gladish, *A History of the Academy of the New Church* (Bryn Athyn: General Church Religion Lessons, 1967-1973), vol. 3, pp. 34f and 57-60, and Academy of the New Church Programme, First Annual Commencement, May 15, 1878. A copy of the commencement program is available in the Academy Archives.

23. The first bachelor of theology degree actually was conferred on a nonresident student, R. J. Tilson of London, in April of 1880. It was at the 1880 commencement that the first two B.Th, degrees were awarded resident theologs.

24. The first initiates were Dr. George R. Starkey, Dr. E. A. Farrington, Captain Alfred Matthias, and E. S. Campbell, Esq. See Carl Odhner in *New Church Life*, vol. 37 (1917), p. 596.

25. See Ormond de Charms Odhner, "The Academy in Crisis," *New*

Church Life, vol. 94 (1974), p. 210f.

26. Gertrude Starkey, "Diary," June 29, 1877. Quoted by Gaskill, p. 8. Miss Starkey became Mrs. John Pitcairn.

27. See William H. Benade, *Conversations On Education* (Philadelphia: Academy of the New Church, 1888), p. 1.

28. See *Convention Journal*, 1882, p. 25. Despite its name, the General Church of Pennsylvania did not include all New Church societies in the Commonwealth, as some were doctrinally allied with the Convention.

29. See *Convention Journal*, 1883, p. 8.

30. *Words for the New Church*, vol. 2 (1880), p. 133f.

31. *New Church Life*, vol. 8 (1888), p. 190.

32. See *Kramph Will Case*, p. 10f.

33. *Journal of the General Church of Pennsylvania*, 1888, p. 84.

34. See *Convention Journal*, 1889, p. 7ff; and *Journal of the General Church of Pennsylvania*, 1889, p. 61.

35. *Convention Journal*, 1889, p. 19.

36. *Convention Journal*, 1890, p. 46.

37. Roger Bernst in *Aurora*, vol. 1 (1799), p. 163.

38. See *Journal of the General Church of Pennsylvania*, 1890, pp. 82 and 92.

39. William F. Pendleton, "The Inauguration and Progression of the Academy," *The Academy of the New Church, 1876-1926: An Anniversary Record* (Bryn Athyn: Academy Book Room, 1926), p. 15.

40. See *Journal of the General Church of the Advent of the Lord*, 1891, p. 6.

41. Carl Th. Odhner, "The History of the General Church," *New Church Life*, vol. 24 (1904), p. 414.

42. Ibid.

43. *New Church Life*, vol. 14 (1894), p. 189.

44. Carl Odhner in *New Church Life*, vol. 24 (1904), p. 415.

45. A verbatim account of the January 20, 1897 meeting with Benade was dictated by Homer O. Synnestvedt to Carl Th. Odhner several hours after it had taken place, and verified at that time by William F. Pendleton. See *A Statement Concerning Recent Disturbances in the Church of the Academy of the New Church and in the General Church of the Advent* (Philadelphia: n. p., March 1, 1897), pp. 13-16. Available in the Academy Archives.

46. Ibid., p. 17.

47. Ibid. pp. 18-24. At a later meeting of the board of directors, Benade denied that he had resigned. See Academy of the New Church Board Minutes, October 9, 1897. Available in the Academy Archives. The

bishop spent the last years of his life in retirement. He died in London in 1905.

48. *Formation of A New General Church* (Huntingdon Valley: n. p., March 1, 1897), p. 6. Available in the Academy Archives.

49. Carl Odhner in *New Church Life,* vol. 24 (1904), p. 417.

CHAPTER 4

1. *New Church Life,* vol. 22 (1902), p. 505f.

2. Bryan Wilson, *Religious Sects,* 1970 (New York: World University Library, 1973), p. 119.

3. See Montgomery County Deeds, Montgomery County Court House, Norristown, Pennsylvania. The total purchase price may have been somewhat higher, as one twenty-three-acre tract is recorded as a one-dollar sale.

4. See *A Statement Concerning Recent Disturbances in the Church of the Academy of the New Church and in the General Church of the Advent* (Philadelphia: n.p., March 1, 1897), p. 6.

5. See Eldric Klein, ''The Village Community Gets a Name: Digest of the Minutes of the Village Association,'' in *Bryn Athyn: From these Beginnings* (Bryn Athyn: Academy Book Room, 1966), pp. 5-11. Quotation, p. 7.

6. Peter Berger and Thomas Luckman, *The Social Construction of Reality,* 1966 (Garden City: Doubleday-Anchor, 1967), p. 126.

7. Liston Pope, *Milhands and Preachers* (New Haven: Yale University Press, 1942), p. 121.

8. De Charms, *New Church Life,* vol. 64 (1944), p. 9.

9. Emanuel Swedenborg, *The True Christian Religion,* no. 434.

10. *New Church Life,* vol. 15 (1895), p. 33f.

11. See *1900 U.S. Census.*

12. Carl Th. Odhner in *New Church Life,* vol. 18 (1898), p. 20.

13. Philadelphia/Bryn Athyn New Churchmen listed in *Who Was Who* include: Francis Bailey; Philip Freneau; Charles Rittenhouse, Louis Beauregard, and Nathaniel Dandridge Pendleton; Harold, John, and Raymond Pitcairn; and Condy Raguet. In the *Dictionary of American Biography* are found: Bailey, Freneau, John Pitcairn, and Raguet. The *National Cyclopedia of American Biography* lists: William Chauvenet; Randolph W. Childs; Freneau; Constantine Hering; William Frederic and Louis B. Pendleton; John Pitcairn; and Arthur and Paul Synnestvedt. Frances and Felix A. Boericke are listed in the *Encyclopedia of Pennsylvania Biography.*

14. *New Church Life,* vol. 12 (1892), p. 18.

15. Ibid., vol 37 (1917), p. 138.

16. Ibid., vol. 19 (1899), p. 98f.

17. See ibid, vol. 15 (1895), p. 31, for descriptions of the three types of ceremonies.

18. Ibid., vol. 19 (1899), p. 98.

19. Emanuel Swedenborg, *Arcana Coelestia,* no. 8998.

20. *New Church Life,* vol. 29 (1909), p. 341, 133, 340, and 55.

21. Ibid., vol. 29 (1909), p. 345.

22. Letter from W. F. Pendleton to Lillian Grace Beekman, July 16, 1913. Available in the Academy Archives.

23. *New Church Life,* vol. 16 (1896), p. 190.

24. Ibid., vol. 32 (1912), p. 421.

25. Ibid., vol. 29 (1909), p. 346f.

26. Ibid., vol. 9 (1889), p. 128.

27. Emanuel Swedenborg, *Heaven and Hell,* no. 384.

28. *New Church Life,* vol. 14 (1894), p. 161.

29. *Journal of the Third General Assembly of the General Church of the New Jerusalem,* 1899, p. 11.

30. *New Church Life,* vol. 22 (1902), p. 294.

31. See ibid., vol. 24 (1904), p. 679f; vol. 25 (1905), p. 297; and especially vol. 26 (1906), p. 162.

32. W. F. Pendleton, "Conception and the Prevention of Offspring," January 1, 1908. Delivered originally at the "Men's Meeting" in Toronto in 1908, it was also given at the "Men's Meeting" held in connection with the General Assembly in Bryn Athyn in June of 1910. The unpublished manuscript is available in the Academy Archives.

33. Letter from W. F. Pendleton to "My Dear Friend," undated pencil draft. Available in the Academy Archives.

34, *New Church Life,* vol. 19 (1899), p. 178.

35. Ibid., vol. 20 (1900), p. 407.

36. *Journal of the Second General Assembly of the General Church of the New Jerusalem,* 1898, pp. 20, 23, and 22.

37. Thomas Worcester, Presidential Address to the Convention, 1853. Quoted in *New Church Life,* vol. 34 (1914), p. 170.

38. Homer Synnestvedt, "Thoughts on Education," *Journal of Education of the Academy of the New Church,* 1902, p. 7.

39. *New Church Life,* vol. 24 (1904), p. 386.

40. Alfred Acton, "New Church Education," *Journal of Education of the Academy of the New Church,* 1912, p. 9.

41. See *New Church Life,* vol. 17 (1897), p. 175.

42. See *The Academy of the New Church* (Bryn Athyn: Academy Book Room, 1926), p. 58.

43. See *New Church Life,* vol. 20 (1900), p. 393; and *Journal of Education,* 1910, p. 63, and 1920, pp. 19, 21, and 24f.

44. See Richard R. Gladish, *A History of the Academy of the New Church* (Bryn Athyn: General Church Religion Lessons, 1967-1973), vol. 4, pp. 122 and 125.

45. *New Church Life,* vol. 21 (1901), p. 70f.

46. See *Journal of the First General Assembly of the General Church of the New Jerusalem,* 1897, pp. 11 and 3-6.

47. Carl Th. Odhner in *New Church Life,* vol. 24 (1904), p. 418.

48. See *Journal of the First General Assembly of the General Church of the New Jerusalem,* 1897, pp. 137-139. Quotations, p. 138f.

49. Ibid., pp. 103 and 29.

50. Ibid., p. 146.

51. See *Journal of the Third General Assembly of the General Church of the New Jerusalem,* 1899, pp. 114f and 7-14.

52. Clifford Geertz, *The Interpretation of Culture* (New York: Basic Books, Inc., 1973), p. 113f.

53. *General Church of the New Jerusalem Reports,* 1900-1905, p. 367.

54. *New Church Life,* vol. 24 (1904), p. 27.

55. Ibid., vol. 28 (1908), p. 548. *Liturgy for the General Church of the New Jerusalem* (Bryn Athyn: Academy Book Room, 1908), p. 11.

56. *Liturgy for the General Church of the New Jerusalem* (Bryn Athyn: Academy Book Room, 1908), p. 11.

57. See W. F. Pendleton, *Notes and Papers on Ritual,* 1919-1922 (Bryn Athyn: Academy Book Room, 1956), p. 156.

58. *Liturgy,* pp. 367, 409, 412, 416, 420, and 437.

59. Pendleton, *Notes and Papers,* p. 160.

60. See Jennie Gaskill, *Biography of Raymond Pitcairn* (Bryn Athyn: Academy Book Room, 1973), p. 156.

61. Raymond Pitcairn, "Christian Art and Architecture for the New Church," *New Church Life,* vol. 40 (1920), p. 618.

62. Otto von Simson, *The Gothic Cathedral* (New York: Bollingen Foundation, Inc., 1956), pp. 8 and 10.

63. See Ralph Adams Cram, "A Note on Bryn Athyn Church," *The American Architect,* vol. 113, (May 29, 1918), p. 710.

64. Ibid., p. 709.

65. See E. Bruce Glenn, *Bryn Athyn Cathedral* (Bryn Athyn: Bryn Athyn Church of the New Jerusalem, 1971), p. 82.

66. Cram, "Bryn Athyn Church," p. 710.

67. Ibid.

68. Benjamin Tweedale, interview with E. Bruce Glenn, 1964. Quoted by Glenn, p. 94.

69. Cram, "Bryn Athyn Church," p. 711.

70. See *New Church Life,* vol. 40 (1920), p. 617f.

71. Glenn, *Bryn Athyn Cathedral,* p. 54.

72. Don Rose, *My Own Four Walls* (New York: Doubleday, Doran and Company, Inc., 1941), p. 72.

73. Glenn, *Bryn Athyn Cathedral,* p. 134.

74. The Academy seal is a quartered shield representing the New Church. On the crest is a lion signifying the Lord's Divine Human, a crown symbolic of His government, and a key representing the opening of the internal sense of the Word. The shield itself depicts the mitre of Aaron to signify the priesthood; an eagle brooding over her young to represent education; a temple with an open door over which is written "Nunc Licet," symbolizing the New Church; and Michael slaying the dragon, which stands for the destruction of falsity by the truth of divine revelation. The seal of the General Church consists of the seven candlesticks and seven stars, which are described in *Revelation* 1:20. Below is a riband bearing the legend in Greek: "Behold I make all things new."

75. See *Bryn Athyn: From These Beginnings,* p. 14ff.

76. The *Kramph Will Case* (Bryn Athyn: Academy of the New Church, 1910), pp. 89 and 104.

77. Philadelphia *Ledger,* July 3, 1908.

78. *Kramph Will Case,* pp. 314, 319, 326, 335, and 332.

79. *Bryn Athyn: From These Beginnings,* p.16.

80. Cram, "Bryn Athyn Church," p. 710.

CHAPTER 5

1. See *Bryn Athyn Church Annual Report,* 1979-80, p. 12. Available in the Academy Archives. Membership statistics are as of June 30, 1980.

2. See Bruce Henderson's "School District Merger Fight," unpublished manuscript, n. d., p. 40. Available in the Academy Archives.

3. Emanuel Swedenborg, *Heaven and Hell,* no. 44. (Reference hereafter *HH.)*

4. See *HH,* no. 399.

5. Kurt H. Asplunch, "The New Church Community in the World Today," unpublished manuscript, 1961. Courtesy of the author. Quotations pp. 9, 10, 11, and 12.

6. See *Bryn Athyn Borough Comprehensive Plan* (Norristown, Pa.: Montgomery County Planning Commission, 1968), p. v-9.

7. See ibid., p. v-3. All land-use figures are based on a 1964 survey made by the Montgomery County Planning Commission, but there has been essentially no change in borough land distribution in the last eighteen years.

8. All figures related to the age, size, and value of housing are drawn from the 1970 census unless otherwise indicated.

9. *Bryn Athyn Comprehensive Plan,* pp. iv-20.

10. Estimates based on 1980 assessed valuation, which in theory is a third of market value, but in Bryn Athyn, as elsewhere in Montgomery County, it is no more than 20 percent.

11. See *Bryn Athyn Comprehensive Plan,* pp. iv-24 and vi-6.

12. See *Bryn Athyn Post,* April 1, 1976.

13. The nonwhite population of Montgomery County is only 4 percent of the total population. All race, age range, income, occupation, and educational level statistics are taken from the 1970 census.

14. *Bryn Athyn Comprehensive Plan,* pp. iii-7.

15. Ibid., p. vi-5.

16. The committee's statistics indicated that some eighty members of the General Church living in or near Bryn Athyn were over seventy-five years of age, and of these old people, twenty-six lived alone, five were in nursing homes, twenty lived with a spouse, relative, or friend in the same age group, and twenty-nine lived with children or younger relatives, in a number of cases with unmarried daughters. See *Theta Alpha Journal,* Spring 1971, p. 13.

17. According to a Department of Commerce estimate made in 1972 and released in 1975, the average annual per capita income in Bryn Athyn was $5,499. See *Philadelphia Inquirer,* February 22, 1976.

18. In 1968 the Montgomery County Planning Commission estimated that approximately a third of the borough labor force was employed by the General Church or the local schools. These institutions employed some 160 persons in 1976, a total which includes individuals living outside the borough.

19. Leon S. Rhodes, "Yeomen of the Board," unpublished manuscript, 1974. Courtesy of the author. Quotation p. 1.

21. See *Bryn Athyn Comprehensive Plan,* pp. iv-2.

21. See Harvey Cox, *The Feast of Fools* (Cambridge: Harvard University Press, 1969), p. 18.

22. Anthony F. C. Wallace, *Religion* (New York: Random House, 1966), p. 126.

23. See *Bryn Athyn Church Annual Report,* 1979-80, p. 11f. Available in the Academy Archives. Arriving at a meaningful statistic related to church attendance in Bryn Athyn is difficult, for while there were 795 members of the Bryn Athyn Society as of June 30, 1980, the congregational pool was 1,514 persons, including 236 members of the General Church who had not signed the roll of the local society, and 470 "others" —a category consisting mainly of New Church college and theological

students and adult members of the community who simply have not joined the General Church. Ushers use crowd counters to tally attendance at cathedral services; in computing average attendance, the secretary of the Bryn Athyn Society excludes special services, which normally attract a far larger congregation than ordinary Sunday liturgies. If one excludes the adults attending the family service as a probable overlap when considering attendance percentages, 68 percent of the members of the Bryn Athyn Society regularly attend church services. But only 36 percent of the congregational pool do so, although aside from Academy students, nonmembers of the General Church have no conceivable attendance obligation. If one excludes 320 nonstudent "others" from consideration, then, as well as allowing for an overlap, an average of 46 percent of the congregational pool attended Sunday services in 1980.

24. Wallace, *Religion,* p. 131.

25. William F. Pendleton, *Notes and Papers on Ritual, 1919-1922* (Bryn Athyn: Academy Book Room, 1956), p. 61.

26. See Martin Pryke, *Our Funeral Customes* (Bryn Athyn: General Church Publication Committee, 1960), p. 14. The author quotes *Psalm* 30:11 ("Thou has turned for me my mourning into dancing, thou hast put off my sack cloth and girded me with joy.") as an appropriate expression of the emotional alteration which ought occur for a New Churchman as he turns from his own sense of loss to a consideration of the dead person's gain.

27. Margaret Mead, *Culture and Commitment* (Garden City, N. Y.: Natural History Press/Doubleday and Company, Inc. 1970), p. 26.

28. *The Publication,* October 1968, p. 3.

29. Ibid., March 1969, p. 6.

30. Peter Berger, Brigette Berger, and Hansfried Kellner, *The Homeless Mind* (New York: Vintage Books, 1974), pp. 205, 209, and 208.

31. See Wallace, *Religion,* pp. 157-163.

32. Yorvar Synnestvedt, personal interview, 1976.

CHAPTER 6

1. Emmanuel Swedenborg, *The New Jerusalem and Its Heavenly Doctrine,* no. 318 in *Miscellaneous Theological Works.* (Reference hereafter *HD.)*

2. See Max Weber, *The Theory of Social and Economic Organizations,* transl. A. M. Henderson and Talcott Parsons (New York: Oxford University Press, 1947).

3. Talcott Parsons, *Politics and Social Structure* (New York: The Free Press, 1969), p. 102.

4. Emanuel Swedenborg, *Heaven and Hell*, no. 226 (Reference hereafter *HH.*)

5. *HD*, nos. 312 and 314.

6. Emanuel Swedenborg, *Arcana Coelestia*, no. 6822.

7. Emanuel Swedenborg, *The True Christian Religion*, no. 746. (Reference hereafter *TCR.*)

8. See *Liturgy and Hymnal for the Use of the General Church of the New Jerusalem*, fifth and revised editioan (Bryn Athyn: General Church of the New Jerusalem, 1966), pp. 98-105.

9. *TCR*, no. 146.

10. *A Statement of the Order and Organization of the General Church of the New Jerusalem*, 1970, p. 9.

11. Emanuel Swedenborg, *The Coronus*, Appendix to *True Christian Religion*, no. 17.

12. Willard D. Pendleton, personal interview, 1975.

13. Anthony F. C. Wallace, *Administrative Forms of Social Organization*, McCaleb Module in Anthropology from the Series, Addison-Wesley Modular Publications, Module 9, 1971, p. 3.

14. See Chester I. Bernard, "A Definition of Authority," in Robert K. Merton, ed. *Reader In Bureaucracy* (Glencoe, Ill.: The Free Press, 1952) for an analysis of authority relationships in which he sets forth the theory that the "decision as to whether an order has authority or not lies with the persons to whom it is addressed, and does not reside in persons of authority' or those who issue these orders." Quotation p. 80.

15. See Robert K. Merton, *Social Theory and Social Structure*, enlarged edition (New York: The Free Press, 1968), p. 394.

16. See W. F. Pendleton, *Notes and Papers on Ritual, 1919-1922* (Bryn Athyn: Academy Book Room, 1956), p. 48.

17. Erik Sandstrom, personal interview, 1975.

18. See *The Academy of the New Church* (Bryn Athyn: Academy Book Room, 1926), p. 53.

19. "Resolutions for the Corporation of the Academy of the New Church Re Nominating Committees and Nominating Procedures," Revised May 15, 1970, p. 2. Courtesy of the Academy of the New Church.

20. At present there is no need for the funds controlled by these committees, and the money is being reinvested.

21. *Academy Journal*, Literary Number, 1974-75, p. 11.

22. See Roland Robertson, *The Sociological Interpretation of Religion* (New York: Schocken Books, 1970), p. 138f, for a discussion of alternative compensation in religious sects.

23. *HD*, no. 106.

24. Emanuel Swedenborg, *Conjugial Love*, no. 33.   Cf. *HH.,* no. 368.
25. *HH,* no. 369.
26. *HH,* no. 367.
27. *CL,* no. 175.
28. Ibid.
29. Bernard, "Definition," p. 182.
30. Harold C. Cranch, "The Uses of Men and Women," *New Church Life,* vol. 94 (1974), p. 300.
31. Robert E. Synnestvedt, Letter to the Editor, *New Church Life,* vol. 95 (1975), p. 463f.
32. E. Bruce Glenn, Letter to the Editor, *New Church Life,* vol. 96 (1976), p. 562f.
33. See *Theta Alpha Journal,* Fall 1974, p. 6; and *New Church Life,* vol. 96 (1976), p. 147.
34. Margit K. Boyeson, "Some Reflections On the Nature of Men and Women," *Sons of the Academy Bulletin,* February, 1975, p. 146f.
35. Alfred Acton, II, Letter to the Editor, *New Church Life,* vol. 96 (1976), p. 146f.
36. Jeanette E. Stroemple, Letter to the Editor, *New Church Life,* vol. 96 (1976), p. 147.
37. The survey was conducted during the first quarter of 1976. One hundred persons represented 13 percent of the membership of the Bryn Athyn Society. While all those surveyed were eligible for membership, the anonymity of the survey precluded checking whether they actually had signed the roll. The questions considered in this chapter constituted five of fourteen included in questionnaires, most of which were distributed to New Churchmen following a Friday supper, a wrestling match at the Academy, and a Civic and Social Club function. The age range of those surveyed was from eighteen to eighty-six; the income range from earnings under $5,000 a year to more than $50,000; occupations varied from college student to professor to salesman to attorney; and the women responding included both housewives and those in the labor force. In other words, although the sample was small, and not a probability sample, it reflected the diversity of the community. It should be pointed out, however, that while the 1970 census indicated 43 percent of the Bryn Athyn population was male, only 36 percent of the Huntingdon Valley New Churchmen surveyed were male and 64 percent were women, whereas the census showed that 56 percent of the borough population was female. Still, sentiment within the community is clear. An overwhelming 78 percent of those surveyed said they believed women should be eligible to vote for members of the boards of the Academy and the General Church, while 15 percent thought women should not have the fanchise, and 7 percent were undecided. There was

not a significant difference in this case between persons under and over thirty, but when the responses of men and women were considered separately, 82 percent of the men, as opposed to 76 percent of the women, favored female suffrage in the New Church. As to whether women should be permitted to serve on the boards of the three principal borough institutions, 57 percent said yes, 31 percent answered no, and 12 percent had not made up their minds. The question elicited a positive reply from two-thirds of those under thirty, whereas 51 percent of the persons over thirty said they believed women should be eligible for board membership. Separation of responses by sex revealed that more women (60 percent) than men (52 percent) favored changing institutional bylaws to make possible female directors of the General Church and the Academy and female trustees of the Bryn Athyn Society. Furthermore, 65 percent of those surveyed said they thought women should be considered eligible to serve on the council which advises the pastor of the Bryn Athyn Society, and which has included women since 1979, whereas 27 percent felt they should not, and 8 percent were undecided. In this case, 69 percent of the women, as opposed to 58 percent of the men, favored council places for women; and when considered by age cohorts, two-thirds of the persons over thirty, as opposed to 56 percent of those under thirty, expressed a desire to see women as formal advisers to the pastor.

CHAPTER 7

1. Emanuel Swedenborg, *The True Christian Religion,* no. 120; and *Theta Alpha Journal,* Fall 1975, p. 7.

2. Emanuel Swedenborg, *Posthumous Theological Works,* vol. 2., p.559.

3. *New Church Life,* vol. 88 (1968), p. 497.

4. A survey of 100 men over twenty-one and women over eighteen indicates that 72 percent of them would date someone outside the General Church who had no interest in becoming a member, while 20 percent would not, and 8 percent are undecided. When considered by age and sex cohorts, the results suggest that 95 percent of those under thirty would date outside the sect, as opposed to 57 percent of persons over thirty; and while 82 percent of all women surveyed would date outside the Church, only 52 percent of the men indicated they would make such social arrangements.

5. A consistent 79 percent of those surveyed said they would not marry a person outside the Church who was not interested in joining it, and no weakening of this opposition to exogamy was reflected in any subgroup.

6. Emanuel Swedenborg, *Heaven and Hell,* no. 378.

7. Douglas Taylor, "Marriage Within the Church," *New Church Life,* vol. 92 (1972), p. 311.

8. Ibid.

9. N. Bruce Rogers, "Marital Separation," *New Church Life,* vol. 94 (1974), p. 415.

10. See U. S. Bureau of the Census, *Statistical Abstract of the United States: 1975* (96th edition), Washington D. C., 1975, p. 51.

11. Emanuel Swedenborg, *Conjugial Love,* no. 468. (Reference hereafter *CL.*)

12. See Willard D. Pendleton, "Divorce," unpublished manuscript, 1974, p. 5ff. Courtesy of the author.

12. See *New Church Life,* vol. 84 (1964), p. 242.

14. Eighty percent of the participants in my survey said they opposed divorce on any grounds except adultery and those disorders the Writings indicate contribute to it. Only 13 percent were willing to admit other bases, mainly incompatibility, and 7 percent replied they were uncertain whether causes other than sexual infidelity justified the termination of a marriage. Greater indecision about the appropriate grounds for divorce was expressed among women and persons under thirty; men and those over thirty took a somewhat more rigid stand in opposition to any cause but adultery.

15. See *CL,* nos. 252-254 and 464-466.

16. *New Church Life,* vol. 8 (1888), p. 190.

17. Rogers, "Marital Separation," p. 419.

18. See *CL,* no. 320.

19. *CL,* no. 321.

20. *New Church Life,* vol. 85 (1965), p. 91.

21. See George de Charms, "Repeated Marriages," *New Church Life,* vol. 95 (1975), p. 539f.

22. See Morton Hunt, *Sexual Behavior in the 1970's* (Chicago: Playboy Press, 1974), p. 150.

23. *CL,* no. 305.

24. Elmo Acton, "A Consideration of Virginity," *Theta Alpha Journal,* Fall 1966, pp. 27, 22, and 24.

25. *CL,* no. 385.

26. Martin Pryke, "The Preservation of the Conjugial," *New Church Life,* vol. 86 (1966), p. 60.

27. See *Population Characteristics and Estimates,* 1973, Montgomery County, Pennsylvania, pp. iv-15.

28. See *Statistical Abstract of the United States: 1975,* p. 11.

29. Questioned as to their views on contraception, only 9 percent of those surveryed expressed the opinion that birth control was impermis-

sible under all circumstances. No men took a position of unalterable opposition, but 6 percent of the women did, and so did 8 percent of those under thirty as opposed to 3 percent of the persons over thirty. A total of 94 percent of the Swedenborgians surveyed said they felt it would be permissible to attempt to limit the size of their family for reasons related to the physical health of the mother; 85 percent would countenance contraception on the basis of her mental health; 63 percent on financial grounds; but only 28 percent said they would practice birth control in order that the mother might continue her education or pursue a career. The main differences among subgroups were generational rather than sexual. The survey revealed that economic considerations were viewed as justifiable grounds for limiting family size by 72 percent of those under thirty as opposed to 56 percent of the persons over thirty, and educational and occupational reasons were judged acceptable by 31 percent of the younger age-cohort, but only by a quarter of the older one.

30. See *Theta Alpha Journal*, Spring 1960, p. 23f.

31. *New Church Life*, vol. 85 (1965), p. 297f.

32. R. L. Soneson, "Birth Control," *Theta Alpha Journal*, Spring 1972, p.14.

33. Emanuel Swedenborg, *Apocalypse Explained*, no. 1005:3. (Reference hereafter *AE.)*

34. See Martin Pryke, "Vasectomy," *New Church Life*, vol. 94 (1974), p. 319ff. Quotation p. 320.

35. Norbert H. Rogers, Letter to the Editor, *Theta Alpha Journal*, Spring 1976, p. 29f.

36. See Willard D. Pendleton, "Abortion," unpublished manuscript, 1974. Courtesy of the author. Quotations pp. 4, 5, 6, and 7. My survey of the residents of Bryn Athyn indicated that the executive bishop's interpretation of the Writings on the subject is shared by a majority, but not all, Swedenborgians. A total of 71 percent of those questioned said they believed abortion to be permissible when conception occurred from felonious intercourse. Only 57 percent, however, agreed that the health of the mother was a consideration justifying pregnancy termination, and 15 percent expressed the opinion that it was not allowable under any circumstances. Fear of a defective child appeared as an acceptable reason for abortion to only 14 percent of those surveyed, and just 8 percent said they would consider it as a method of birth control. The Swedenborgians appeared to believe, moreover, that their moral judgments should be written into the criminal code, as 74 percent said they opposed the permissive court ruling which allows abortion on demand during the early months of pregnancy.

37. Emanuel Swedenborg, *Arcana Coelestia*, nos. 2220 and 2322.

38. Letter from Willard L. D. Heinrichs to his colleagues, January 1975, accompanying a preliminary study, "The Word on Homosexuality." The letter and unpublished manuscript were made available to me through the courtesy of the author.

39. Heinrichs, "The Word," pp. 5 and 7.

40. Emanuel Swedenborg, *The Spiritual Diary*, nos. 1979 and 2675.

41. See Robert W. Katzbauer, "Greener Pastures," Philadelphia *Bulletin*, December 7, 1975. Ranking based on statistics gathered from the "Unified Crime Report," published by the Pennsylvania State Police Bureau of Research and Development in 1974.

42. Harold C. Cranch, "The Third Use of the Church," *New Church Life*, vol. 73 (1953), p. 156f.

43. Ibid., p. 160.

44. *AE*, no. 764: 2.

45. Cranch, "Third Use," p. 162f.

46. See Douglas Taylor, "Gates to the New Jerusalem" *Missionary Memo*, April 1975, pp. 3-6.

47. Academy Journal, Theological School and College Catalog, 1975-76, p. 29.

48. See Erik Sandstrom, "One Kingdom," *New Church Life*, vol. 91 (1971), pp. 490-502. Quotations pp. 501, 499, 498, and 501.

49. See *Theta Alpha Journal*, Spring 1972, pp. 20-23.

50. B. David Holm, "An Offering In A Clean Vessel," *New Church Life*, vol. 94 (1974), p. 285.

51. My survey of 100 adults residing in the Huntingdon Valley community revealed, moreover, that 78 percent felt that it was time for the General Church to increase its missionary activity in the United States, only 6 percent were opposed, and 16 percent had not made up their minds.

52. Louis B. King, personal interview, 1975, and *Academy Journal*, annual number, 1974-75, p. 16.

53. See Kurt Simons, "Cluster Communities: Why and How," *New Church Life*, vol. 95 (1975), pp. 24-30. Quotations p. 27f.

54. See E. Bruce Glenn, Letter to the Editor, *New Church Life*, vol. 95 (1975), p. 128ff. Quotations p. 129.

55. Douglas Taylor, personal interview, 1975.

56. *Missionary Memo*, September 1975. Available in the Academy Archives.

57. Peter Berger, *The Sacred Canopy, 1967* (Garden City: Doubleday-Anchor, 1967), p. 138.

58. See ibid., pp. 139ff and 144-147.

CHAPTER 8

1. See Mark P. Leone, *Roots of Modern Mormonism* (Cambridge, Mass: Harvard University Press, 1979), p. 169.

2. See Henri Desroche, *The American Shakers* (Amherst, Mass.: The University of Massachusetts Press, 1911), p. 39.

3. See Rufus Bishop, ed., *Testimonies of the Life, Character, Revelations and Doctrines of Mother Ann Lee,* 2nd ed. (Albany, N. Y.: n. p., 1888), p.13.

4. Edward Deming Andrews, *The People Called Shakers* (New York: Dover Roots, Publications, Inc., 1963), p. 228.

5. Leone, *Roots,* p. 27.

6. Ibid., p. 223.

7. As an experiment, New Churchman George F. Dale has produced a translation of *Heaven and Hell* rendered in modern English. It was published in New York by the Swedenborg Foundation, Inc. in 1976.

Bibliography

WORKS BY EMANUEL SWEDENBORG

The Apocalypse Explained (ms. 1759). 6 vols. New York: Swedenborg Foundation, 1928.

The Apocalypse Revealed (Amsterdam, 1766). 2 vols. New York: American Swedenborg Printing and Publishing Society, 1915.

Arcana Coelestia (London, 1749-1756). 12 vols. New York: American Swedenborg Printing and Publishing Society, 1905.

Conjugial Love (Amsterdam, 1768). Translated by Alfred Acton. Bryn Athyn: Academy of the New Church, 1953.

Corpuscular Philosophy in Brief (ms. 1740). In *Scientific and Philosophical Treatises*. Bryn Athyn: Swedenborg Scientific Association, 1905.

Divine Providence (Amsterdam, 1764). New York: Swedenborg Foundation, 1928.

Divine Providence Amsterdam, 1764). New York: Swedenborg Foundation, 1928.

The Doctrine of the New Jerusalem Concerning the Lord (Amsterdam, 1763). In *The Four Doctrines.* New York: Swedenborg Foundation, 1941.

The Economy of the Animal Kingdom (London and Amsterdam, 1740-1741). 2 vols. New York: New Church Press, n. d. [1919].

Heaven and Hell (London, 1758). New York: Swedenborg Foundation, 1944.

*Available in various editions

The Journal of Dreams (ms. 1744). Translated by Carl Th. Odhner. Bryn Athyn: Academy Book Room, 1918.

**Last Judgment* (London, 1758). Translated by P. H. Johnson. London: The Swedenborg Society, 1951.

Messiah About to Come (ms. 1745). Translated by Alfred Acton. Bryn Athyn: Academy of the New Church, 1949.

**The New Jerusalem and Its Heavenly Doctrine* (London, 1758). In *Miscellaneous Theological Works*. New York: Swedenborg Foundation, 1928.

On the Infinite (Dresden and Leipzig, 1734). Translated by James John Garth Wilkinson. London: The Swedenborg Society, 1908.

Posthumous Theological Works. 2 vols. Edited and translated by John Whitehead. New York: Swedenborg Foundation, 1928.

The Spiritual Diary (ms. 1747-1765). 5 vols. London: James Speirs, 1883-1902.

Summary of the Principia (ms. 1734). Translated by Alfred H. Stroh. Bryn Athyn: Swedenborg Scientific Association, 1904.

**The True Christian Religion* (Amsterdam, 1771). 2 vols. London: The Swedenborg Society, 1950.

The Way to A Knowledge of the Soul (ms. 1738 or 1739). In *Psychological Transactions*. Translated by Alfred Acton. Philadelphia: Swedenborg Scientific Association, 1920.

The Word Explained (ms 1746-1747). 8 vols. Translated by Alfred Acton. Bryn Athyn: 1928-1948.

The Worship and Love of God (London, 1745). Translated by Alfred H. Stroh and Frank Sewall. Boston: Trustees of Lydia S. Rotch-Massachusetts New-Church Union, 1914.

GENERAL WORKS

The Academy: A Portrait. Edited by John Raymond and Robert Scott. Bryn Athyn: Sons of the Academy, 1957.

The Academy Journal. Bryn Athyn. 1959-1982.

The Academy of the New Church, 1976-1926: An Anniversary Record. Bryn Athyn: Academy Book Room, 1926.

Acton, Alfred. "New Church Education," *Journal of Education of the Academy of the New Church*, 1912, pp. 3-10.

Acton, Alfred, II. Letter to the Editor, *New Church Life*, vol. 96 (1976), pp. 143-147.

Acton, Elmo. "A Consideration of Virginity," *Theta Alpha Journal*, Fall 1966, pp. 21-27.

Adler, E. Gordon. *The Montgomery Country Story*. Norristown, Pa.: Commissioners of Montgomery County, 1951.

Ahlstrom, Sydney E. *A Religious History of the American People.* New Haven, Conn.: *Yale University Press, 1972.*

Alden, Karl. "The New Church Missionary Tour," *New Church Life,* vol. 36 (1916), pp. 782-788.

Andrews, Edward Deming. *The People Called Shakers.* New York: Oxford University Press, 1953.

Asplundh, Kurt H. "The New Church Community in the World Today." Unpublished Manuscript, 1961.

Aurora, or Dawn of Genuine Truth. London, 1799-1801.

Baltzell, E. Digby *Philadelphia Gentlemen: The Making of A National Upper Class.* (1958) Philadelphia: The University of Pennsylvania Press, 1979.

Benade, William Henry. *Conversations On Education.* Philadelphia: Academy of the New Church, 1888.

———. "Prospectus of a School for Boys" (1847). *New Church Life,* vol. 29 (1909), pp. 658-661.

———. "Report On the Priesthood and Grades in the Priesthood," *Convention Journal,* 1875, pp. 53-93.

Berger, Peter, Brigette Berger, and Hansfried Kellner. *The Homeless Mind.* New York: Vintage Books, 1974.

Berger, Peter. *The Sacred Canopy: Elements of A Sociological Theory of Religion.* (1967) Garden City: Doubleday-Anchor, 1969.

——— and Thomas Luckmann. *The Social Construction of Reality.* (1966) Garden City: Doubleday-Anchor, 1967.

Berger, Peter. "The Sociological Study of Sectarianism," *Social Research,* vol. 21 (1954), pp. 467-485.

Bernard, Chester I. "A Definition of Authority." In Robert K. Merton, ed., *Reader In Bureaucracy.* Glencoe: The Free Press, 1952, pp. 180-185.

Block, Marguerite Beck. *The New Church in the New World.* New York: Henry Holt and Company, 1932.

Boyeson, Margit K. "Some Reflections On the Nature of Men and Women," *Sons of the Academy Bulletin,* February 1975, pp. 11-18.

Bryn Athyn Borough Comprehensive Plan. Norristown, Pa.: Montgomery County Planning Commission, 1968.

Bryn Athyn Church Annual Report, 1979-1980. Bryn Athyn Church.

Bryn Athyn: From These Beginnings. Bryn Athyn: Academy Book Room, 1966.

Burnham, N. C. and William Henry Benade. *Circular to the Receivers of the Heavenly Doctrine of the New Jerusalem in the United States.* Philadelphia: n. p., 1855.

Case, Shirley Jackson. *The Millennial Hope.* Chicago: University of Chicago Press, 1918.

Clark, Elmer T. *The Small Sects in America.* (1937) New York: Abington-Cokesbury Press, 1949.

Cohn, Norman. *The Pursuit of the Millennium.* Fairlawn, N. J.: Essential Books, Inc., 1957.

Cox, Harvey. *The Feast of Fools.* Cambridge: Harvard University Press, 1969.

Cram, Ralph Adams. "A Note On Bryn Athyn Church," *The American Architect,* vol. 113 (May 29, 1918), pp. 709-712.

Cranch, Harold C. "The Third Use of the Church," *New Church Life,* vol. 73 (1953), pp. 152-164.

__________. "The Uses of Men and Women," *New Church Life,* vol. 94 (1974), pp. 294-301.

Cuno's Memoirs On Swedenborg. Edited by Alfred Acton. Bryn Athyn: Academy of the New Church, 1947.

Curricular Studies. Bryn Athyn: Academy of the New Church, 1955.

Confederate Memoirs: Captain W. F. Pendleton. Edited by Constance Pendleton. Bryn Athyn: n. p., 1958.

De Charms, George. "The Distinctiveness of the New Church," *New Church Life,* vol. 64 (1944), pp. 97-108.

__________. *The Growth of the Mind.* Bryn Athyn: Academy Book Room, 1932.

__________. "The Hague Views Examined," *New Church Life,* vol. 57 (1937), pp. 241-269.

__________. "Repeated Marriages," *New Church Life,* vol. 95 (1975), pp. 538-540.

De Charms, Richard. "Autobiography." Unpublished Manuscript, 1857.

Desroche, Henri. *The American Shakers: From Neo-Christianity to Pre-socialism.* Amherst: University of Massachusetts Press, 1971.

The Dew-Drop. Philadelphia, 1852-1854.

Documents Concerning the Life of Emanuel Swedenborg. Edited by Rudolf L. Tafel. 2 vols. London: The Swedenborg Society, 1875 and 1877.

Documents Concerning the Separation of the Rev. Ernst Pfeiffer from the General Church of the New Jerusalem. Bryn Athyn: n. p., April 7, 1937.

Evans, Frederick W. "Autobiography of A Shaker," *The Atlantic Monthly,* vol. 23 (1869), pp. 415-425 and 593-605.

Formation of a New General Church. Huntingdon Valley, Pa.: n. p., March 1, 1897.

Gaskill, Jennie. *Biography of Raymond Pitcairn.* Bryn Athyn: Academy Book Room, 1973.

Geertz, Clifford. "The Impact of the Concept of Culture on the Concept of Man." In Yehudi A. Cohen, ed., *Man In Adaptation: The Cultural Present.* Chicago: Aldine Publishing Company, 1968.

________. *The Interpretation of Culture.* New York: Basic Books, Inc., 1973.

General Church of the New Jerusalem Reports, 1900-1905.

Gladish, Richard R. *A History of the Academy of the New Church.* 4 vols. Bryn Athyn: General Church Religion Lessons, 1967-1973.

Glenn, E. Bruce. *Bryn Athyn Cathedral: The Building of a Church.* Bryn Athyn Church of the New Jerusalem, 1971.

________. Letter to the Editor, *New Church Life,* vol. 95 (1975), pp. 128-130.

________. Letter to the Editor, *New Church Life,* vol. 96 (1976), pp. 561-564.

Green, Calvin, and Seth Young. *The Millennial Church.* Albany, N. Y. C. Van Benthuysen, 1848.

Gunther, Ariel. *Opportunities, Challenge and Privilege.* New York: Vantage Press, 1973.

Gunther, Carl. "Post Road Airlines." Unpublished Manuscript, 1975.

Harvey, Van A. *A Handbook of Theological Terms.* London: George Allen and Unwin Ltd., 1966.

Heinrichs, Willard L. D. "The Word on Homosexuality." Unpublished Manuscript, 1975.

Henderson, Bruce. "School Merger Fight." Unpublished Manuscript, n. d.

Hindmarsh, Robert. *The Rise and Progress of the New Jerusalem Church.* London: Hodson and Sons, 1861.

Holm, B. David. "An Offering In A Clean Vessel," *New Church Life,* vol. 94 (1974), pp. 281-285.

Hunt, Morton. *Sexual Behavior in the 1970's.* Chicago: Playboy Press, 1974.

Jamison, A. Leland. "Religion On the Christian Perimeter." In James Ward Smith and Leland A. Jamison, eds., *The Shaping of American Religion,* vol. 1 in *Religion in American Life.* Princeton: Princeton University Press, 1961.

Journal of the Central Convention, 1840-1852.

Journal of Education of the Academy of the New Church. Bryn Athyn, 1901-1959.

Journals of the General Assembly of the General Church of the New Jerusalem, 1897-1899.

Journals of the General Church of the Advent of the Lord, 1891-1892.

Journals of the General Church of Pennsylvania, 1883-1890.

Journals of the General Convention of the New Jerusalem in the U.S.A., 1817-1976.

Journal of the Pennsylvania Association of the New Jerusalem, February 22, 1861. In *Journals of the General Church of Pennsylvania,* 1845-1883.

Katzbauer, Robert W. "Greener Pastures." Philadelphia *Bulletin,* December 7, 1975.

The Kramph Will Case: The Controversy in Regard to Swedenborg's Works on Conjugial Love. Bryn Athyn: Academy of the New Church, 1910.

Leone, Mark P. *Roots of Modern Mormonism.* Cambridge: Harvard University Press, 1979.

Liturgy and Hymnal for the Use of the General Church of the New Jerusalem. Fifth and Revised Edition. Bryn Athyn: General Church of the New Jerusalem, 1966.

Liturgy for the General Church of the New Jerusalem. Bryn Athyn: Academy Book Room, 1908.

Main, Jackson Turner, *The Social Structure of Revolutionary Virginia.* Princeton: Princeton University Press, 1965.

Mays, David John. *Edmund Pendleton, 1721-1803: A Biography.* Cambridge: Harvard University Press, 1952.

Mead, Margaret. *Culture and Commitment.* Garden City, N. Y.: Natural History Press/Doubleday and Company, Inc., 1970.

Meade, William. *Old Churches, Ministers and Families of Virginia* (1857). Baltimore: Genealogical Publishing Company, 1966.

Merton, Robert K. *Social Theory and Social Structure.* Enlarged Edition. New York: The Free Press, 1968.

Missionary Memo. Bryn Athyn, 1974-1982.

New Church Life. Philadelphia and Bryn Athyn, 1881-1982.

Newchurchman. Philadelphia, 1841-1844.

New Church Repository and Monthly Review. New York, 1849.

New Jerusalem Magazine. Boston, 1827-1893.

New Church Messenger (titled *New Jerusalem Messenger* from 1853-1884 and *The Messenger* since 1970). Brooklyn, 1884-1970.

New Philosophy. Bryn Athyn, 1898-1982.

Niebuhr, H. Richard. *The Social Sources of Denominationalism.* (1927) New York: The World Publishing Company, 1957.

O'Dea, Thomas F. "Sects and Cults." *International Encyclopedia of Social Sciences,* vol. 14, pp. 130-136.

Odhner, Carl Th. *Annals of the New Church,* 1688-1850. Bryn Athyn: Academy of the New Church, 1904.

______."The History of the General Church." *New Church Life,* vol. 24 (1904), pp. 403-419.

______. "John Pitcairn: A Biography." *New Church Life,* vol. 37 (1917), pp. 1-21, 79-84, 151-161, 229-234, 280-301, 414-428, 515-546, and 505-601, and vol. 38 (1918), pp. 19-21.

______. "The New Church and the Gentiles." *New Church Life,* vol. 33 (1913), pp. 458-478.

______. "Richard de Charms." *New Church Life,* vol. 22 (1902), pp. 2-9 and 129-137, and vol. 23 (1903) pp. 76-83, 245-250, 359-363, and 595-599.

______. "Swedenborg and Ernesti." *New Church Life,* vol 32 (1912), pp.133-151 and 197-209.

______. "William Henry Benade." *New Church Life,* vol. 25 (1905), pp. 449-618 and 721-731, and vol. 26 (1906), pp. 65-77.

______. "William Henry Benade." *New Church Life,* vol. 25 (1905), pp. 449-618 and 721-731, and vol. 26 (1906), pp. 65-77.

Odhner, Cyriel L. "Swedenborg's Hobby." *New Church Life,* vol. 43 (1923), pp. 65-72.

Odhner, Ormond de Charms. "The Academy in Crisis," *New Church Life,* vol. 94 (1974), pp. 208-213.

______. "The Origins of the New Church Priesthood." Unpublished Manuscript, 1975.

Odhner, S. C. "A New Document Concerning Swedenborg." *New Church Life,* vol. 34 (1914), pp. 45-53.

Parsons, Talcott. *Politics and Social Structure.* New York: The Free Press, 1969.

Pendleton, Willard D. "Abortion." Unpublished Manuscript, 1974.

______. "Divorce." Unpublished Manuscript, 1974.

Pendleton, William Frederick. *Notes and Papers on Ritual,* 1919-1922. Bryn Athyn: Academy Book Room, 1956.

Pitcairn, Raymond. "Christian Art and Architecture for the New Church." *New Church Life,* vol. 40 (1920), pp. 611-624.

Pope, Liston. *Millhands and Preachers: A Study of Gastonia.* New Haven: Yale University Press, 1942.

Population Characteristics and Estimates, 1973. Montgomery County, Pa.

The Precursor. Cincinnati, 1836-1842.

Pryke, Martin. *Our Funeral Customs.* Bryn Athyn: General Church Publications Committee, 1960.

______. "The Preservation of the Conjugial." *New Church Life,* vol. 86 (1966), pp. 54-65.

______. "Vasectomy." *New Church Life,* vol. 94 (1974), pp. 319-321.

The Publication. Bryn Athyn, 1968-1973.

Reichel, William G., and William H. Bigler. *A History of the Moravian Seminary for Young Ladies at Bethlehem, Pennsylvania.* Bethlehem: Moravian Seminary, 1901.

"A Report On A Distinctive Social Life." Academy College, January 24, 1967.

"Resolutions for the Corporation of the Academy of the New Church Re: Nominating Committees and Nominating Procedures." Revised May 15, 1970. Academy of the New Church.

Rhodes, Leon S. "Yeomen of the Board." Unpublished Manuscript, 1974.

Robertson, Roland. *The Sociological Interpretation of Religion.* New York: Schocken Boks, 1970.

Robinson, John A. T. *Jesus and His Coming: The Emergence of a Doctrine.* New York: Abington Press, 1957.

Rogers, N. Bruce. "Marital Separation," *New Church Life,* vol. 94 (1974), pp. 414-421.

Rogers, Norbert H. Letter to the Editor, *Theta Alpha Journal,* Spring 1976, pp. 29-30.

Rose, Don. *My Own Four Walls.* New York: Doubleday, and Company, Inc. 1941.

Sandstrom, Erik. "One Kingdom." *New Church Life,* vol. 91 (1971), pp. 490-502.

__________. "The Women's Lib Movement." *New Church Life,* vol. 95 (1975), pp. 541-546.

__________. "Women Priests?" *New Church Life,* vol. 95 (1975), pp. 98-109.

Schwedenberg, T. H. "The Swedenborg Manuscripts." *Archives of Neurology,* vol. 2 (1960), pp. 407-409.

Sessler, John Jacob. *Communal Pietism Among Early American Moravians.* New York: Henry Holt and Company, 1933.

Seventy-fifth Birthday Celebration. (Raymond Pitcairn's) Bryn Athyn, n. p., 1960.

Sigstedt, Cyriel O. *The Swedenborg Epic.* New York: Bookman Associates, 1952.

Simons, Kurt. "Cluster Communitites: Why and How." *New Church Life,* vol. 95 (1975), pp. 24-30.

Simson, Otto von. *The Gothic Cathedral: Origins of Gothic Architecture and the Medieval Concept of Order.* New York: Bollingen Foundation, Inc. 1956.

Snook, John B. "An Alternative to Church-Sect." *Journal for the Scientific Study of Religion,* vol. 13 (1974), pp. 191-204.

Soneson, R. L. "Birth Control." *Theta Alpha Journal,* Spring 1972, pp. 11-14.

Sons of the Academy Bulletin. Bryn Athyn, 1912-1982.

Stark, Werner. *Sectarian Religion.* vol. 2 in *The Sociology of Religion: A Study of Christendom.* New York: Fordham University Press, 1967.

A Statement Concerning Recent Disturbances in the Church of the Academy of the New Church and the General Church of the Advent. Philadelphia: n. p., 1897.

A Statement of the Order and Organization of the General Church of the New Jerusalem. General Church of the New Jerusalem, 1970.

Statistical Abstract of the U. S.: 1975. U. S. Bureau of the Census, 96th Edition. Washington, D. C., 1975.

Stroemple, Jeanette E. Letter to the Editor. *New Church Life,* vol. 96 (1976), p. 147.

Synnestvedt, Homer. "Thoughts On Education." *Journal of Education of the Academy of the New Church,* 1902, pp. 5-14.

Synnestvedt, Robert E. Letter to the Editor. *New Church Life,* vol. 95 (1975), pp. 463-464.

Taylor, Douglas. "Gates of the New Jerusalem." *Missionary Memo,* April 1975, pp. 3-6.

______."Marriage Within the Church." *New Church Life,* vol. 92 (1972), pp. 305-312.

Testimonies of the Life, Character, Revelations and Doctrines of Mother Ann Lee. Second Edition. Edited by Rufus Bishop. Albany, N. Y.: n. p. 1888.

Theta Alpha Journal. Bryn Athyn, 1910-1982.

Toksvig, Signe. *Emanuel Swedenborg: Scientist and Mystic.* New Haven: Yale University Press, 1948.

Troeltsch, Ernst. *The Social Teachings of the Christian Churches.* 2 vols. Translated by Olive Wyon. New York: The Macmillan Company, 1931.

Two Centuries of Nazareth, 1740-1940. Nazareth, Pa.: Bi-Centennial, Inc. 1940.

Wallace, Anthony F. C. *Administrative Forms of Social Organization.* McCaleb module in Anthropology from the Series, Addison-Wesley Modular Publications, module 9, 1971, pp. 1-12.

______. *Religion: An Anthropological View.* New York: Random House, 1966.

Weber, Max. *The Sociology of Religion (1922).* Translated by Ephraim Fischoff. Boston: Beacon Press, 1964.

______. *The Theory of Social and Economic Organizations.* Translated by A. M. Henderson and Talcott Parsons. New York: Oxford University Press, 1947.

Whitehead, William. *Annals of the Academy,* 1874-1896. Bryn Athyn: Academy Book Room, 1976.

Wilson, Bryan. *Religious Sects.* (1970) New York: World University Library, 1973.

Words for the New Church. Philadelphia, 1879-1883.

Index

About the Author

MARY ANN MEYERS is Secretary of the University and Lecturer in American Civilization at the University of Pennsylvania. She specializes in the study of the changing role of religious leaders in America, and has written extensively on the subject of death in religion.